Injecting Illicit Drugs

This book is dedicated to the following people:

To Epa for helping me to gain an understanding of some difficult issues related to the subject
Richard Pates

To Ida and Cameron McBride
Andrew McBride

Injecting Illicit Drugs

Edited by

Richard Pates
BSc, DClinPsy, AFBPsS, CPsychol
Consultant Clinical Psychologist and Clinical Director
of the Community Addictions Unit
Cardiff, UK

Andrew McBride
MB, ChB, MSc, FRCPsych
Consultant Psychiatrist
Oxford, UK

Karin Arnold
Community Addictions Unit
Cardiff, UK

Blackwell
Publishing

Addiction
Press

Editorial offices:
Blackwell Publishing Ltd, 9600 Garsington Road, Oxford OX4 2DQ, UK
    Tel: +44 (0)1865 776868
Blackwell Publishing Inc., 350 Main Street, Malden, MA 02148-5020, USA
    Tel: +1 781 388 8250
Blackwell Publishing Asia Pty Ltd, 550 Swanston Street, Carlton, Victoria 3053, Australia
    Tel: +61 (0)3 8359 1011

First published 2005 by Blackwell Publishing Ltd

Library of Congress Cataloging-in-Publication Data

Injecting illicit drugs/edited by Richard Pates, Andrew McBride, Karin Arnold.
    p. ; cm.
  Includes bibliographical references and index.
  ISBN-13: 978-1-4051-1360-1 (pbk. : alk. paper)
  ISBN-10: 1-4051-1360-X (pbk. : alk. paper)
  1. Intravenous drug abuse.
  [DNLM: 1. Substance Abuse, Intravenous. 2. HIV Infections—transmission.
3. Hepatitis C—transmission. 4. Needle Sharing—adverse effects.] I. Pates, Richard.
II. McBride, Andrew III. Arnold, Karin.

  RC564.I525 2005
  362.29—dc22   2004029555

ISBN-10: 1-4051-1360-X
ISBN-13: 978-14051-1360-1

A catalogue record for this title is available from the British Library

Set in 10/12.5pt Ehrhardt
by Graphicraft Limited, Hong Kong
Printed and bound in India
by Replika Press Pvt Ltd, Kundli

For further information on Blackwell Publishing, visit our website:
www.blackwellpublishing.com

Contents

Series Foreword

Addiction represents one of the most significant challenges to modern society. Addiction to cigarettes is currently estimated to cause some 3 million deaths in the world per year, and this figure is set to rise to 10 million in the next decade. Alcohol dependence is believed to account for more than a million premature deaths each year, while dependence on opiates and illicit simulants, with its associated crime, is a scourge which affects the lives of all of us directly or indirectly, and the problem is not receding – if anything it is growing.

Our knowledge and understanding of what addiction is and what can be done to mitigate the problems has also increased in leaps and bounds in the past 50 years and important new findings are emerging all the time. Addiction Press encompasses the Society for the Study of Addiction's journal *Addiction* and a new book series, of which this is the third volume to be published. Addiction Press was set up with the express purpose of communicating current ideas and evidence in this expanding field, not only to researchers and practising health professionals but also to policy makers, students and interested non-specialists.

The study of addiction involves many academic disciplines, including psychology, psychiatry, public health, epidemiology, pharmacology, physiology, genetics, sociology and history. Therefore this series is, of necessity, multi-disciplinary in scope and style. No artificial constraints have been imposed on the type of book that will be included – if the idea is fresh and there is a need for a volume of a particular type, it will be considered to form part of the series.

The series is intimately linked with Blackwell Publishing's major journal in the field, *Addiction*, and it is hoped that my involvement in the editorial staff of the latter will help with developing ideas for topics and authors for the former.

Finally, it is my fervent hope that the series will do more than communicate ideas in this important field; it will be part of the process for generating and stimulating thought and debate and so play some role in taking the field forward.

Robert West
Series Editor
University College, London

Contributors

Karin Arnold
BSc, MPhil
Researcher Community Addictions Unit, Cardiff, UK

David Best
BA Hons (1st Class), MSc (with Distinction), PhD
Senior Lecturer in Addictions, National Addiction Centre, Institute of Psychiatry,
London, UK

Nick Crofts
MB BS (Melb), MPH, FAFPHM
Director, Turning Point Alcohol and Drug Centre, Melbourne, Victoria, Australia

Kate A Dolan
BSc, PhD
Senior Lecturer, National Drug and Alcohol Research Centre, UNSW, Sydney,
Australia

Jimmy Dorabjee
BA Sociology; Founding Member/ex Chairman, The Asian Harm Reduction
Network, Chiang Mai, Thailand; Member, UN Reference Group on HIV Prevention
and Care among Injecting Drug Users
Deputy Director, The Centre for Harm Reduction, Macfarlane Burnet Institute for
Medical Research and Public Health, Melbourne, Victoria, Australia

Pim Gregory
Research Assistant, Community Addictions Unit, Cardiff, UK

Jean-Paul Grund
PhD
Senior Researcher, Addiction Research Centre (CVO), Utrecht, The Netherlands

Robert B Haemmig
MD, Psychiatrist & Psychotherapist FMH; President of Swiss Society of Addiction
Medicine SSAM
Medical Director of Integrated Drug Service, University Psychiatric Services Berne,
Social and Community Psychiatry, Berne, Switzerland

Robert Heimer
PhD
Associate Professor, Department of Epidemiology and Public Health, Yale University
School of Medicine, New Haven, CT, USA

Andrew McBride
MB ChB MSc FRCPsych
Consultant Psychiatrist, Oxford, UK

Mark D. Norman
RMN, BSc (Hons)
Community Psychiatric Nurse, Leeds Addiction Unit, Leeds, UK

Dr Rossana G. Oretti
BSc (Hons), MB, BS, MSc, MRC Psych
Consultant Psychiatrist in Substance Misuse, Community Addictions Unit, Cardiff,
UK

Richard Pates
BSc DClin Psy AFBPS, CPsychol
Consultant Clinical Psychologist and Clinical Director of the Community Addictions
Unit, Cardiff, UK

Trudi J Petersen
RMN, BSc, PgDip
Researcher/practitioner, Pembrokeshire and Derwen NHS Trust, UK

Jennifer Scott
BSc, PhD, MRPharmS
Lecturer in Pharmacy Practice, University of Bath, UK

Dr David Shewan
MA (Hons), PhD
Reader in Psychology; Research Director, Glasgow Centre for the Study of Violence,
Glasgow Caledonian University, UK

Matthew Southwell
BA (Hons)
Managing Director, Traffasi, London, UK

Heino Stöver
PhD
Associate Professor, University of Bremen, Faculty of Law, Germany

Ingrid van Beek
MB.BS MBA FAFPHM FAChAM
Medical Director, Sydney Medically Supervised Injecting Centre, NSW, Australia

Jan Jakob Wichter
BSc Applied Psychology, MPhil Psychology
Psychologist, Teichland, Germany

Helen Williams
RMN, BSc (Hons)
Team Leader, PRISM (The Mid and West Wales Alcohol and Drug Advisory Service), Carmarthen, UK

Acknowledgements

We would like to thank all the authors for their time and knowledge so generously given, and Rachel Wheeler, without whom this book would never have been finished.

Introduction

Andrew McBride, Richard Pates and Karin Arnold

To the best of our understanding this is the first book ever compiled that focuses specifically on injecting drug use and the health consequences of this behaviour. It cannot claim to be exhaustive or comprehensive, but seeks to cover as wide a range of relevant issues as the editors could fit into the available space and our expert contributors could supply.

Animal and human psychoactive drug use can be traced back into pre-history. But it took the sophisticated tool making skills and boundless experimental enthusiasm of the human to work out how to optimise recreational drug delivery. Every mucous membrane, skin surface and orifice has been tried as a means of getting drugs into the human organism and thus inside the mind. Efforts at transfusion can be traced back centuries, and the injection of drugs back to the nineteenth century. Crane (1991) concluded that the practice of the non-medical intravenous injection of drugs originated in Egypt, supporting this with the report of Biggam (1929), a British Army physician, who first described the technique among a group of Cairo heroin addicts. On balance it seems more likely that intravenous injection arose over time in different places for a range of reasons.

O'Donnell and Jones (1968) concluded that drug use has become more deleterious to the addict and society because injecting has replaced less effective routes of administration. Because injecting tends to become highly ritualised (see Chapters 4 and 10) and 'rituals are often central to the occurrence of infections' (Crane, 1991), it is perhaps unsurprising that injecting has become a major public health problem.

After considering the history of the technology and the spread of injecting drug-using behaviour around the globe, most of the chapters address different health consequences of injecting from a number of perspectives. It may help to orient oneself in considering these risks as they might arise for the drug injector, starting with the injecting equipment and the contents of the syringe, then working through local and systemic complications and the immediate and longer-term consequences. One possible framework is presented in Table I.1. As can be seen, the book could be entitled 'If something can go wrong it will' as there is probably no hazard that one can imagine which hasn't befallen some hapless injector.

For the individual user, there are clearly multiple risks from the act of injection itself as well as from the drugs used. In addition to negative drug effects, the lifestyle of drug

Table I.1   A simple categorisation of complications of injecting.

The Equipment
  The environment
  The cooker/water/filter
  The syringe
  The needle
The Injected 'Drug'
  The Drug itself
  Drug interactions
  Allergy
  Contaminants
    Deliberate and accidental contaminants
    Inorganic
    Particulate embolism
    Air embolism
    Fat embolism
    Infectious agents
      Prions
      Viruses
      Bacteria
      Other organisms
At the Site of Injection
  Trauma and infection
    Skin – abscess, scarring and tattooing
    Subcutaneous tissues – fat necrosis
    Veins
    The 'simple' miss
    Connective tissue, tendons and muscles
    Arterial injection
    Nerves
    Lungs, breasts, penises and necks
Distant and Systemic Effects
  Overdose
  Poisoning
  Infection
  Thrombosis – superficial and in deep veins
  Emboli

users is often detrimental to health. Poverty, poor nutrition, poor sanitation, social exclusion, criminal sanctions and, in many countries, limited access to medical care, will all have a negative impact on health.

We hope that this overview of the issue of injecting drug use will stimulate continued interest in injecting drug use, those who inject, and the individual and public health issues that injecting raises.

References

Biggam, A.G. (1929) Malignant malaria associated with the administration of heroin intravenously. *Transactions of the Society of Tropical Medicine and Hygiene*, **23**, 147–153.

Crane, L.R. (1991) Epidemiology of infections in intravenous drug abusers. In D.P. Levine (ed.): *Infections in Intravenous Drug Abusers*, pp. 3–26. New York: Oxford University Press.

O'Donnell, J.A. & Jones, J.P. (1968) Diffusion of the intravenous technique among narcotic addicts in the US. *Journal of Health and Social Behaviour*, **9**, 120–130.

Chapter 1

History of Injecting

Richard Pates and Jan Wichter

Introduction

The history of injecting will never be attributed to just one person because of the involvement of very old practices and the number of people involved in the development over the centuries. What is important is the coming together of two principles; that of introducing a substance into the body and the mechanisms by which the syringe acts as a pump and creates a vacuum to suck liquid into the barrel. It is interesting to note that Christopher Wren, in the description of his early experiments, called the device a syringe, although at this stage it was a crude device consisting of a quill and a bladder (Wren, 1665).

Blaise Pascal (1623–1662), a French physicist and mathematician, discovered the law of physics known as Pascal's Law, which states that when pressure is applied to any part of a liquid the pressure is distributed equally to all parts of the liquid. This principle is the foundation of modern hydraulics of which the syringe is one example.

The method of introducing substances into the body other than by oral routes cannot be traced back to a specific place and time, as weapons such as poison-tipped darts and blowpipes have been in existence since before recorded history. However, when the history of the needle and syringe as a means of administering substances into the body is considered, Macht (1916) gives as the earliest explicit record, transfusion of blood under intravenous injections, in the treatment of Pope Innocent VIII in 1492.

Bugnicourt (2003) quotes many early descriptions on his website, including a mention by Philon in 230 BC of a syringe with a piston for introducing rose water into the aural canal. He also quotes the use of clysters by Celse in the period from 53 BC onwards to apply various substances, including salt water, and oils as a treatment for worm infestations. In his anatomical research, Leonardo da Vinci (1452–1519) was known to have used injections to explore bronchial vessels and other cavities.

The Transactions of The Royal Society (Wren, 1665) record the experiment by Christopher Wren of transfusing blood into a dog. The article asserts that Wren was the inventor of this practice and claims that in 'some books printed beyond the seas, treating of the Way of Injecting liquors into veines; in which books the original seems to be ascribed to others'. . .' 'Tis notorious that at least six years since (a good while before it was heard off (sic), that anyone did pretend to have so much as thought of it.' The paper goes on to describe the process. Wren thought that 'He could easily contrive a way to conveigh any liquid thing immediately into the mass of blood; videl: By making Ligatures on the Veines, and then opening them on the side of the Ligature towards the Heart, and by putting into them slender Syringes or quills, fastened to Bladders (in the manner of clyster pipes) containing the matter to be injected; performing that Operation upon pretty big and lean doggs, that the vessels might be large enough and easily accessible.'

Wren, in the company of other members of the Royal Society, experimented by injecting opium and *crocus metallorum* (a mixture of antimony oxide and antimony oxysulphate) into the hind legs of dogs. The success of the experiment showed that the opium was soon circulated into the brain, and 'did within a short time stupify though not kill the Dog; but a large dose of the *crocus metallorum* made another dog vomit up life and all.' The paper continues to describe that the success of this method became known and a foreign ambassador who was curious, tried with some *crocus metallorum* 'upon a malefacto, that was an inferior servant of his; with this success that the Fellow, as soon as ever the injection began to be made, did, either really or craftily, fall into a swoon.' The article concludes that liquors injected into the veins may make 'odde commotions in the blood, disturb nature and cause strange symptoms in the body', but that besides the medical uses that may be made of this invention it may also serve for anatomical purposes, both observations being somewhat prescient.

If Wren invented this in the 1650s, the method clearly spread. Samuel Pepys (1664) writes on 16th May 1664 that with his friend Mr Pierce the surgeon 'went to see an experiment of killing a dog by letting opium into his hind leg. He and Dr Clerke did fail mightily in hitting the vein and in effect did not do the business after many trials; but with the little they got in the dog did presently fall asleep'.

Crude injecting devices persist to the present day, especially in areas where there is a lack of availability of needles and syringes, for example in prisons or areas without needle exchanges and where there are laws prohibiting the possession of injecting equipment. Courtwright *et al.* (1989) showed that even at the beginning of widespread availability of syringes, a replacement in the form of a medicine dropper with a bulb or a pacifier on the end was used. The needle was attached to the device with a cigarette paper serving as seal between the components.

A syringe was defined in *The Edinburgh Medical and Surgical Dictionary* (Morris & Kendrick, 1807) as 'a well known instrument, serving to imbibe or suck in a quantity of fluid and afterwards expel the same with violence. A syringe is used for transmitting injections into cavities and canals'. In the early nineteenth century, syringes were mainly used for injecting corpses to trace the blood vessels for anatomical study (Derricott *et al.*, 1999).

Subcutaneous methods of the application of drugs were made popular by Lafargue, who, in 1836, devised a technique called inoculation: a vaccination lancet was dipped into morphine and then forced almost horizontally under the skin, retained for a few seconds and then withdrawn. Howard-Jones (1947) also describes Lafargue (1836) developing a 'dry syringe', an apparatus where medicated pellets were pushed under the skin with a needle. (Also see Lafargue (1861).) At the beginning of the nineteenth century, another attempt to introduce drugs into the body via the skin was by use of a plaster containing an active agent which was placed onto an artificially induced, open blister.

Development of the modern hypodermic syringe

The credit for inventing the modern syringe seems to be divided between a Frenchman, Charles Pravaz; an Irishman, Francis Rynd; and a Scot, Alexander Wood. However, Kane (1880) in his discussion on the development of the syringe states that two Americans, Isaac Taylor and Washington claimed to have used a practice in 1839. They made an incision in the skin and used a syringe to inject a drug into the subcutaneous cellular tissue of the patient, the syringe being thrust into the cut. Taylor and Washington did not claim to be the first to use this method having read about the technique in a French journal, the name of which they could not remember!

Pravaz has been credited by some with the invention of the hypodermic syringe. Howard-Jones (1947) states quite firmly that although Pravaz did use a fine trocar-and-cannula to inject iron perchloride into the lumen of an aneurysmal sac to produce a clot, this apparatus was very different from the modern syringe. Howard-Jones also points out that syringes had long been used for therapeutic and experimental purposes, but these were different from the modern hypodermic syringe.

In 1845, Rynd described a new treatment of treating neuralgia with injections from a retractable trocar. He claimed great success for his method, but did not describe the apparatus until after the invention of the hypodermic syringe (Rynd, 1861). Again Rynd's apparatus was an elaborate trocar-and-cannula and not a syringe as such (Howard-Jones, 1947).

Kane (1880) states that in 1843 Rynd and Wood both almost simultaneously used an Anel's syringe for injection after an incision had been made. Howard-Jones (1947) suggests that the dating of Wood's work with a syringe to 1843 was erroneously quoted by Charles Hunter in his correspondence about the localisation of effect of the subcutaneous injection of morphia. Wood's first paper on his work was published in 1855 and it is clear in this paper that it was in 1853 he introduced his syringe. The needle used by Wood was not pointed and had no lateral opening, thus necessitating the opening of the skin prior to injection. In 1853, Wood used an adapted syringe developed by Ferguson to inject morphia hypodermically. In 1858, Charles Hunter improved on Wood's syringe by adding a pointed needle with a lateral opening. This was the real forerunner of the modern syringe. In the next 20 years the use of the syringe for hypodermic injections spread rapidly as did knowledge of the technology of the syringe.

Kane (1880) said that the best syringe was probably that made of glass with a protective casing of metal. The instrument was either graduated on the glass or on the piston rod. The end of the piston rod (the plunger) was packed with leather kept moist with carbolised oil; the needles were of steel, gold plated or of pure gold. Kane thought that steel needles properly cared for were the best. Through each needle a fine wire should be pushed and kept *in situ* after each time of using. He commented that hard rubber syringes were poor and inaccurate, and that glass syringes were readily broken. Rubber syringes had been used during the American Civil War to irrigate wounds and to inject powder into wounds and ears.

The rise in the practice of injecting

From the invention of the hypodermic syringe in 1853, the popularity of its use spread in the latter part of the nineteenth century. Many papers were published in the medical literature on the use of subcutaneous injections, often of morphia to treat various conditions. Anstie (1868) discussed his 10 years' experience of the subcutaneous administration of medicines and stated that there was absolutely no danger with this method of administration provided one was aware of the increased potency of drugs administered in this way, and that substances that were neither too acid or alkaline should be used. He did concede that he had one case of abscess among the hundreds of injections given, but this he attributed to the injection of chloroform 'an agent entirely unfit to be used in this way, as I am now aware'. Anstie described a wide variety of substances that may be used and a wide range of illnesses to be treated in this way.

Allbutt (1869) discussed the use of morphia via injection in the treatment of heart disease. He wrote, 'So strongly am I convinced of its importance that I feel I ought not to delay the publication of my observations' and 'in the latter stages of heart disease I believe we have in the morphia syringe an invaluable ally'. Anderson (1875) described the treatment of asthma by use of subcutaneous injection of morphia; he described his success with these methods and ventured that 'the plan is so simple and so obvious, that I cannot but think that it must have occurred to others beside myself'.

Crombie (1873) described a technique of coating silk thread with morphia, puncturing the skin with a needle and then drawing the impregnated thread under the skin. He advocated this as he thought that the syringe was too expensive and too delicate for the poor, and they should not be disadvantaged in the use of morphia in treatment.

Kane (1880) in his survey of the use and problems of injections of morphia said in the preface of his work that 'A physician of the present day without a hypodermic syringe in his pocket or close at hand, would be looked upon as would a physician fifty years ago, did he not own and use a lancet'. He went on to state that 'no therapeutic discovery has been so great a blessing and so great a curse to mankind as the hypodermic injection of morphia'.

Concern over the rise of hypodermic injections of morphia was first raised by Allbutt (1870), who complained that patients were 'now injecting themselves daily or more than daily during long periods of time, for neuralgias, which are as far from cured as they were at the outset'. Levinstein (1878) described the problems of morphine addiction and ascribed part of the problem to allowing the patient to have access to the syringe and thus inject at will. He proposed that it would need an edict from the Prussian Government to halt the practice of allowing syringes to be used other than by physicians.

Needles were also used for non-medical purposes, which led, besides the administration of drugs, to some bizarre situations. The *British Medical Journal* (Anon., 1898) cites 'the custom of scenting the breath and body by the use of hypodermic injections of scent injected under the skin'. Establishments were opened solely for this purpose, and the author expressed the hope that 'the apparatus is aseptic or at all events that it is occasionally washed for if this precaution is neglected there is likely to be a pretty general dissemination of disease'.

The debate on the 'localisation of effect'

A debate took place in the medical literature of the time between Charles Hunter and Alexander Wood (Howard-Jones, 1947) as to the localisation of effect for subcutaneous injection of opiates for the relief of local pain. Hunter showed that injections had a systemic action, meaning the drug had effects on the whole body. Wood, who advocated local action, disputed this position. This debate continued from 1858 when Hunter first questioned Wood's assertion regarding the localisation of effect until as late as 1895 when there was still evidence being proposed in favour of local action.

According to Howard-Jones (1947), the use of cocaine as a local anaesthetic was exploited by Koller in 1884; Wood and his adherents thought that they had already stumbled upon the possibilities of local anaesthesia. As Howard-Jones (1947) says of local anaesthesia, the only thing lacking before Koller was an agent that really worked! He concluded that 'The modern reader is tempted at first to place some reliance upon the reports of therapeutic results achieved with morphine in various "neuralgic" conditions. But when he reads of identical results with other drugs which could not possibly have effected the results attributed to them, and even with pure water, his confidence is shaken.'

Astonishing claims were once made for injecting water as a therapeutic procedure. Howard-Jones (1947) describes Lafitte (1875) conceding 'that there may be a psychological effect in some patients, but he inclines more to the view that the injected water exerts a physical action upon the cutaneous nerve-endings, and he concludes by suggesting that water should replace morphine by injection'.

One of several responses to Lafitte's paper in the form of a published letter to the *British Medical Journal*, by people who had previously practised water injections, was from Lelut (1875), who told of a careless servant mixing-up bottles of morphine and water for an injection of a patient with sciatica. Hence Lelut injected water and the patient was cured. A letter from Dr Burney Yeo (1875) claimed that a Dr G.W. Moore had substituted water for morphine and atropine injections, with results that were 'entirely successful'. Howard-Jones (1947) reported that many other papers on the therapeutic value of water were published in the following years. There were other peculiar substances injected, which were less likely to be harmless from today's perspective: in his 1845 treatment, Rynd dissolved the morphia in creosote and, in Wood's case, one of his first hypodermic injections of 1853 was sherry! Shortly afterwards, Wood (1858) described his reason for doing so: 'I thought it would not irritate and smart so much as alcohol, and it would not rust the instrument as a water solution of opium would do'.

The role of intravenous injection

Subcutaneous injection has now generally been superseded by intravenous and intramus-cular injections. However, the early experiments by Wren were intravenous, and Macht (1916) in his review mentioned a book published in 1665 in which Escholtz described intravenous injections, including three patients treated by him. Macht also refers to a number of papers describing intravenous injecting in the eighteenth and nineteenth centuries, including the first warning of the danger of introducing large quantities of air into the vein, and attempts to treat tetanus and hydrophobia by intravenous injection. Macht concluded, 'However useful intravenous medication may be in special cases, its field of application is certainly more limited than that of hypodermic injection'.

Kane (1880) discussed the possibility of accidental entrance of the needle into a vein, describing a number of cases where this may have happened and the symptoms that followed. This is what we would now describe as the 'rush' but were then uncomfortable feelings for the unfortunate patients. It is clear from Kane's discussion that intravenous injection was not considered usual by American doctors in the nineteenth century.

The practice of intravenous injection by drug users is an interesting phenomenon. Before the 1920s this practice was unknown despite the knowledge among medical practitioners. It may be that the practice appeared simultaneously in Egypt and America. Biggam (1929), who first described the technique among a group of Cairo heroin addicts, suggested that this may have been an accidental discovery which spread among heroin users.

O'Donnell and Jones (1968) stated that in the United States, it took less than 20 years for the diffusion of the intravenous route. Few addicts used the intravenous route before 1925, then by 1935 it had become quite frequent, used by almost 50% of addicts, and by 1945 it had become the preferred route of administration. This raises the question of how this diffusion occurred.

O'Donnell and Jones (1968) suggested that several factors added to the rapid spread of intravenous injecting. Before 1925, eating, sniffing and smoking were the most common ways of administration in addicts who used drugs for pleasure. But 'hypodermic use was most frequent among addicts who had started drug use in the context of medical treatment'. Those who were 'consciously using drugs for pleasure would be the most likely to note and to adopt a more pleasurable technique'.

Interviews by O'Donnell and Jones (1968) and Courtwright et al. (1989) confirm the hypothesis that intravenous use started with 'skin poppers' accidentally hitting veins. However, in the early twentieth century addicts were taking doses that were enormous by today's standards and mostly had overdose experiences when they accidentally hit a vein. When narcotics started to become more difficult to obtain and the doses became smaller, communication in the drug subculture facilitated the diffusion of the intravenous technique. The fact that injecting is more economical and the enjoyable rapid effect, or 'rush', contributed to the quick diffusion. This could, as O'Donnell and Jones (1968) suggest, be explained by Wikler's (1965) conditioning theory: the effects of a pleasurable intravenous administration of a drug were more reinforcing than the earlier routes of administration. There is also a suggestion that the route may have been popularised following the treatment of syphilis in the early years of the century by using intravenous injections of salversan (J. Derricott, personal communication).

Twentieth century injecting

In a biography of Lady Diana Cooper (Ziegler, 1981), it was revealed that she used morphia by injection intermittently in 1915 as a diversion. Her future husband, Duff Cooper commented that, 'I hope she won't become a morphineuse, it would spoil her looks'. The 'morphineuse', i.e. the woman, often of the middle or upper class, was a feature of late nineteenth- and early twentieth-century Europe, particularly in Paris. The subject of the novel *Felix* (Hichens, 1903) was a morphineuse and included the description of the downfall of a society woman through injections of morphine. André Gide was told by a Swiss journalist during a visit to Zurich in 1927 (Davenport-Hines, 2001) that students began to inject themselves in their final years of grammar school when aged 16 or 17. The journalist knew someone whom the professor had caught using a syringe in a final examination. The student acknowledged that he had got the habit in class and commented, 'Do you think anyone could endure the dullness of X's teaching without shooting up?'

Howard and Borges (1971) described needle sharing in San Francisco, indicating that the practice of injecting was widespread among the amphetamine users of California; biographical works of the 1960s and 1970s certainly include injecting as a route of drug administration.

In Britain, the number of drug addicts in the 1960s was known to be tiny compared to the present day, the number of injecting drug users having increased massively since 1980. Syringes used nowadays are almost universally disposable and made of plastic, and since the late 1980s have been available free from needle and syringe exchanges. This is not true in some countries where needle and syringe exchange is still proscribed or unavailable for other reasons.

Cobb (2003) attributes the invention of the disposable plastic syringe to Colin Murdoch, a New Zealand pharmacist, who obtained a patent for it in 1956, but was not supported by the New Zealand Department of Health who refused to buy his invention. Cobb reports that an American inventor, Phil Brooks, received a patent for a disposable syringe in 1974.

The future of injecting

The disposable plastic syringe has achieved dramatic success since its introduction. However, reuse and sharing of syringes, especially in places like prisons where still no needle-exchange facilities are provided, or in situations where drug injectors have no alternative but to reuse or share a syringe, have given rise to attempts to introduce one-shot or autodestruct syringes. One example of a single-use syringe is given by Mahurkar (2001), who introduced the 'smart syringe' to minimise needle-stick injuries. The needle is automatically retracted into the plunger after use, and all components are interlocked, which leads to a 100% reduction in needle stick injuries.

However, the advent of difficult-to-reuse syringes has been criticised by Caulkins *et al.* (1998) who developed a mathematical model which investigated whether these syringes reduced the spread of HIV from which they concluded that introducing a certain number of difficult-to-reuse syringes and simultaneously reducing the consumption of regular syringes by the same number will increase, not decrease, the proportion of infectious injections. As difficult-to-reuse syringes are more expensive than regular syringes, they suggested that there is little justification in substituting them for regular syringes.

A common problem for injectors after a prolonged history of injecting is the difficulty of finding veins. Dobson (1998) describes the introduction of a 'smart needle', which can find a vein every time, and which has been tested by Mansfield and colleagues at Texas University. The Doppler effect is harnessed to pick up changes in sound frequency caused by blood flowing through a vein. The Doppler apparatus is contained in the cavity at the top of a standard 18-gauge needle, and a continuous auditory feedback allows users to find a vein quickly. Its main use so far has been to allow catheters to be inserted easily and with little preparation.

Other techniques have been developed to help those patients who require repeated injections for health reasons. Patients with diabetes, for example, need to administer insulin to keep their blood sugar levels in balance, and have traditionally used self-administered injections, although sub-cutaneously rather than intravenously, but a number of problems may occur, such as needle phobia. In order to overcome these barriers, new methods of needle-free drug administration have been invented in recent years. The homepage of the National Institute of General Medical Sciences (2002) describes medicated skin patches, bioerodible implants, and patient-activated implants, which can be regulated with an ultrasound pulser. Research is also cited concerning the development of pill-pumps. Here the pill is coated with a water-absorbing membrane, which has a tiny laser-drilled hole through which water seeps and dissolves the gradually leaking medicine during digestion. The thickness of the pill's coat regulates the rate of drug release. These new ways of drug administration seem to be of less use to illicit drug users, as they are expensive and require access to these new technologies. The rush, which is a desired part of the drug experience, is absent when the drug is released gradually.

Other alternatives are the so-called jet injectors. Mendosa (1998) describes the advantages and disadvantages of these innovations in the administration of insulin to people with diabetes. Jet injectors release a tiny stream of a drug forced through the skin under high pressure, penetrating the skin through an opening much smaller than the size of a conventional needle. The active substance then spreads through the tissue at the injection site. Depending on the pressure applied and the model of injector used, injections can be intramuscular, subcutaneous or intradermal. Jet injectors are now much less expensive, making them viable for more widespread use. There are a variety of different models competing in a rapidly growing market. Examples of companies selling them can be viewed in a regularly updated website hosted by Mendosa (2003). Models serving different users have been introduced, such as low pressure models for children and high pressure models for people with thicker skin, to overcome bruising and to ensure the right depth of penetration. There are also gas-pressured models, which have advantages over spring-controlled models containing a click-counting dosage wheel, being easier to use for physically weaker and sight-impaired people. There are powder injectors, which have the finely powdered particles of the drug travelling at high velocity, induced by a gas cartridge, which delivers the drug through the skin at the dose required. Drug addicts wanting to make use of this system would not currently have access to the technology to fill the special capsules. However, there are alternative jet injectors which can be loaded from conventional medication vials containing liquid medication, and so open possibilities for injectors wanting a change in the way they administer their drug of choice.

Most of the new devices and methods discussed above may be suitable for delivering pharmaceutical drugs, but are probably decades away from the street injector or the budget of needle and syringe exchanges.

References

Allbutt, T.C. (1869) On the hypodermic use of morphia in diseases of the heart and great vessels, *Practitioner*, **3**, 342–346.

Allbutt, T.C. (1870) On the abuse of hypodermic injections of morphia, *Practitioner*, **5**, 327–331.

Anderson, J.K. (1875) On the treatment of spasmodic asthma by the subcutaneous injection of morphia, *Practitioner*, **15**, 321–322.

Anonymous (1898) Editorial. *British Medical Journal*, **ii**, 827.

Anstie, F. (1868) The hypodermic injection of remedies, *Practitioner*, **1**, 32–41.

Biggam, A.G. (1929) Malignant malaria associated with the administration of heroin intravenously. *Transactions of the Society of Tropical Medicine and Hygiene*, **23**, 147–153.

Bugnicourt, A. (2003) http://alain.bugnicourt.free.fr/cyberbiologie/seringue/seringue.html

Caulkins, J.P., Kaplan, E.H., Lurie, P., O'Connor, T. & Ahn, S.H. (1998) Can difficult-to-reuse syringes reduce the spread of HIV among injection drug users? *Interfaces*, **28**(3), 23–33.

Cobb, D. (2003) The hypodermic needle, commonly known as 'the syringe!' (http://www.irmc.org/news/news22503.html).

Courtwright, D., Joseph, H. & Des Jarlais, D. (1989) *Addicts who Survived*. Knoxville: University of Tennessee Press.

Crombie, J.M. (1873) A simple method for the subcutaneous application of morphia, *British Medical Journal*, 16 August, 194.

Davenport-Hines, R. (2001) *The Pursuit of Oblivion, A Global History of Narcotics 1500–2000*. London: Weidenfeld and Nicholson.

Derricott, J., Preston, A. & Hunt, N. (1999) *The Safer Injecting Briefing*. Liverpool: HIT.

Dobson, R. (1998) Smart needle hones in on veins to make injections painless. *Sunday Times*, 6th December.

Hichens, R. (1903) *Felix*, New York: Frederick A. Stokes.

Howard-Jones, N. (1947) A critical study of the origins and early development of hypodermic medication, *Journal of the History of Medicine and Allied Sciences*, **2**(2), 201–249.

Howard, J. & Borges, P. (1971) Needle sharing in the Haight: some social and psychological functions, *Journal of Psychedelic Drugs*, **4**(1), 71–80.

Hunter, C. (1858) On narcotic injections in neuralgia. *Medical Times and Gazette*, **2**, 408–409.

Kane, H.H. (1880) *The Hypodermic Injection of Morphia*. New York: Chas. Bermingham.

Lafargue, G.V. (1836) Notes sur les effets de quelques médicaments introduits sous l'épidermie. *Comptes Rendus Hebdomadaires des Séances de l'Académie des Sciences Paris*, **2**, 397–398, 434.

Lafargue, G.V. (1861) Inoculation hypodermique par enchevillement des substances actives telles que le sulfate de morphine, le sulfate de strychnine, dans le traitement des névralgies, des paralysies partielles. . ., *Bulletin de Générale Thérapie, Médecine et Chirurgie*, **60**, 20–26, 150–159.

Lafitte, L. (1875) Des injections sous-cutanées d'eau distilée ou d'eau pure; leur bons éffets thérapeutiques. *L'Union Médicale*, **20**, 445–48, 458–61.

Lelut, E. (1875) Les injections sous-cutanées d'eau distillée ou d'eau pure. *L'Union Médicale*, **20**, 513.

Levinstein, E. (1878) *The Morbid Craving for Morphia*. London: Smith, Elder and Co.

Macht, D.I. (1916) The history of intravenous and subcutaneous administration of drugs, *Journal of the American Medical Association*, **56**(12), 856–860.

Mahurkar, S.D. (2001) (http://www.smartsyringe.com).

Mendosa, R. (1998) The jet injector paradox. *Diabetes Wellness Letter*, February, pp. 1–3.

Mendosa, R. (2003) Diabetes monitor: on-line diabetes resources: company web sites (http://www.diabetesmonitor.com/company.htm).

Morris, R. & Kendrick, J. (1807) *The Edinburgh Medical and Surgical Dictionary*. Edinburgh: Bell and Bradfute; Mundell, Doyle and Stevenson.

National Institute of General Medical Sciences (2002) (http://www.nigms.nih.gov/news/science_ed/medbydes.html).

O'Donnell, J.A. & Jones, J.P. (1968) Diffusion of the intravenous technique among narcotic addicts in the US. *Journal of Health and Social Behaviour*, **9**, 120–130.

Pepys, S. (1664) *The Diary of Samuel Pepys*, Vol. 5, 1664 (eds R. Latham & W. Matthews) London: Harper Collins (published 2000).

Rynd, F. (1845) *Dublin Medical Press*, **13**, 167–168.

Rynd, F. (1861) Description of an instrument for the subcutaneous introduction of fluids in affections of the nerves. *Dublin Quarterly Journal of Medical Science*, **32**, 13.

Wikler, A. (1965) Conditioning factors in opiate addiction and relapse. In D.M. Wilner & G.G. Kassebaum (eds): *Narcotics*, pp. 85–100. New York: McGraw-Hill.

Wood, A. (1855) A new method of treating neuralgia by the direct application of opiates to the painful points. *Edinburgh Med. Surg., Journal*, **82**, 265–281.

Wood, A. (1858) Treatment of neuralgic pains by narcotic injections. *British Medical Journal*, **1858**, 721–723.

Wren, C. (1665) An account of the rise and attempts, of a way to conveigh liquors immediately to the mass of blood, *Philosophical Transactions of the Royal Society*, **1**, 128–130.

Yeo, T.B. (1875) *British Medical Journal*, **2**, 702.

Ziegler, P. (1981) *Diana Cooper*, London: Hamish Hamilton.

Chapter 2

The Eye of the Needle: an Ethno-Epidemiological Analysis of Injecting Drug Use

Jean-Paul Grund

Introduction

The global diffusion of injecting drug use

In Chapter 1, Pates and Wichter trace the birth and development of the needle and syringe, and the first medical and recreational experiences with this technical innovation – famous and infamous at once, because of its association with both the global eradication and diffusion of life-threatening infectious diseases. Recreational or non-medical drug injecting remained a primarily Western phenomenon until late into the twentieth century. But globalisation and global drug prohibition have resulted in the worldwide diffusion of drug injection, most strikingly into drug production areas and adjacent sub-regions, where traditionally milder preparations of the same alkaloids (or their precursors) were being consumed through less hazardous modes of administration.

In 1992, 80 countries reported injecting drug use to the World Health Organization (WHO) (Anon., 2002; Stimson & Choopanya, 1998); in 1995, this number had increased to 121 (Stimson & Choopanya, 1998) and by 1999 to 134 (Anon., 2002). In 2003, 136 countries reported injecting drug use (WHO, 2004). Thus, over a period of 11 years, WHO has witnessed a 70% increase in the number of countries reporting drug injecting.

As Stimson and Choopanya (1998) note, these reports do not contain information on the actual scale and nature of this largely underground activity. There may be some countries with isolated cases, but studies conducted in countries reporting drug injecting for the first time suggest that these reports reflect recently emerged changes in drug use patterns, and not previous under-reporting. In the 1990s drug injecting diffused rapidly in many countries, in Asia and the former Soviet Union in particular, and it has also taken a strong foothold in South America (Stimson *et al.*, 1998).

Injecting vs other routes of administration: a comparison of effects

Injecting is only one of several possible routes of self-administration for heroin and many other drugs, albeit the most efficient one. Despite the global increase in injecting, only a minority of opiate and other powder drug users employ the intravenous route. There are three ways one can inject a drug: subcutaneously, intramuscularly and intravenously. Most 'powder drug' injectors (the term 'powder drug' – American drug slang – refers to drugs that can potentially be injected, in particular heroin and other opioids, the amphetamines and cocaine) prefer intravenous injecting (mainlining), the most direct way of ingesting any drug into the body, whereas, for example steroid users such as body builders favour intramuscular injection.

Opiates, amphetamines and cocaine can be taken into the body via its various mucous membranes, for example those under the tongue, in the nose (sniffing), stomach and intestines (swallowing), rectum (suppositories, enemas) and on the (female) genitals. Amphetamines are mostly sniffed or swallowed, while smoking methamphetamine ('ice') has recently gained popularity in the US and elsewhere. Many amphetamine users in Australia and Northern Europe inject the drug. Sniffing is the most common mode in cocaine use. Smokable cocaine (base) or crack was deemed of epidemic proportions in the US in the 1990s and continues to be part of the drug menu of many heavy drug users in South America, the US and Western Europe. Heroin is mostly inhaled ('chasing the dragon') in many Asian countries and The Netherlands, while many 'new' users in the US take the drug intranasally. In their respective production areas, opium is traditionally smoked and ingested as part of folk medicine, while coca leaves are chewed and used in folk preparations (from tea to toothpaste).

Beyond the initial impact effect or 'rush', all methods produce similar states of intoxication. But administration routes differ in several ways. First, the speed with which a drug's effects become noticeable varies by the mode of administration: oral ingestion is characterised by gradual onset (anywhere between 15 and 60 minutes); applied intranasally, rectally or under the tongue, a dose will take noticeable effect after 5 to 10 minutes; while smoking, vapour inhalation (chasing and basing) and injecting produce their effects within seconds (Strang & Wells, 1988). Second, there are marked differences in overall bioavailability, with injecting giving clearly the most 'bang for the buck'. When chasing, the actual absorption of heroin is much lower and varies by the drug's chemical form (hydrochloride or base) of the heroin, processing impurities, diluents, inhalation technique and environment (Huizer, 1987; Mo & Way, 1966). Rectal insertion, recently promoted in Britain as a harm reduction alternative to injecting, apparently results in relatively greater and faster absorption than intranasal application, while oral administration is hampered by stomach contents (see Chapter 10).

Health consequences of powder drug use vary with route of administration; in that respect an important matter is that the various routes of administration have different overdose potential. For a comparison of the health consequences of injecting and chasing see, for example, Grund (1993a).

Overdose potential is a function of the total amount of drugs ingested over a given time period and individual tolerance for the ingested substance. Overdose does not depend entirely on the speed of onset, as a lethal dose can be absorbed over an extended period or built up in more than one dose (Garriot & Sturner, 1973). Although injecting carries the greatest risk for fatal overdose, anal insertion, oral ingestion and sniffing probably compete for second place, because, just as when injecting, a certain dose is entered into the body in one go and then gradually but definitely crosses the mucous membranes, even after the consumer goes into a 'nod'. In contrast, when chasing or smoking, the drug is administered in small incremental doses, which are felt instantly. Thus, chasers reach their desired high by sequentially administering small quantities of the drug. In theory this could add up to a lethal dose, but in practice the chance of overdose is small due to the steady and controlled titration inherent to this mode. Chasers may smoke themselves into a light state of unawareness, a nod, but as illustrated by the following statement of a Dutch chaser, this gradual build-up normally prevents fatalities:

When you nod, you nod. And you can't add on to that level anymore.

Theoretically, smoking heroin from a 'bong' (a chambered pipe, in which fumes are collected before being ingested in one inhalation) could increase the risk of overdose significantly, but this method is not prevalent.

Injecting drug use and the spread of infectious diseases

Injecting drug users (IDUs) have always been at risk of exposure to a wide range of blood borne viruses (BBVs) (Selwyn, 1993). Syringe-mediated malaria epidemics among IDU populations in non-tropical areas were reported as early as 1920 in Cairo, Egypt, and the 1930s in New York, while more recently Brazil witnessed the re-emergence of malaria among people who injected drugs in areas where the disease had become rare (Donoghoe & Wodak, 1998). The first needle/syringe programmes (NSPs) in The Netherlands were in response to outbreaks of hepatitis B virus (HBV) infection in the late 1970s.

Of the 80 countries reporting injecting drug use in 1992, 65% reported HIV infection associated with injection drug use (Anon., 2002). By 1999, 85% of 134 countries reported HIV infection in IDUs (Anon., 2002). According to the most recent data on the World Health Organization website, only 68% of 136 countries reporting injecting drug use also reported HIV infection (WHO, 2004). The decrease between 2004 and 1999 is probably not an actual reduction and may be explained by inconsistencies in data collection.

The secretariat of the UN Reference Group on HIV/AIDS Prevention and Care Among IDU in Developing and Transitional Countries reports a systematic review of data pertaining to 130 countries with documented cases of drug injecting, of which 78 countries (60%) report HIV; data on 119 countries could not be obtained (Aceijas *et al.*,

2004). The secretariat has presented its data with caution but views them as an improved baseline measure. Based on the available data, at the end of 2003 there were an estimated total of 13.2 million IDUs worldwide (0.3% of the estimated 4 billion adult population). The majority of those (10.3 million, 78%) live in developing and transitional countries (Aceijas et al., 2004). In the absence of appropriate and sufficient prevention measures, which is still the case in most developing and transitional countries, these populations are at risk of large-scale generalised HIV epidemics in the next 10 to 20 years, kindled by presently uncontrolled epidemics among IDUs (UNAIDS, 2004).

Injecting drug use and public health

Before the potential for widespread uncontrolled HIV epidemics among IDUs was recognised, drug injecting was a fringe issue in global public health policy making. In most countries, drug users were (and unfortunately remain) almost entirely dealt with by repressive, mandatory and otherwise intrusive policies that are fundamentally at odds with basic human rights, in particular the rights to health and privacy, and the protection against cruel, inhuman or degrading treatment or punishment, as defined in the Universal Declaration of Human Rights (United Nations, 1948; UNHCR/UNAIDS, 1998).

Taking the international scientific literature and UN documents as examples, the emergence and rapid spread of HIV among communities of drug injectors around the world has changed the way that the self-injection of psychoactive drugs for non-medical purposes is considered by societies. From a fringe issue, non-medical drug injecting has become a major (international) public health focus. Unfortunately, a quarter century into the HIV epidemic, only in a minority of countries has this increased attention and research resulted in sufficient action to avert the spread of HIV among drug injectors. Most prevention efforts have focused on what David Moore has called 'technologies of the body', behavioural strategies aiming to reduce individual exposure risks, while largely ignoring the 'social, cultural and economic production and reproduction' of vulnerability (Moore, 2004).

Furthermore, the increased attention of policy makers to drug injecting has already started fading in many places. What is more, the increased knowledge resulting from all the attention for HIV among IDUs has not helped to prevent the same thing happening all over again across the globe. As is documented in Chapter 7, the HIV epidemic among drug injectors has long overshadowed the even more rapid spread of another blood borne pathogen, the hepatitis C virus (also see Calafat & Montse, 2004; Craine et al., 2004; Davis & Rhodes, 2004; Edlin, 2004; Long et al., 2004; Loughlin et al., 2004; Macalino et al., 2004; Rahbar et al., 2004; Wood et al., 2004). As yet, there has not been an example of an IDU-driven HIV epidemic evolving into a large-scale generalised epidemic to focus the attention of policy makers on the deplorable health and human rights situation of the large numbers of people who inject drugs, and the social, economic and (international) legislative determinants of these problems. Unfortunately, in countries such as Ukraine and several Asian countries, such a transition may well be underway, but weaknesses in national surveillance systems make it extremely hard to measure this process accurately. For example, cases of sexual transmission among the officially registered HIV cases in Ukraine have increased, while transmission among IDUs apparently decreased (UNAIDS/WHO, 2003). However, a secondary analysis of the Ukrainian case registration and surveillance data concluded that most of this shift resulted from changes in testing patterns and testing saturation among IDUs. In two of the most affected oblasts (Donetsk and Odessa) about three-quarters of established cases of sexual transmission concerned infections from IDUs and their sexual partners (Grund et al., 2003; UNAIDS, 2004).

Limitations of epidemiology

Epidemiologists spend much time on trying to track epidemics. Epidemiology provides us with valuable information on the course and, in particular, the *agents* of the spread of infectious diseases. But, despite their relevance to public health monitoring and planning, epidemiological data tell us little about the behaviours and the real-life contextual correlates that are at their core.

For example, traditional epidemiology has not kept pace with the consequences of rapidly advancing globalisation during the past 30 years, which has become a powerful social and economic force. Globalisation and, in particular, the resulting increase in intercontinental mobility, has had a tremendous impact on the spread of infectious diseases. Increased mobility has resulted in the spread of previously more-or-less localised BBVs and has also contributed significantly to the global diffusion of drug injecting. But beyond merely contributing to the expansion of both of these public health threats, globalisation has truly resulted in what Rodrick Wallace has called a 'synergy of plagues' (Wallace, 1988) by bringing stow-away viral travellers into contact with a new, faster vector of transmission: the intravenous needle and syringe. HIV is a textbook example.

In essence, epidemics are social processes. Despite their differences, HIV, tuberculosis or hepatitis C all follow this rule. In her noteworthy paper on the relationship between ethnography and epidemiology, Lisa Maher (2002) writes that, 'the politically loaded categories of epidemiological risk groups have essentialized entire populations, obscured the complex realities of risk practices and left little room for understanding how social conditions shape individual lives.' She refers to the late Jonathan Mann who noted that, 'applying classical epidemiological methods to HIV/AIDS ensures (pre-determines) that "risk" will be defined in terms of individual determinants and individual behavior' (Mann, 1996). In the epidemiology of HIV and drug injecting this has resulted in a rather narrow focus in which the physical instruments of transmission (the syringe and needle) have been fetishised (Grund et al., 1992), at the expense of understanding the social and cultural settings in which these instruments are used.

Epidemiological data may alert us to a shift in vulnerability underlying these numbers, 'but they cannot tell us what is happening here or why. Even where the risk or patterning of a disease is known and quantifiable, the logic of its distribution or the reasons behind shifts and increases are not always apparent' (Maher, 2002). Thus, epidemiology has done remarkably poorly in including the other two cornerstones of the 'epidemiological Triad', *host* and *environment*, into its analysis of disease spread.

While ethnography is not designed to quantify shifts in the burden of disease, it is particularly useful for identifying the human interactions that result in disease transmission. Ethnographic research offers compelling explanations of epidemiological phenomena by positioning the *agent* (e.g. HIV) and *vector* of spread (e.g. collective use of injecting equipment) in a dynamic interaction with the *host* (the IDU) and the risk *environment* (see, for example, Rhodes, 2002), the social networks of IDUs and the larger social structures that shape these, including underdevelopment, poverty, conflict, racism, drug legislation and its enforcement. As Maher (2002) writes, 'Ethnographic research has the capacity to "unpack" the vulnerabilities flagged by epidemiological data, to identify the dynamic contexts of belief and action and the role of cultural disjunctions and local/ global linkages in determining the health of populations.'

Participant observation of drug injecting

When preparing this chapter, literature searches for participant observation and other descriptive studies of drug injecting behaviours found very few first-hand accounts. Therefore, much of what follows is based on my own ethnographic research and that of a few other researchers who have directly observed people inject recreational drugs.

Between 1985 and 1992, I observed several hundred people inject drugs in Rotterdam, The Netherlands, first as an outreach worker running a peer-based needle exchange programme and then as part of fieldwork of an ethnographic study of the drug use patterns of heavy heroin and cocaine users. A key part of this study concerned participant observation of and informal interviews about actual drug using sessions (Grund, 1993b). In 1990 and 1991, I observed people in a shooting gallery in New Haven, Connecticut, and on the streets of the Bronx, New York, when working with the then underground needle exchange programme of Act Up. From 1993 to 1995, I conducted fieldwork for a National Institute on Drug Abuse (NIDA) funded study of a peer-driven HIV prevention intervention among IDUs in Connecticut. Furthermore, over the years I have met quite a large number of educated, more privileged people who inject drugs, with whom I have frequently engaged in discussions on drug injecting patterns, associated risk behaviour and their determinants.

Since 1995, I have been privileged to visit a large number of countries that have recently emerged following the dissolution of the 'Soviet Bloc'. My work in these countries was to support the implementation of harm reduction approaches towards the (in some sub-regions rapidly) emerging twin epidemics of drug use and HIV. During the daytime I talked with politicians, health and law enforcement policy makers, psychiatrists, drug specialists, infectious disease specialists, non-governmental organisation (NGO) representatives and church officials about drugs, HIV, harm reduction and effective drug treatment approaches.

In the evenings and sometimes during the night I hung out and talked with drug users. Whenever possible, I observed and discussed their drug preparation and use patterns. Contacts were mostly made through the local Soros Foundations and sometimes at needle exchange programmes, of which there were only a handful: too few to stop the epidemic, despite the good intentions.

Thus, in early 1995 I was sitting in a car on a hill in Skopje, Macedonia, with the presidential villa just 200 metres up the road. Behind the wheel was a 19 year old sleek Macedonian clubber who, when we met, kept his cravings for smoking heroin under control with very expensive Naltrexone®. His father was an important public figure, whom I had met through the local Soros foundation. Naltrexone® was apparently not an option for his two friends in the back seat, Albanian Macedonians, because as soon as the car stopped they pulled out half a gram of heroin and showed me the various ways they smoked their drug, chasing it from tinfoil and in joints.

Whenever I got the chance, I tried to engage in such 'quick and dirty' fieldwork during my travels through Central and Eastern Europe. I observed and talked with drug users about their drug use in Macedonia, Slovenia, Croatia, the Czech and Slovak republics, Poland, Russia, Ukraine, Moldova, Kazakhstan and the three Baltic countries. Where I could not undertake fieldwork myself, I urged doctors and outreach workers to go out into the field to document drug preparation and injecting patterns. This resulted in viewing many hours of video of mostly young people preparing and injecting drugs. In 1999, I conducted weeklong site visits to needle exchange programmes in five Russian cities, as part of an evaluation study of needle exchange programmes. In four of them I minutely documented the self-preparation of injectable opiates and stimulants, taking photographs and writing detailed field notes.

Descriptive ethnography of drug injecting

Globally, a significant minority of non-medical drug users prefer to inject their drugs. They do so for various reasons, which I will discuss further below. First, we will take an ethnographic tour of the mechanics of the injecting ritual (Agar, 1977; Grund, 1993b).

Opiate injection

Heroin

> The man starts to prepare a shot. He puts his spoon on the table and throws in a knife tip of brown heroin. He adds some lemon juice and with his syringe he gets some water, which he carefully squirts in the spoon, around the heroin powder just under the edge of the spoon. He heats the spoon and when the stuff has dissolved he stirs and draws the solution in the syringe through a piece of cotton. After checking the syringe for air bubbles, he puts his syringe on the table. Then he takes his belt and puts it

around his left arm. Making a fist he pumps up his veins. He looks carefully at his arm and then sticks in the needle. When he pulls the piston back, blood immediately runs into the syringe. He then pushes the piston about halfway home. Then he draws up some blood and pushes the mixture into his vein again. He moves the syringe a little, draws ± 1.5 cc blood and pushes it in once more. All the time his hand is a fist. Then he unties the belt, pulls the needle out, puts it down and waits about two minutes, concentrating on the rush.

Grund (1993b)

This extract from my field notes, recorded at the end of the 1980s in Rotterdam, The Netherlands, provides us with a good impression of the intravenous self-administration of heroin. The entire behavioural sequence did not take more than a few minutes. It can be even quicker, as I witnessed while doing field research in New London, Connecticut, in 1993–1994. I had just picked up Gregg (not his actual name), a local drug injector, who was interested in the study and helped me with the fieldwork which had just commenced. We were driving to the projects on the edge of town, for me not yet familiar territory. Gregg pointed me to a quiet, somewhat bushy side street. Gregg had asked me before whether it was okay to get straight, but it was not quite clear to me where and when he intended to do so. As soon as the car halted, Gregg did his thing:

Gregg pulls out a sealed 1 ml B&D Insulin from the seam of his jacket. In his other hand he has a (typical east coast) glassine one-unit heroin bag, stamped with the dome of the White House and the brand name *President*. After traveling up the I-95, *President* sells for $20 a bag in New London. That is a 100% markup compared to the streets of New York, from where this *Brand* originates. But, according to Gregg, the dope currently around is of excellent quality, that is, if you know the right places and people. As if to make a case in point, Gregg tears open the glassine and carefully empties it in the small plastic cap that protects the back of the plunger of the syringe. He squirts in a few units of water, which he had drawn from a tiny bottle (received from the intervention I was studying). Then he pulls the plunger from the syringe and uses it to stir the heroin into solution, which happens instantly. He reinserts the plunger, puts a little cotton ball in the cap and pulls the liquid into the syringe. After checking for air, Gregg simply rolls up his left sleeve, makes a fist and injects in his armpit. As soon as the blood registers, he pushes the heroin into his vein and pulls out, covering the injection site with an alcohol pad, which I did not see him use pre-injection. Immediately, he rinses the needle and puts it back in the seam of his pocket. The empty bag is tossed out of the window. Within a minute after halting the car, Gregg is ready for fieldwork.

J.-P. Grund, unpublished field note, New London, CT (1994)

Kompot and cheornaya (black)
The situation I observed across Eastern Europe and Central Asia seemed quite different from what I had witnessed elsewhere. My observations suggested that young people

throughout the former Soviet Union (FSU) engaged in very similar collective drug preparation and injecting patterns, which seemed engineered for the transmission of HIV and other BBVs. Outreach workers and doctors working in the initial harm reduction programmes in the region reported that these were not isolated cases, but part of a widespread practice among youth in most cities and increasingly in rural areas.

While the use of (imported) heroin has increased rapidly in many cities, illicit drug use patterns in this region are characterised by a tradition of kitchen production of drugs. At the end of the 1970s, chemical students in Gdansk, Poland, boiled down the chemical process to prepare heroin to its basics: they 'cooked' the dried poppy heads into an injectable concoction of opium alkaloids, using readily available household and industrial chemicals. This process came to be known by the name 'kompot' and diffused rapidly across Poland. In the 1980s, Poland experienced a rapidly escalating HIV epidemic among kompot injectors. In the early 1980s a simplified version of the process, which can be conducted on an ordinary kitchen stove, spread through the FSU under names, such as 'cheornaya' and 'shirka'.

The tradition of self-production is rooted in two related and older traditions. First, the poppy flower has been prepared for culinary, (self-) medicinal and, presumably, recreational purposes, throughout the region since time immemorial. Second, the regional tradition of 'zamogon' (moonshine) seems to have provided a model for the self-preparation of a number of psychoactive substances other than alcohol. Thus, for many years, drug users throughout the region used relatively simple 'kitchen chemistry' to produce potent injectable opiates and amphetamines. In the former Czechoslovakia, Russia, Ukraine and other FSU countries, drug injectors also cooked up ephedrine-based medications into injectable methamphetamine ('piko', 'vint') and methcathinone ('jeff'), both powerful psychostimulants. The following field note documents the self-production of cheornaya:

Belii starts cooking 7 bags of opium in the living room. He scrapes the plastic bags and puts the gum into an enamel bowl. He adds a little water and with a teaspoon he mixes the two while heating the bowl on a hot plate. Then he covers the mixture in 'Razvoritel 646' (ethyl acetate) and adds quite a lot of soda. He explains that he uses about one teaspoon of soda for every gram of opium. He stirs the lot while the ethyl acetate is boiling. He does not put a saucer with cold water on top of the bowl (as I have observed in various other places) and soon the room is filled with ethyl acetate fumes. Then he pours the ethyl acetate into a glass, careful not to get any of the opium sludge into the glass. Adding more solvent and soda to the opium sludge, he repeats this process 3 times. Then he puts the content of the glass in another enamel bowl. And now he starts to boil this until almost all of the ethyl acetate has evaporated. By now the smell of the ethyl acetate – cf. acetone – is almost intolerable: both fieldworker Vitalic's and my eyes hurt and are running.

When almost all of the ethyl acetate has evaporated, he adds a little water and resumes heating for a while. At a certain moment, he gets up and brings the bowl into the kitchen. He puts it on the stove and goes on with heating it until only a film is left. He adds acetic anhydride and a little water and while wiggling the bowl constantly he evaporates all liquid again. They call this 'second stage cleaning' (which is in fact not cleaning, but acetylising the morphine into mono- and diacetylmorphine). Then he adds water to dissolve the film and draws it into a 20 ml 'viborka' (working syringe), using cotton on the hub as a filter. Subsequently, the liquid is shared among eight users by squirting it into their syringes (frontloading) and, while 'Girl, you'll be a woman soon' from the *Pulp Fiction* soundtrack blares from the stereo, everybody starts getting busy with getting off. They inject in couples, helping each other looking for and bringing up veins. Denis shouts 'Tarentino, Cool!' After he got off, he tells me how much he loves this director's work and that he has many videos of his films. While speaking, he makes a self-injection gesture with a smirk on his face.

> J.-P. Grund, unpublished field note, Nizhniy Novgorod, Russia (1999)

Nizhniy Novgorod is located on an important drug trafficking route, and by the summer of 1999, when this field note was recorded, opium gum had replaced the poppy straw that is still commonly used in many parts of the region. When poppies are used, the heads are ground, mixed with a few spoons of soda and a little water and then immersed in the ethyl acetate. From that point on the process is basically the same. Cooking poppies may be more characteristic for the Eastern European region, while in Central Asia, closer to the opium production areas, opium is more widely used.

Processing poppies into crude injectable opioid cocktails may also be practised by some users in the US, as witnessed by discussions on poppy growing and chemistry on Internet user groups. The following is an excerpt from one of those discussions:

I always cook the opium latex that I get from my fresh pods (this batch is hens and chicks, and Persian whites) when nice and ready. This cooked opium is definitely better for use in isolating the morphine with glacial acetic acid, then turning that morphine into heroin via acetic anhydride. Or you could just use the cooked opium itself, but my tolerance dictates at the very least the isolation of the morphine, even for injection purposes . . . It is surprising the quality and potency of the heroin that one can make in a garage with relatively little equipment . . . I almost wish heroin wasn't so easy to make from these pods, no I don't . . .

> Negrogesic (2003)

Opium solution and blackwater in Asia

The old Chinaman dips river water into a rusty tin can, washes down a yen pox hard and black as a cinder.

> (Burroughs, 1959)

Just as Europeans can look back at an ancient and rich viniculture, in Asia recreational and medicinal opium consumption (smoking and oral ingestion) is part of an ancient tradition that took roots in all classes of society in countries as distant and diverse as Persia and China (Berridge & Griffiths, 1981). Throughout history, opium has been the principal if not the only national drug in many Asian countries. While poppies are traditionally cultivated on a small scale throughout Asia, nowadays the 'Golden Triangle' (Burma/Myanmar, Laos and Northern Thailand) and the 'Golden Crescent' (Afghanistan) produce the majority of the world's opium and heroin. While smoking remains the primary mode of opium and heroin use in these production areas and elsewhere in Asia, in the past decade drug injecting has made an important inroad. Heroin injecting has diffused along trafficking routes into the majority of Asian countries. China, for example, has become a main destination market for Golden Triangle heroin and reportedly now imports Golden Crescent heroin as well. There may now be 2–3.5 million heroin users in China, who consume about 200 tons of heroin every year (Fabre, 2003). But injecting opium has a longer history in the region.

Injecting liquefied opium surfaced in the twentieth century, most likely introduced by Western sailors. Two preparations have been described in the literature: a solution of raw opium and 'blackwater' or 'yen pox'. These practices remain prevalent today, with recent reports coming from, for example, Afghanistan, Brunei, Darussalam, Cambodia, China, Iran, Laos, Pakistan and Viet Nam (CHR/AHRN, 2003; Reid & Costigan, 2002). While a number of authors mention the practice of blackwater injecting (CHR/AHRN, 2003; Doussantousse & Thanh Hoa, 2001; Reid & Costigan, 2002; Tran et al., 2004), detailed ethnographic descriptions, such as those by Power (1996), are rare.

Raw opium is prepared for injecting by boiling in water and filtering out the solid particles with cheesecloth or muslin, cotton wool or other filtering material. Blackwater opium is a residual product from smoking prepared opium. Although Burroughs (1959) refers to the Chinese 'yen pox' as the ash that remains in the bowl of the opium pipe, it is not. Blackwater opium results from scraping out the stems of the opium pipe. Yen pox or 'thuoc phien', Vietnamese for blackwater, is built up during smoking, as the smoke is deposited on the inside of the pipe. It contains ash particles drawn into the pipe, but its solid content is very low, as most of the solid plant material in the smoking opium has been burned in the bowl. Therefore, when heated it quickly liquefies, which makes it unsuitable for smoking from an opium pipe.

As Berger (1979) wrote, nothing is wasted in survival economies and the 'hard black cinders' have significant currency value. Opium den staff regularly clean out the opium pipes and the yen pox collected is subsequently re-entered into the lowest echelon of the drug economy, where proprietors catering for opium smokers meet their colleagues who service injectors. Robert Power observed in Hanoi and Ho Chi Minh City in 1993 that the residue was bought by shooting gallery managers, who seemed to collect thuoc phien from a network of opium smoking dens around the city. After their collection round, these independent entrepreneurs prepared the blackwater opium for injecting (Power, 1996).

As with raw opium, blackwater opium is prepared for injecting by first boiling it in water. After the first water extraction, the suspension is filtered through a muslin cloth and the residue is reboiled and refiltered up to three times. Subsequently all the extractions are mixed into one and the resulting solution is stored in a 'pot', which could be a cup, mug or beer bottle. This refining process reportedly removes most of the impurities

(Power, 1996). Opium injectors rate blackwater over solutions made from raw opium. In Power's study of Vietnamese IDUs only a minority purchased raw opium as it was deemed to be weaker than blackwater (Power, 1996). (Heroin smokers in The Netherlands and crack smokers in New York consider the drug deposit recovered from their smoking implements as a precious delicacy as well (Grund, 1993b).) Reportedly, blackwater opium contains up to 8% morphine (CHR/AHRN, 2003), which is more than average quality raw opium.

The blackwater was subsequently served to the customers of the 'shooting-galleries', 'take out' being an exception in Power's study. Customers would buy some 3 ml of blackwater, whereupon the 'chu' (dealer/gallery keeper) would mostly use a (glass) gallery syringe to draw the opium solution from the common 'pot' and would then, reportedly routinely, inject the drug into the customer's body, often mixed with a range of diverted psychoactive pharmaceuticals (narcotic analgesics, benzodiazepines, barbiturates), which were on offer as well. Power (1996) provides vivid case notes of the goings-on at shooting galleries in Hanoi and Ho Chi Minh City in 1993, in which one can read *disease transmission* between every pair of lines.

The proliferation of heroin use in Asia and the repression of the cottage industry that developed around the venues where opium solutions are traditionally injected have resulted in their decline (Doussantousse & Thanh Hoa, 2001; Tran *et al.*, 2004). Law enforcement is probably implicated in both the diffusion of opium injecting and its decline, in both Asia and Western Europe. Westermeyer (1976), for example, documented the relationship between the repression of opium smoking with the emergence of both injecting drug use and heroin use within months of the establishment of anti-opium laws in Hong Kong, Laos and Thailand. In the 1960s in The Netherlands, opium injecting was prevalent among 'cultural rebels', who obtained their supplies in the Chinatowns of Amsterdam and Rotterdam. This ended abruptly in 1972, when, after Dutch law enforcement declared a major victory against the Chinese opium trafficking rings, heroin flooded the drug markets of Amsterdam and Rotterdam (Grund & Blanken, 1993).

Morphine

There are case reports of morphine injection (including diverted ampoules of pharmaceutical morphine and illicit morphine-base) from several Asian countries, but this does not seem to be widespread (Reid & Costigan, 2002). Early drug injectors in the Soviet Union reportedly injected diverted morphine (called 'steklo') (Balakireva, personal communication). A significant proportion of IDUs in Vienna, Austria, inject morphine. The centrally located Karlsplatz houses a lively market in diverted pharmaceutical grade morphine, which is prescribed in oral slow-release preparations as part of substitution treatment for heroin addiction, mostly provided by general practitioners. While official statistics are unavailable, quite a few doses of Compensan®, Kapanol CSR®, Mundidol®, Substitol® and Vendal® end up being injected. One user explained how to isolate the morphine from a Compensan® tablet:

It is quite simple: first you wash off the tablet's pink coating and then you crush it really fine. Put about 3–4 ml in a spoon and bring it to a boil. Only when it boils, you throw in the powder, not before; otherwise it becomes custard.

(J.-P. Grund, conversation with seller, Karlsplatz, Vienna, 2003)

Cocaine injection

Cocaine hydrochloride dissolves in water without the necessity of additional chemicals or heating. Little preparation is required to inject (relatively pure) cocaine, as can be seen in the following field note:

While talking, Alex peeled some cotton threads from the lining of his jacket. Between his fingers he rolled them into a little ball. From his pocket he took a spoon and a little package containing cocaine. He put the coke in the spoon with a little water and stirred it. Next he put in the little ball, which he used as a filter. He drew up the cocaine and took his shot.

Grund (1993b)

When the cocaine is of relatively poor quality users may heat the solution.

In the past few years, reports of crack injection have emerged from the US and some European cities. Crack is cocaine specifically prepared for smoking (generally by the dealer) by separating the base from the hydrochloride. To inject crack, it must be reacidified by the end-consumer (who probably was unable to find powder cocaine). When prepared for injection, crack is acidified in the same manner as the Southwest Asian heroin base in the field note from Rotterdam above.

Cocaine is sometimes combined with heroin, called a 'speed ball' or 'cocktail':

Doug starts to prepare a cocktail of heroin and cocaine. He puts some heroin in the spoon and adds some lemon juice and water. Then he boils the contents with his disposable lighter. When the heroin has dissolved he puts the spoon back on the table and waits a few moments. Then he carefully puts his fingertip in the solution in the spoon: 'it's okay now', he says, referring to the temperature of the solution. He holds the package with cocaine above the spoon and with a knife he shoves the cocaine into the spoon. He then stirs the cocaine through the heroin solution with the plastic needle-protector from his syringe and draws it into his syringe.

Grund (1993b)

Amphetamines

Like cocaine, powder amphetamine of sufficient purity dissolves in water at room temperature, but often it is of poor quality and must be heated to go into solution.

IDUs in several former 'Eastern-Bloc' countries have also produced two stimulants – methamphetamine ('vint') and methcathinone ('jeff') – from ephedrine, either distilled from ephedrine-based medications (e.g. Solutan®) or from ephedrine crystals bought on the black market. Vint is produced by reducing ephedrine, using the following chemicals: red phosphor, black 'crystal' iodine, H_2SO_4, household soda and H_2O. The next field note documents the process when starting with ephedrine crystals:

> Dima mixes the ephedrine and the red phosphor in the wrapper. Then he puts the mixture and some lumps of black iodine in a 'reactor' (a small glass medication bottle). He closes the bottle with a rubber stopper with a little glass tube through it and shakes it, heating it shortly with a lighter a number of times. The reaction is visibly going on in the bottle: the three chemicals are forming into a little expanding ball (all-in-all this takes some 10 minutes). Then he adds H_2SO_4 and on-and-off he heats the mixture for at least 30 minutes. Several times he cleans the soot from the flame from the outside of the 'reactor'. Several times, he smells the fumes that come out of the bottle. He explains that he can determine whether the reaction is completed, based on the smell. (I smelled the fumes once, and it did not smell pleasant.) At the beginning of the process the solution was very red; at the end it was light reddish-brown.
>
> When the reaction is completed, Dima adds about 4 ml of H_2O and the solution is light yellowish with a residue of black particles. In the meantime, his pal Denis has cut a 20 ml syringe in two and melted the hub closed. From this moment he takes over. He wraps cotton wadding around a large bore needle and draws up the liquid from the reactor and squirts it into the prepared 20 ml barrel. He adds a few 'needles' of household soda and the solution starts bubbling, neutralizing the acidic solution. He makes a new cotton filter around another needle and he draws the solution into three 2 ml syringes. One he gives to Dima, who walks away a few meters to shoot up. With the second, he injects himself. The third is later divided with another 2 ml syringe. When they shoot up both men seem to experience an intensive rush (both cover their eyes with a cloth and lay down for some minutes).
>
> J.-P. Grund, unpublished field note, Pskov, Russia (1999)

When starting with ephedrine-based medications, the ephedrine needs to be isolated first and this is done by mixing the medication together with a base into gasoline. After adding HCl, the ephedrine crystals or 'flakes' precipitate at the bottom of the container. The crystals are subsequently removed from the gasoline and dried. While the described production of methamphetamine seems rather complicated, this field note was recorded in a field near the river Pskova, demonstrating that it can be done anywhere. (It is interesting to observe that home production of methamphetamine ('crank' or 'bathtub speed') using pseudoephedrine-based medications is a similar process that evolved in the Mid-West of the US in the 1990s. Over the past 10 years, production and distribution have become professionalised and methamphetamine use has spread all over the US.) Turning ephedrine into methcathinone is much easier: ephedrine is simply mixed with permanganate in acidic water at room temperature for about 15 to 20 minutes. Both these processes end with liquid drugs that are subsequently injected. While both drugs could be simply dried and ingested by other modes, reportedly this seldom happens.

Other drugs

Few IDUs limit themselves to one class of drugs. In addition to cocktails of opiates and stimulants, many use prescription drugs, benzodiazepines in particular. Some Australian injectors reportedly injected ecstasy and LSD in the early 1990s (Moore, 1993). In many Asian countries, IDUs inject pharmaceutical drugs, either diverted from legal distribution channels or simply bought over the counter. In India, heroin effectively replaced opium and cannabis as the drug of choice, but most users chased the drug. Injecting increased rapidly when users discovered buprenorphine, which reportedly was injected during medical treatment for heroin addiction. During the 1990s, injection of (cheap) Tidigesic® (buprenorphine) quickly spread throughout most major urban centres of the Indian subcontinent. Most users inject cocktails of illicit and diverted psychoactive drugs, including heroin, buprenorphine, diazepam, pentazocine and pheniramine maleate. (Burrows, et al., 2001; CHR/AHRN, 2003; Reid & Costigan, 2002). During the 1990s, some heroin injectors in Skopje, Macedonia, were observed dissolving their black market heroin in diverted ampoules of diazepam (Grund & Nolimal, 1995). A large proportion of heroin and/or cocaine injectors in Western Europe consume benzodiazepines, often to overcome the side effects of heavy cocaine use. It is worth mentioning that not all of them inject these prescribed or diverted medications. Thus, in The Netherlands, where by comparison the prevalence of injecting is very low, most heavy heroin/cocaine users take benzodiazepines, such as diazepam (Valium®) and flunitrazepam (Rohypnol®), orally, whereas less than 500 km to the south-east, in Frankfurt am Main, the same drugs are mostly injected.

Conclusions

Injecting has been the predominant route of self-administration among opiate (heroin) users in Western societies, while smoking has been the most common route in Eastern societies. However, there has been a process of continual 'crossover' with Western routes appearing in the East and Eastern routes appearing in the West. But despite its ongoing diffusion across continents and cultures, globally injecting opiate users remain out-numbered by those who ingest these drugs by sniffing, smoking or inhalation. Neither is injecting drug use the inescapable end stage of a progressive sequence towards more efficient administration modes, as is frequently suggested in both scientific and lay publications. This observation has merit at both the level of the individual consumer (see, for example, Chapter 10) and that of 'drug culture'. In the last quarter of the twentieth century, shifts away from injecting have appeared in the US (towards sniffing) (Grund,

1998) and Europe (towards 'chasing the dragon') (EMCDDA, 2001), most notably in The Netherlands (Grund & Blanken, 1993).

The observations presented in this chapter suggest a wide range of behavioural patterns around the injection of opiates, which are primarily determined by the practical considerations of getting high, preparing drugs, even producing drugs by means of 'kitchen chemistry', and injecting these into the body. Obviously, injecting drugs in Russia and other post-Soviet countries requires a larger set of paraphernalia and ingredients, specific knowledge of organic chemistry and a much more controlled, indoor environment (while heroin injection has less demanding environmental requirements). Novice IDUs must learn the knowledge and skills to bring this sequence to the desired end. Such knowledge and skills are communicated through social learning processes within the networks of drug using young people. Indeed, drug injecting is often, if not mostly, a social activity in which drug users work together towards the shared goal of getting high. This is especially obvious in Eastern Europe where the practical reasons for collaboration are most demanding:

> It is very seldom when you use alone. At minimum you use with two or three people . . . Somebody has money for drugs, a second knows where to get good drugs, a third has some anhydride or a place to cook and yet another has syringes . . . It is also much cheaper to use in groups.

Why inject?

Given the range of health problems associated with injecting (see Chapters 3, 7–9 and Grund (1993a)) and that there are viable alternatives, why would people opt to inject their drugs? This is not an easy question to answer, as it mostly concerns an intricate mesh of factors and motivations, which are perhaps best understood within Zinberg's framework of 'drug, set and setting' (Zinberg, 1984).

Drug

When probed, many IDUs will mention their appreciation of the immediate pharmacological impact or rush following an injection of heroin, amphetamines or cocaine. This is especially apparent among cocaine injectors.

> Karel is shooting up cocaine. He puts the coke in the spoon, stirs, pulls it up through a piece of cotton and shoots the coke without using a belt. The rush makes him sweat very much. 'It's an extreme flash, it's very good coke', he says, 'I always take the coke first, cause I want to enjoy the coke-flash. A little later I take the brown.'

But freebasing cocaine reportedly can produce a similarly intense rush (Gawin & Kleber, 1986; Wallace, 1990). Likewise, in some drug scenes (in various European cities, for example) users inject their heroin, but smoke their cocaine. Therefore, the pharmaco-logical properties are not a sufficient explanation for the dominance of injecting among certain populations of heavy users.

Set

Quite a few users will tell that personal factors, such as curiosity about the rush, drove them to their first injection. Curiosity or experimentation is also mentioned as a reason for injecting other drugs, such as ketamine or ecstasy, or psychedelics such as LSD, but in most places these concern isolated cases, although the injection of 'calypso' (diverted medical ketamine) gained quite a level of popularity among Russian university students in the 1990s. Probably a small minority of injectors seems to have fallen in love with the needle as such, and several case reports can be found in the literature of IDUs booting for extended periods (just pumping blood up and down the syringe/vein several times, without an objective pharmacological effect as there is no measurable drug left in the content) and injecting liquor or merely water, just to experience the act of injecting. Such Pavlovian conduct has led to the formulation of a psychological theory of 'needle fixation' (see Chapter 4) which, without doubt, has some resonance in certain drug cultures. For example, in the Frankfurter 'Bahnhofsvierteil', the main station area where most Frank-furt street users congregate, I observed a man in his thirties inject. He was dressed in a black leather jacket and trousers, the trousers round his ankles. He wobbled on his spot for at least 15 minutes, enjoying his high and, as it seemed, flashing the syringe hanging from his femoral vein, while his girlfriend (heavy stoned and also sparsely dressed in leather) snuggled up against one of his legs. 'Nadelgeil', murmured the worker of the injection room just around the corner, who accompanied me. However, during my various fieldwork periods I have seen quite some people busy with injecting for extended periods, but in all but one case this was associated with problems finding a suitable vein. Given the relative rarity of such idiosyncratic behaviours, it is unlikely that curiosity or other individual motivations or traits fully account for the adoption of injecting by majorities of consumers in certain places and not in others.

Setting

The shifts away from injecting in The Netherlands (towards chasing heroin and basing cocaine) and the US (towards snorting heroin) have been explained as an interaction of economic and social cultural variables. For example, over the past 25 years the purity of heroin and cocaine in The Netherlands has been at a level high enough to allow for non-injecting administration modes. Combined with community norms rejecting injecting, this resulted in the gradual decline of the prevalence of injecting among heroin users. In the second half of the 1990s, this also seemed to be the case in Macedonia (which remains an important hub on the Balkan Route along which Afghan heroin is transported to Europe). Although I met several injectors in Macedonia, and although the prevalence of injecting drug use has reportedly increased over the years, injecting appeared to be perceived as unattractive among young people:

Ali and Mohammed are uncertain which mode is practised most, chasing or smoking in cigarettes. 'We do it both. I guess it depends on where you are or who you are with. Sometimes I snort it', explains Ali. When I ask him whether he has ever injected, Ali almost gets upset. He vehemently shakes his head and very resolutely says he never did and never will inject: 'That's very bad, it's dirty. You will never see an Albanian injecting'. He rapidly translates my question to Mohammed, who underscores his partner's assertion in German: 'Nein, nein, nicht gut. Man soll das nimmer machen'. (No, no, not good. One should never do that.)

(Grund & Nolimal, 1995)

Conversely, the specific self-preparation practices of opiate and stimulant drugs in Eastern Europe result in the availability of liquid drugs that are easily injected. The ubiquitous practice of injecting medical drugs (which could be administered orally or by other modes with similar treatment outcomes) in the FSU may well have contributed to lowering the stigma associated with recreational injecting. During the Soviet times young kids were taught not to fear the needle. Health promotion posters of an infant hand-in-hand with a syringe and with the text 'I am not afraid of injecting and, if needed, will inject right away', were hanging in many kindergartens.

Many studies point towards the policy environment associated with the use of illicit drugs, in particular to the effects of consumer level drug supply reduction strategies. When, as a result of supply reduction measures, heroin is very expensive and, in particular, of low purity, its users are driven towards injecting the drug. Within months of the establishment of anti-opium laws in Hong Kong, Laos and Thailand, injecting heroin use appeared suddenly (Westermeyer, 1976). In contrast, when opiates are relatively inexpensive and of reasonable quality, users feel no pressure to initiate injecting. Interestingly, already in 1998, the United Nations pointed towards the relationship between drug availability (and drug supply reduction measures) on the one hand and HIV risk behaviours on the other:

Where injecting drug use already exists, reducing the supply of illegal drugs alone does not necessarily help. In fact, it can even increase risky injecting behaviour. When drugs are plentiful, many users choose to smoke rather than inject. However, injecting delivers a 'high' with a smaller drug dose than smoking, so people may switch from smoking to injecting if their usual supplies shrink. A study in Calcutta showed that huge seizures of heroin in the city were followed by a sharp rise in the proportion of drug users choosing to inject.

(UNAIDS/WHO, 1998)

As expressed by Des Jarlais et al. (1991), '[p]olicy choices form the environment in which illicit drug use patterns will evolve, but do not completely determine those patterns'. Thus, while we may be unable to prevent the use of certain substances, certain policy choices and interventions may influence whether these are injected or taken into the body by less hazardous administration modes, and perhaps limit the harm experienced by users, their families and the rest of society.

References and further reading

Aceijas, C., Stimson, G.V., Hickman, M. & Rhodes, T. (2004) Global overview of injecting drug use and HIV infection among injecting drug users. *AIDS*, **18**(7), 2295–2303.

Agar, M.H. (1977) Into that whole ritual thing: ritualistic drug use among urban American heroin addicts. In B.M. Du Toit (ed.), *Drugs, Rituals and Altered States of Consciousness*, pp. 137–148. Rotterdam: Balkema.

Anonymous (2002) HIV/AIDS and injection drug use epidemics: international trends. *CDUHR News*, **5**(1), 1–3 (editorial). (Center for Drug Use and HIV Research National Development and Research Institutes)

Berger, J. (1979) *Pig Earth, Historical Afterword*, pp. 195–213. New York: Pantheon.

Berridge, V. & Griffiths, E. (1981) *Opium and the People*. New York: St. Martin's Press.

Burroughs, W.S. (1959) *Naked Lunch*. Paris: Olympia Press.

Burrows, D., Panda, S. & Croft, N. (2001) *HIV/AIDS Prevention Among Injecting Drug Users in Kathmandu Valley*. Melbourne: Center for Harm Reduction (http://www.chr.asn.au/freestyler/gui/files//NepIDUKathValley.pdf).

Calafat, A. & Montse, J. (2004) Health and safety problems in recreational nightlife in the Island of Mallorca. *International Journal of Drug Policy*, **15**(2), 157–162.

CHR/AHRN (2003) *Manual for Reducing Drug Related Harm in Asia*. Melbourne: Centre for Harm Reduction, Macfarlane Burnet Centre for Medical Research and Asian Harm Reduction Network.

Craine, N., Walker, M., Carnwath, T. & Klee, H. (2004) Hepatitis C testing and injecting risk behaviour: the results of a UK based pilot study. *International Journal of Drug Policy*, **15**(2), 115–122.

Davis, M. & Rhodes, T. (2004) Beyond prevention? Injecting drug user narratives about hepatitis C. *International Journal of Drug Policy*, **15**(2), 123–131.

Des Jarlais, D.C., Courtwright, D.T. & Joseph, H. (1991) The transition from opium smoking to heroin injection in the United States. *AIDS & Public Policy Journal*, **6**(2), 88–90.

Donoghoe, M.C. & Wodak, A. (1998) Health and social consequences of injecting drug use. In G.V. Stimson, D.C. Des Jarlais & A. Ball (eds) *Drug Injecting and HIV Infection*. London: UCL Press/WHO.

Doussantousse, S. & Thanh Hoa, N. (2001) The life and times of the Hanoi drug user: some recent insights from field research. A research report for the UNDCP, UNAIDS Vietnam, April 2001 (http://www.undp.org.vn/projects/vie98006/RDU.htm).

Edlin, B.R. (2004) Hepatitis C prevention and treatment for substance users in the United States: acknowledging the elephant in the living room. *International Journal of Drug Policy*, **15**(2), 81–91.

EMCDDDA (2001) *Annual Report 2001 on the State of the Drugs Problem in the European Union*. Luxembourg: Office for Official Publications of the European Communities (http://ar2001.emcdda.eu.int/en/download/index.html).

Fabre, G. (2003) The black hole of China white. Paper presented at the TNI/BCN Conference on Burma, Drugs and Conflict, December 2003, Amsterdam.

Garriott, J.C. & Sturner, W.Q. (1973) Morphine concentrations and survival periods in acute heroin fatalities. *New England Journal of Medicine*, **289**, 1276–1278.

Gawin, F.H. & Kleber, H.D. (1986) Abstinence symptomatology and psychiatric diagnosis among cocaine abusers. *Archives of General Psychiatry*, **43**, 107–113.

Grund, J.-P.C. (1993a) Health consequences of chasing and injecting: a comparison. In Grund, J.-P.C. (ed.): *Drug Use as a Social Ritual: Functionality, Symbolism and Determinants of Self-Regulation*, Chapter 10. Rotterdam: Addiction Research Institute (IVO) (http://www.drugtext.org/library/books/grund01/grund10.html).

Grund, J.-P.C. (1993b) *Drug Use as a Social Ritual: Functionality, Symbolism and Determinants of Self-Regulation*. Rotterdam: Addiction Research Institute (IVO) (http://www.drugtext.org/library/books/grund01/grundcon.html).

Grund, J.-P.C. (1998) From the straw to the needle? Determinants of heroin administration routes. In J.A. Inciardi & L.A. Harrison (eds): *Heroin in the Age of Crack-Cocaine*. Drugs, Health, and Social Policy Series, Vol. 6, pp. 215–258. Thousand Oaks: Sage Publications.

Grund, J.-P.C. & Blanken, P. (1993) *From 'Chasing the Dragon' to 'Chinezen': the Diffusion of Heroin Smoking in The Netherlands*. Rotterdam: Addiction Research Institute (IVO).

Grund, J.-P.C. & Nolimal, D. (1995) *A heroin epidemic in Macedonia: a report to the Open Society Institute New York and the Open Society Institute Macedonia*. New York: Lindesmith Center (http://www.drugpolicy.org/library/tlcmaced.cfm).

Grund, J.-P.C., Stern, L.S., Kaplan, C.D., Adriaans, N.F.P. & Drucker, E. (1992) Drug use contexts and HIV-consequences: the effect of drug policy on patterns of everyday drug use in Rotterdam and the Bronx. *British Journal of Addiction*, **87**, 381–392.

Grund, J.-P., Botschkova, L., Kruglov, Y., Martsynovskaya, V., Scherbinskaya, A. & Anduschak, L. (2003) *Quo vadis? A case study of the Ukrainian HIV case registration system*. Kiev: Ukrainian AIDS Center, Ministry of Health (in Ukrainian).

Huizer, H. (1987) Analytical studies on illicit heroin. V. Efficacy of volatilization during heroin smoking. *Pharmazeutische Weekblad* (scientific edition), **9**, 203–211.

Long, J., Allwright, S. & Begley, C. (2004) Prisoners' views of injecting drug use and harm reduction in Irish prisons. *International Journal of Drug Policy*, **15**(2), 139–149.

Loughlin, A.M., Schwartz, R. & Strathdee, S.A. (2004) Prevalence and correlates of HCV infection among methadone maintenance attendees: implications for HCV treatment. *International Journal of Drug Policy*, **15**(2), 93–102.

Macalino, G.E., Hou, J.C., Kumar, M.S., Taylor, L.E., Sumantera, I.G. & Rich, J.D. (2004) Hepatitis C infection and incarcerated populations. *International Journal of Drug Policy*, **15**(2), 103–114.

Maher, L. (2002) Don't leave us this way: ethnography and injecting drug use in the age of AIDS. *International Journal of Drug Policy*, **13**(4), 311–325.

Mann, J.M. (1996) Human rights and AIDS: the future of the pandemic. In I.I. Schenker, G. Sabar-Friedman & F.S. Sy (eds), *AIDS Education: Interventions in Multicultural Societies*, pp. 1–7. New York: Plenum.

Mo, B.P. & Way, E.L. (1966) An assessment of inhalation as a mode of administration of heroin by addicts. *Journal of Pharmacology and Experimental Therapeutics*, **154**, 142.

Moore, D. (1993) 'Speeding, ecking and tripping': ethnographic notes from a small world of psychostimulant use. In D. Burrows, B. Flaherty & M. MacEvoy (eds), *Illicit Psychostimulant Use in Australia*, pp. 71–90. Canberra: Australian Government Printing Service.

Moore, D. (2004) Governing street-based injecting drug users: a critique of heroin overdose prevention in Australia. *Social Science and Medicine*, 59(7), 1339–1559.

Negrogesic (from Southern California) on opium chemistry. Posted: 29-10-2003 07:33 (posting #1364413) at http://www.bluelight.nu/vb/showthread.php?threadid=105008.

Power, R. (1996) Rapid assessment of the drug-injecting situation at Hanoi and Ho Chi Minh City, Viet Nam. UNDCP.

Rahbar, A.R., Rooholamini, S. & Khoshnood, K. (2004) Prevalence of HIV infection and other blood-borne infections in incarcerated and non-incarcerated injection drug users (IDUs) in Mashhad, Iran. *International Journal of Drug Policy*, 15(2), 151–155.

Reid, G. & Costigan, G. (2002) *Revisiting 'The Hidden Epidemic'. A situation assessment of drug use in Asia in the context of HIV/AIDS*. Australia: Centre for Harm Reduction, Burnet Institute.

Rhodes, T. (2002) The 'risk environment': a framework for understanding and reducing drug-related harm. *International Journal of Drug Policy*, 13, 85–94.

Selwyn, P.A. (1993) Illicit drug use revisited: what a long, strange trip it's been. *Annals of Internal Medicine*, 119(10), 1044–1046.

Stimson, G.V. & Choopanya, K. (1998) Global perspectives on drug injecting. In G. Stimson, D.C. Des Jarlais & A. Ball (eds), *Drug Injecting and HIV Infection: Global Dimensions and Local Responses*, pp. 1–21. London: UCL Press.

Stimson, G., Des Jarlais, D.C. & Ball, A. (1998) *Drug Injecting and HIV Infection: Global Dimensions and Local Responses*. London: UCL Press.

Strang, J. & Wells, B. (1988) Amphetamine abuse update. *Journal of Postgraduate General Practice*, 2, 1618–1625.

Tran, T.N., Detels, R., Hien, N.T., Long, H.T. & Nga, P.T.H. (2004) Drug use, sexual behaviours and practices among male drug users in Hanoi, Vietnam – a qualitative study. *International Journal of Drug Policy*, 15(3), 182–188.

UNAIDS/WHO (1998) *Report on the Global HIV/AIDS Epidemic*. Geneva: UNAIDS/WHO (http://www.who.int/emc-hiv/global_report/rep_html/report5.html).

UNAIDS/WHO (2003) *Annual AIDS Epidemic Update*. Geneva: UNAIDS/WHO (http://www.unaids.org/Unaids/EN/Resources/Publications/corporate+publications/aids+epidemic+update+-+december+2003.asp).

UNAIDS (2004) *Report on the Global AIDS Epidemic*. Geneva: UNAIDS (http://www.unaids.org/bangkok2004/report.html).

UNDCP (2000a) Russian Federation: Country Profile. Moscow: UNDCP Regional Office Russian Federation.

UNDCP (2000b) Annual Field Report 2000 – Russia. Moscow: UNDCP Regional Office Russian Federation (http://www.unodc.org/russia/en/report_2000-12-31_1.html).

UNHCR/UNAIDS (1998) *HIV/AIDS and Human Rights: International Guidelines*. New York & Geneva: United Nations.

United Nations (1948) *Universal Declaration of Human Rights, adopted and proclaimed by General Assembly resolution 217 A (III) of 10 December 1948* (http://www.unhchr.ch/udhr/index.htm).

UNODC (2003) Country Report Russian Federation. Moscow: UNODC Regional Office Russian Federation (http://www.unodc.org/pdf/russia/russia_country_profile_2003.pdf).

Wallace, B.C. (1990) Treating crack cocaine dependence: the critical role of relapse prevention. *Journal of Psychoactive Drugs*, **22**(2), 149–158.

Wallace, R. (1988) A synergism of plagues: planned shrinkage, contagious housing destruction and AIDS in the Bronx, *Environmental Research*, **47**, 1–33.

Westermeyer, J. (1976) The pro-heroin effects of anti opium laws in Asia. *Archives of General Psychiatry*, **33**, 1135–1139.

WHO (2004) Website Department of Mental Health and Substance Abuse (http://www.who.int/substance_abuse/facts/en/).

Wood, E., Montaner, J.S.G., Braitstein, P., Yip, B., Schecter, M.T., O'Shaughnessy, M.V. & Hogg, R.S. (2004) Elevated rates of antiretroviral treatment discontinuation among HIV-infected injection drug users: implications for drug policy and public health. *International Journal of Drug Policy*, **15**(2), 133–138.

Zinberg, N.E. (1984) *Drug, Set, and Setting: The Basis for Controlled Intoxicant Use*. New Haven: Yale University Press.

Chapter 3

Pharmaceutical Aspects of Injecting

Jennifer Scott

There are several key pharmaceutical factors that relate to injecting drug use, from the injection preparation stage through to administration. The manufacture of pharmaceutical injections is well understood in terms of quality control and risk management. Application of this understanding to injecting drug use points to possible harm reduction interventions. This chapter aims to give the reader a baseline overview of these matters by describing the key principles of pharmaceutical preparation and use of the intravenous route, and relating this to injecting drug use. It is divided into three sections, the first considers the use of the intravenous route in healthcare and relates this to injecting drug use. The second section covers pharmaceutical aspects that relate to injection preparation and the third section covers pharmaceutical aspects that relate to injection administration.

Principles of using the intravenous route in healthcare

Only use the intravenous route when essential

As a general rule in healthcare, medicines are only given by injection when no other route of administration is suitable. For example, when the patient is acutely ill and the medicine needs to get into the bloodstream immediately, an intravenous injection will be used. Other routes of administration are preferable because they offer some form of defence against potential hazards such as microbiological or chemical contaminants, whereas injecting straight into the bloodstream bypasses the body's natural defence mechanisms. For example, acid in the stomach can destroy bacteria that may be present on the surface of a tablet after handling. Drugs applied to the skin as creams may pass through the defensive layers of the skin, but bacteria and particles are kept out. Using the intravenous route presents increased risks compared to other routes of administration. Contamination of injections can cause serious infections; the presence of tiny particles can damage veins and internal organs. Hence it is preferable, in terms of harm reduction, for drug users to take drugs by routes other than injection, for example 'chasing' heroin or smoking crack.

Use ready-made injections where at all possible

If the intravenous route does have to be used in healthcare, it is preferable to use a medicinal product that has been manufactured by a pharmaceutical company in a ready-to-use form. This minimises the chance of administration errors. Ready-to-use products only need to be transferred into the syringe or connected to the infusion device to enable administration. This limits their exposure to the environment where they could be contaminated with bacteria or particles. They also require minimal calculation of dose or volume, reducing the chance of human error. A pharmaceutical company will have manufactured the product in a large batch in a clean environment and will have used some form of preservative or sterilisation. They will also have undertaken rigorous quality control checks to ensure that the product complies with all legal requirements placed upon it. Ready-to-use injections are the type that medical staff draw into syringes on wards prior to administration. Some are not quite 'ready-to-use' but require only dilution with water for injection before use. This can be compared with the prescribing of injectable substitute drugs such as diamorphine. Although the injectable route still carries a risk of infection and the risk of vascular damage, the risks presented from injecting pharmaceutical diamorphine in a clean environment with clean equipment are less than those from injecting street heroin, due to the quality control procedure in place during the manufacture of pharmaceutical diamorphine, new sterile equipment and the clean environment of a supervised injecting room.

Injections that need to be made should be prepared in a clean environment following strict procedures

In healthcare settings where no ready-to-use or ready-to-dilute product exists, for example because sterilisation would destroy the drug, but the patient must receive the drug by the intravenous route, the injection or infusion has to be manufactured 'from scratch' for the individual patient. As a concept, this is comparable to the preparation of street drug injections by injecting drug users (IDUs).

In healthcare, when injections have to be made this is done in area called an 'aseptic suite' which is located within a hospital pharmacy. The aseptic suite is a clean environment where the risks of contamination are minimised by controlling factors such as air quality, worker protective clothing and by designing the room so there are no sharp corners so the surfaces can be kept ultra clean. All materials and equipment used are of very high quality to minimise contamination. The people doing the manufacturing are trained and wear special protective clothing and 'scrub and glove up' before handling anything. Aseptic manufacturing within hospitals is strictly controlled and closely audited to ensure that quality standards are high.

IDUs usually prepare their injections from street drug powders using makeshift materials such as teaspoons and pieces of cigarette filters. Injections will be prepared in an uncontrolled air environment such as inside a house or outside in open-air. As no quality assurance procedures are in place, the injection may be contaminated with a range of solid particles and infectious agents that pose risks to health. These risks and ways to reduce them will be considered in the subsequent sections of this chapter.

Use the intravenous route for as short a time as possible

If the intravenous route is used in healthcare, it is used for as short a time as necessary. The longer the intravenous route is used the greater the chances of irritation at the site of injection and of infection. The body has less defence against the intravenous route than other methods of medicine administration, particularly if the person is in poor health anyway. Complications that have arisen in healthcare from the use of the intravenous route include infection at the site of injection, systemic infection, irritation of veins, leakage of liquid out of veins and into surrounding muscle and the formation of granulomas ('lumps') on internal organs. As IDUs often inject frequently, some over long periods of time, the risk of complications is high, particularly if the person has co-existing illness that may compromise their immune system such as HIV. Safer injecting advice attempts to reduce the incidence of complications associated with injecting drug use as well as limiting the spread of blood borne viruses.

Pharmaceutical aspects of injection preparation

The methods used by IDUs to prepare injections will depend on several factors, including the drug itself, available equipment, the methods learned from others and past experience of 'what works'. Unlike pharmaceutical manufacturing, because of the nature of illicit drug use, there will be no preparation protocol to follow and no quality assurance of the final product. Research has found common steps followed by IDUs in the preparation of street drugs (Scott *et al.*, 1998; Ponton and Scott, 2003). Figure 3.1 illustrates the steps identified for heroin injection preparation and Figure 3.2 shows the steps identified for crack cocaine injection. Note that within each step a large amount of variation was identified, e.g. quantity of acid added, volume of water used, and in some cases the steps were undertaken in a different order. For heroin, stirring was only included by some IDUs. IDUs who reported preparing injections from tablets largely did so by crushing the tablets and mixing them with water in the syringe barrel. Few people heated or added acidifiers to tablets.

Safer injecting advice attempts to encourage IDUs to follow step-wise procedures that will theoretically reduce harm. Comparisons with the pharmaceutical preparation of injections can be made to support the safer injecting advice that is given to IDUs. Let us consider the factors involved in the preparation process of illicit injections in turn, to examine the risks to which the IDU may be exposed and the advice that can be given to reduce such risks. The extent to which research evidence has demonstrated the benefit of advice will be given.

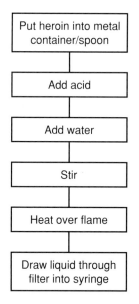

Figure 3.1   Stages identified in the preparation of street heroin for injection (Scott *et al.*, 1998; Ponton & Scott, 2003).

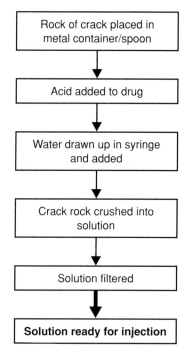

Figure 3.2   Stages identified in the preparation of crack cocaine for injection (Ponton & Scott, 2003).

The environment

The environment around us, including the air we breathe and the surfaces we touch, contains small particles and microorganisms, requiring that pharmaceutical injections are manufactured in clean controlled environments. The environments in which IDUs prepare injections will vary greatly, making research into the environmental risks to IDUs problematic. The basic principles of pharmaceutical manufacturing can be applied, but have yet to be researched, for harm reduction properties amongst IDUs.

Particulate contamination is increased by draughts, so preparing injections away from open doors and draughts is advisable, not least because any strong wind is likely to blow away the drug if it is in powder form! Avoidance of preparation on visibly dirty surfaces is also advocated. In healthcare, the preparation surface is usually contained by means of a physical boundary such as a tray. This tray is wiped down with alcoholic cleaning fluid and all equipment kept within the tray boundary. Translating this into the IDU environment, a tray can also be used on which to prepare injections. Ideally the surface would be wiped down with an alcohol swab and allowed to dry before any equipment is placed on it. A further benefit of the tray is that it can be used to promote the 'own space' concept – encouraging IDUs to use all their own equipment and not to share it with others. One way to reduce the chances of equipment getting mixed up in social situations where several people are preparing injections is to encourage IDUs to keep their own equipment within the boundaries of their tray. A magazine cover has also been advocated as an 'own space' area. Although paper is a known source of contamination, the benefits of preventing the sharing of equipment are likely to outweigh the risks.

The preparer

In pharmaceutical manufacturing, the workers can present significant risk of contamination to injectable products. Hence special protective suits are worn, hand washing is imperative, and people with colds and skin problems such as psoriasis are excluded from manufacturing areas.

IDUs should be encouraged to wash their hands before preparing injections to reduce contamination risks. Hot soapy water should be used, but if this is not possible alcohol swabs can be used as hand wipes. The hands should be allowed to dry before preparation begins. In practice, a towel is likely to be used to dry hands. IDUs should be encouraged to use their own clean towel only, in case blood from other users has contaminated the towel. Having dry hands is important as water can carry infection. Homeless IDUs may be at particular risk from the environment and from infection from their skin; access to hand washing facilities may be limited in this group, so that the use of swabs should be advocated.

IDUs often prepare injections for other people and some may also administer injections to others, particularly new and inexperienced injectors. Such practice poses particular risks for the transmission of blood borne viruses and should be discouraged whenever possible.

The equipment

The sharing of needles, syringes and other injecting paraphernalia is associated with the transmission of blood borne viruses such as HIV and hepatitis C and other infections. Sharing of any item should be strongly discouraged. See Chapters 7–9.

Drugs

Control of contaminants in street drugs is probably impossible. McLauchlin *et al.* (2002) studied the microflora of heroin samples, finding at least one bacteria type in each sample. The literature contains several accounts of outbreaks amongst IDUs attributed to drugs contaminated with microorganisms; for example, the deaths in Glasgow and elsewhere due to heroin contaminated with *Clostridium novyi* type A (McGuigan *et al.*, 2002); *Clostridium botulinum* infections have also been reported (Anon., 2002). As such organisms are subvisible, the appearance of drugs gives no guide to whether or not they are infected.

Contamination with insoluble materials is also a problem. The appearance of street drugs will vary and the amount of insoluble materials present change. Insoluble materials may come from the original source, such as the opium poppy plant, or from added bulking agents such as magnesium silicate (talc). IDUs report that they judge the end-point in preparation from the visible appearance of the material they are trying to dissolve, sometimes adding more and more acid until all the material has dissolved. As the insoluble material may be contaminant rather than drug, excessive and potentially harmful amounts of acid may be used for no good reason. Unfortunately, there is no alternative way to 'see' the end-point of preparation in this context. More research is needed in this area. IDUs should be advised to add a little acid at a time and to use a filter to remove remaining insoluble materials. For more information, see section entitled Acidifiers, below.

The use of crushed tablets or the contents of capsules to make injections is particularly risky. Tablets and capsules are formulated to be swallowed; they are obviously not intended for injection. As a consequence, materials used to assist in the formulation may be harmful if injected. Such materials do not need to be soluble in small amounts of water, such as the amounts used to prepare injections. The use of tablets and capsules by IDUs to prepare injections is widely reported in the literature, usually in case reports of adverse heath consequences (e.g. Makower *et al.*, 1992; Ruben & Morrison, 1992; Robertson *et al.*, 1994; Bittner *et al.*, 2002; Ganesan *et al.*, 2003). One study has examined the particle content of injections prepared with Diconal tablets and Temgesic tablets (Scott *et al.*, 1998), which have both been reported as being injected by IDUs (Robertson *et al.*, 1994). When compared to the particle content of street heroin injections prepared and analysed using the same experimental method, the greater particle content of the injections made with tablets can be clearly seen (Figure 3.3). As a sampling method was used, the total number of particles in the injection would be much larger in all cases and also have a

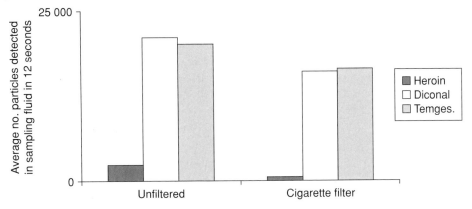

Figure 3.3   Number of particles detected by analysis of a 50 μl sample of injection prepared using street heroin powder, Diconal tablets and Temgesic tablets using a Coulter Multisizer IIe. Data are shown for unfiltered injections and injections filtered through a piece of cigarette filter (Scott *et al.*, 1998).

great deal of variation. These experiments support the observations in case studies that injecting tablets carries higher risks because of the high number of particles present.

Acidifiers

As shown in Figures 3.1 and 3.2, IDUs add acids when preparing heroin and crack cocaine for injection because these street drugs usually exist in the chemical form known as the base form. Bases are volatile and prepared for smoking, not injecting. Bases are not very soluble in water and therefore do not dissolve in the small amounts of water used to prepare injections. Acids are added to convert street drugs that are present in the base form to a more soluble form known as a salt. For example, citric acid added to street heroin produces diamorphine citrate (a 'salt'). The heroin salt will dissolve in the small amount of water needed to prepare an injection. If the drug purity (and therefore the weight of diamorphine to be converted) is known, the amount of acid needed to convert the base can be calculated. However, since this will not be the case for IDUs, the amount added is commonly based on past experience of what works and visual change indicating that the drug has dissolved (Ponton & Scott, 2003). As only a small amount of acid is usually needed, it is likely that excess acid is probably used by many IDUs.

A variety of acids have been reported to be used by IDUs, including citric acid, ascorbic acid and acid-containing household items such as lemon juice, vinegar and kettle descaler (Garden *et al.*, 2003). Experiments that have copied the ways in which IDUs prepare heroin, using ascorbic and citric acids, showed that the resulting injections have a lower pH (i.e. are more acidic) than pharmaceutical diamorphine injections (Scott *et al.*, 2000). These experiments also showed that the addition of acid is necessary to dissolve base heroin, contradicting the suggestion made in some safer injecting leaflets that heating the mixture for longer is an alternative.

The literature does contain some evidence about the risks from using acids. The risk of candidal infection from lemon juice has been reported by several authors (Newton-John *et al.*, 1984; Etienne *et al.*, 1986; Hay, 1986; Bisbe *et al.*, 1992; Friess *et al.*, 1997). In some cases, only ophthalmic infection resulted, leading to loss of vision, but in others systemic infection led to severe illness and death.

The use of acidic products which contain other ingredients, such as non-brewed condiment and 'Jif' lemon is not recommended. As well as the risks of these water-based products carrying microbial contamination, the presence of additives could also increase harm.

What then are the physiochemical risks from injecting acidic solutions? The body has several biochemical ways of neutralising acid in the bloodstream, so that in a healthy individual it is likely that the injection of small quantities of acid can be tolerated systemically. This applies only to the acid itself, and not to other toxic substances that the preparation may contains as contaminants. Locally, the injection of acids will cause irritation at the site of injection, damaging veins and surrounding tissue. Injecting into muscle causes particular concern as absorption of liquid from muscle tissue into the bloodstream is slow and variable, potentially giving the solution time to damage the muscle. Muscle damage caused by acidic solutions contributed towards the consequences of the *Clostridium novyi* type A outbreak (McGuigan *et al.*, 2002), although the acid itself was not the source of infection.

The use of kettle descaler by IDUs as a source of acid is of particular concern. Kettle descaler contains strong acids which vary between brands. Different products contain citric acid, formic acid and phosphoric acid, and some may also contain perfumes. The use of kettle descaler is likely to cause severe irritation to veins.

More research is needed to explore which acids present the least risk of harm to the IDU.

Water

Injections administered intravenously must be aqueous, i.e. water-based. The intravenous injection of oils is very dangerous and can lead to vein blockage and thrombosis. Water from most sources will contain various chemicals, including minerals and organic compounds. These may react chemically with injection formulations, so water used to prepare medical injections has been treated to remove most chemicals. Water can also be a source of bacterial, fungal and viral infection, and particulate contamination. Water for injection is therefore sterilised to kill microorganisms and filtered.

One of the main concerns in the injection of water is the presence of pyrogens. Pyrogens are substances capable of producing a fever. They may come from bacteria, fungi, viruses and non-microbial sources. After injecting pyrogens, the person may have an acute fever. Depending on the type of pyrogen and the amount present, consequences can be mild or serious. High levels of contamination with some pyrogens can cause coagulation of the blood and medical shock. Pyrogens are removed from water by distilling it to remove the pyrogens and then sterilising it shortly afterwards. Sterilisation is very important to avoid pyrogen build-up on cooling and storage. As well as water, pyrogens may also come from the drug substance, the hands of the preparer, or equipment.

Water for Injections BP is the sterile water medical product used to prepare most medical injections. Under amendments to Section 9A of the *Misuse of Drugs Act* (1971) which came into force in August 2003, IDUs can lawfully be supplied certain items of injecting paraphernalia for harm reduction purposes (Siddiqui, 2003). Water for Injections is included in these items; however, as it remains a prescription only medicine under the *Medicines Act* (1968) in the UK, supply without a prescription needs to be done under a Patient Group Direction (PGD) (previously known as group protocols). For information of PDGs see www.groupprotocols.org.uk. Although 'Water for Injections BP' is prescription only, sterile water labelled as 'sterile water' as opposed to 'Water for Injections BP' is not prescription only.

Cookers

The term 'cooker' is used to describe any metal container in which an injection is prepared Commonly used items include spoons, the bottom of drinks cans and purpose-made items such as the Stericup®, which is produced in France and supplied to discourage the sharing of paraphernalia. Cookers raise two main issues. The first is cleanliness – the cooker should be cleaned before and after use to minimise contamination. In the absence of hot clean water and detergent, alcohol swabs can be used, as long as the cooker is allowed a few minutes for the alcohol to evaporate afterwards. The second is the material from which the cooker is made. It is probable that in the presence of hot, acidic solution, some metals may corrode, introducing dissolved metal molecules into the solution. Injection of these may cause harm. However, there is a need for more research in this area before any advice on suitable and unsuitable materials can be given. In the interim, it is advocated that any cooker which shows signs of metal degradation should be discarded.

Filters

IDUs use filters to remove insoluble materials from the prepared solution, the main reason being to avoid needle blockage, which would interrupt the administration of the injection. From a harm reduction perspective there is a further potential benefit in the removal of insoluble material that could precipitate blood clots and aggravate veins.

Filters used are usually makeshift, such as a piece of filter tip removed from a cigarette or a piece of hand rolling cigarette filter. Other materials cited include cotton wool, pieces of clothing and tissue paper (Scott *et al.*, 1998, Ponton & Scott, 2003). A study of the effects of makeshift filters on injections prepared with street heroin found that

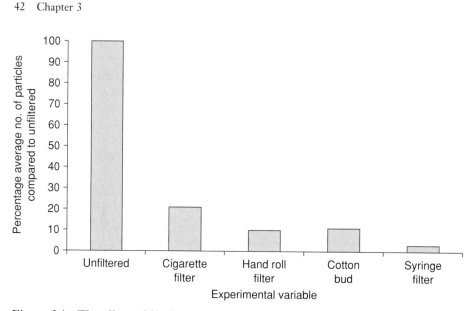

Figure 3.4 The effects of filtering heroin injections with various types of filter.

particulate contamination was reduced after filtering. Figure 3.4 shows the data from this research (Scott, 2000). Analysis was performed on 50 μl samples of heroin injections prepared copying the methods of IDUs. Taking the particle content of the unfiltered sample as 100%, the graph shows the reduction in average particle content when filtered using the various means listed. The syringe filter is a commercially available 5 μm pre-syringe filter, called the Acrodisk® made by Gelman Sciences for laboratory use. This research plus previous work using tablets supports the use of filters, in that they reduce the particle content of injections and hence probably reduce the risks of clinical complications due to the injection of insoluble materials.

   The sharing of filters, and other paraphernalia, has been implicated in the transmission of hepatitis C (Hagan *et al.*, 2001, Thorpe *et al.*, 2002). The sharing of filters is challenging for needle exchange providers. People may share filters because they retain some of the drug. In the work reported by Scott (2000) illustrated in Figure 3.4, the amount of heroin retained by the filters was also measured. Injections were prepared with 250 mg of street heroin which had a 56% diamorphine content. The average amount of heroin retained in the filters was as follows: cigarette filter 9 mg, hand rolling filter 11 mg, cotton bud 8 mg and syringe filter 18 mg. The latter is highest because it drew most insoluble material from the spoon into the filter. This work confirms what IDUs have known for years, filters do retain drug. By reusing filters or using several of them to prepare further injections, IDUs are able to avoid wasting drug. Filters have a value and may be donated to others who do not have any money or drugs but are in withdrawal. Telling people not to reuse or share filters would be better supported if an alternative method of filtration, acceptable to the IDU but that does not retain drug, could be offered. Research is underway in the area (Imbert, 2002).

Attention needs to be paid to the material from which the filter is made. Filters made from cotton have been associated with infection in IDUs by the bacteria *Enterobacter agglomerans* present in cotton and identified within the filters linked to the cases (Ferguson *et al.*, 1993). The moist conditions within used filters, especially if kept warm, for example next to the body in a pocket, provide ideal growing conditions for microbiological contaminants. The use of used filters is associated with 'cotton fever' or 'dirty hits', a benign acute febrile condition seen in IDUs that resolves spontaneously (Harrison & Walls, 1990). It is sometimes seen after reusing old filters. The acute reaction could be a response to pyrogens.

There is also concern around the shedding of fibres from filters. The use of loose fibrous materials such as cotton wool should be avoided. Makeshift filters are, almost by definition, not fit for the purpose of filtering injections and hence are likely to be associated with problems, despite offering some protection against the harm from injecting large amounts of solid materials.

Injection administration

For detailed discussion of safer injecting techniques, the reader is referred to Chapter 11. To avoid duplication, this section will focus on pharmaceutical aspects of injection administration and relate them to IDUs.

The injectable routes

Most IDUs will use the intravenous route; however, other injectable routes might be used when venous collapse has occurred impairing venous access. Two routes known to be used are: the subcutaneous route (termed 'skin popping') where the injection is delivered into the subcutaneous skin layer, and the intramuscular route (termed 'muscle popping') where the injection is deposited into a muscle. Drug needs to be absorbed into the bloodstream from the site of injection to exert an effect. Absorption from under the skin or from muscle is variable. Factors such as movement will influence the rate at which the drug gets into the bloodstream. Additionally, some of the drug will be metabolised in the tissues as it is absorbed; hence the effects felt may be less for an equivalent dose when taken by one of these routes rather than intravenously.

Pharmacokinetics

If the same drug is given at the same dose to two different people, the effects of the drug and how their body handles that drug may be different. This is because individual 'people factors' can alter the way the drug is 'processed' in the body. Pharmacokinetics is the study of these 'people factors'. It allows the use of mathematical models to predict how someone's body will handle a drug, depending on their individual variables. This can be an important tool in minimising side effects and maximising benefit, by keeping the amount of drug in the bloodstream within the therapeutic range. However, since the purity and content of street drugs change, such predictions cannot be made for IDUs.

When a drug is taken, there are four processes that the drug undergoes in the body:

(1) *Absorption* This is the absorption of the drug from the formulation in which it is taken, into the bloodstream. For example, a drug formulated as a tablet dissolves in the gastrointestinal tract and is absorbed across many biological layers into the bloodstream. When an intravenous injection is administered, there are no biological barriers through which the drug must pass before getting into the bloodstream – the drug is directly administered into the bloodstream. This maximises the effects of any drug taken as none is lost in the absorption process. It also increases the risk of overdose, should a larger than tolerated dose be taken.

(2) *Distribution* This is the distribution of the drug from the bloodstream to the tissues where it exerts its effect. In the case of psychoactive drugs, this will mean the distribution of the drug from the bloodstream into the central nervous system, where action of neurological receptors occurs. Drug may be extensively distributed in many tissues, not simply those in which the effect is desired; hence side effects such as constipation occur in opiate users due to drug actions on the gut. Factors that can affect distribution include the presence of other drugs and also some illnesses.

(3) *Metabolism* This is the chemical alteration and breakdown of the drug into a form that can be excreted. Drugs may go through several stages of metabolism and some metabolites (chemically altered drug products) can have an effect themselves. Different people metabolise the same drug differently, due to genetic and other factors. Some people may break down drugs very quickly and hence can tolerate larger doses; others may break drugs down slowly and hence get toxic effects from small doses. In some cases the body can get rid of the drug without changing it chemically in any way. The liver is the main organ involved in drug metabolism, although other organs can play a role too. People with liver disease, such as hepatitis, may not be able to metabolise drugs as efficiently as those with a healthy liver and in such cases a smaller dose may be needed to avoid toxicity. A larger dose may be needed if the drug is a pro-drug (that itself does not exert an effect but relies on metabolism to change it to an active drug).

(4) *Excretion* This is the process of excreting the drug from the body. The main organ involved in excretion is the kidney, which filters out metabolites and unchanged drug from the bloodstream and excretes them in the urine. Other organs may also be involved in excretion, including the lungs and skin. People with kidney disease may need their dose of drug changed to compensate for altered excretion.

Pharmacokinetics of street drugs are difficult to study because of variations in doses administered and formulation. What is clear is that if drugs that exert similar effects, such as central nervous system depressants (e.g. heroin, alcohol and benzodiazepines) are taken together, the chances of overdose are increased (this is called a pharmacodynamic interaction). That some drug users seem to tolerate higher levels of poly drug use than others, depends on factors such as dose, tolerance, health and their individual pharmacokinetics. As research into genetic variation increases, more information may become available to guide drugs professionals on overdose prevention amongst IDUs.

Concluding remarks

In summary, many areas of understanding arising from pharmaceutical research and practice are of relevance to injecting drug use, but the variability in, and unregulated nature of, drug use makes it difficult to be exact in utilising this knowledge. The challenge lies in relating this information to IDUs in a way that promotes the adoption of safer injecting techniques.

References

Anonymous (2002) Cluster of wound botulism cases in injecting drug users. *CDR Weekly*, **12**(44) (http://www.phls.org.uk/publications/cdr/archive02/News/news4402. html#bot).

Bisbe, J., Miro, J.M., Latorre, X. *et al.* (1992) Disseminated candidiasis in addicts who use brown heroin: report of 83 cases and review. *Clinical Infectious Diseases*, **15**(6), 910–923.

Bittner, C., Zuber, M. & Eisner, L. (2002) Acute ischaemia of the right hand after inadvertent intra-arterial injection. *Swiss Surgery*, **8**(6), 281–284.

Etienne, M., Nemery, A., Darcis, J.M. *et al.* (1986) Disseminated candidiasis in heroin addicts. Report of two cases and review of the literature. *Acta Clinica Belgica*, **41**(1), 18–22.

Ferguson, R., Feeney, C. & Chirurgi, V.A. (1993) *Enterobacter agglomerans*-associated cotton fever. *Archives of Internal Medicine*, **153**(20), 2381–2382.

Friess, S., Herbrecht, R., Kuntz, J.L. *et al.* (1997) *Candida albicans* vertebral osteomyelitis treated successfully with fluconazole. *Journal de Mycologie Médicale*, **7**(4), 207–211.

Ganesan, S., Felo, J., Saldana, M. *et al.* (2003) Embolized crospovidone (poly[N-vinyl-2-pyrrolidone]) in the lungs of intravenous drug users. *Modern Pathology*, **16**(4), 286–292.

Garden, J., Roberts, K., Taylor, A. & Robinson, D. (2003) *Evaluation of the provision of single use citric acid sachets to injecting drug users* (research report). Edinburgh: Effective Interventions Unit, Scottish Executive.

Harrison, D.W. & Walls, R.M. (1990) 'Cotton fever': a benign febrile syndrome in intravenous drug abusers. *Journal of Emergency Medicine*, **8**, 135–139.

Hagan, H., Thiede, H., Weiss, N.S. *et al.* (2001) Sharing of drug preparation equipment as a risk factor for hepatitis C. *American Journal of Public Health*, **91**(1), 42–46.

Hay, R.J. (1986) Systemic candidiasis in heroin addicts. *British Medical Journal*, **292**, 1096.

Imbert, E. (2002) *A Steribox New Filter*. Ivry-sur-Seine: Apothicom (http://www.steribox.tm.fr/english/new_filter/index.htm).

McGuigan, C.C., Penrice, G.M., Gruer, L. *et al.* (2002) Lethal outbreak of infection with *Clostridium novyi* type A and other spore-forming organisms in Scottish injecting drug users. *Journal of Medical Microbiology*, **51**, 971–977.

McLauchlin, J., Mithani, V., Bolton, F.J. *et al.* (2002) An investigation into the microflora of heroin. *Journal of Medical Microbiology*, **51**, 1001–1008.

Makower, R.M., Pennycook, A.G., Moulton, C. (1992) Intravenous drug abusers attending an inner city accident and emergency department. *Archives of Emergency Medicine*, **9**(1), 32–39.

Newton-John, H.F., Wise, K. & Looke, D.F.M. (1984) Role of the lemon in disseminated candidiasis of heroin abusers. *Medical Journal of Australia*, **140**(13), 780–781.

Ponton, R. & Scott, J. (2003) Heroin and crack – injection preparation and user variations. Paper presented at the 14th International Conference on the Reduction of Drug Related Harm, 9 April 2003, Chiang Mai, Thailand.

Robertson, J.R., Ronald P.J.M., Raab, G.M. & Parpia, T. (1994) Deaths, HIV infection, abstinence, and other outcomes in a cohort of injecting drug users followed up for 10 years. *British Medical Journal*, **309**, 369–370.

Ruben, S.M. & Morrison, C.L. (1992) Temazepam misuse in a group of injecting drug users. *British Journal of Addiction*, **87**(10), 1387–1392.

Scott, J. (2000) *Development, implementation and evaluation of harm reduction techniques for drug users*. PhD thesis. Aberdeen: Robert Gordon University.

Scott, J., Kennedy, E.J., Winfield, A.J. & Bond, C. (1998) Investigation into the effectiveness of filters for use by intravenous drug users. *International Journal of Drug Policy*, **3**(2), 181–186.

Scott, J., Kennedy, E.J., Winfield, A.J. & Bond, C. (2000) Laboratory study of the effects of citric and ascorbic acids on injections prepared with brown heroin. *International Journal of Drug Policy*, **11**(6), 417–422.

Siddiqui, N. (2003) *An Amendment to Section 9A of the Misuse of Drugs Act 1971 – to permit the supply of injecting paraphernalia*. Home Office Circular HOC 35/2003. London: Home Office.

Thorpe, L.E., Ouellet, L.J., Hershow, R., Bailey, S.L., Williams, I.T., Williamson, J., Monterroso, E.R. & Garfein, R.S. (2002) Risk of hepatitis C virus infection among young adult injection drug users who share injection equipment. *American Journal of Epidemiology*, **155**(7), 645–653.

Further reading

CPPE (1998) *Open Learning Pack: Drug Use and Misuse*. Manchester: Centre for Pharmacy Postgraduate Education.

Derricott, J., Preston, A. & Hunt, N. (1999) *The Safer Injecting Briefing*. Liverpool: HIT.

Obadia, Y. (2001) Injecting misuse of buprenorphine among French drug users. *Addiction*, **96**(2), 267–272.

SCPPE (1998) *Distance Learning Pack: Pharmaceutical Care of the Drug Misuser*. Glasgow: Scottish Centre for Post Qualification Pharmaceutical Education.

SCPPE (2001) *Distance Learning Pack: Pharmaceutical Aspects of Methadone Prescribing*. Glasgow: Scottish Centre for Post Qualification Pharmaceutical Education.

Sheridan, J. & Strang, J. (eds) (2002) *Drug Misuse and Community Pharmacy*. London: Taylor & Francis.

Chapter 4

Needle Fixation

Richard Pates, Andrew McBride and Karin Arnold

Introduction

Needle fixation, or the habit of injecting compulsively, is well known to both injection drug users (IDUs) and to the agencies that treat people with drug problems. There is a paucity of literature on the subject and there are those who deny the existence of any such phenomenon. This chapter will explore what is known about needle fixation and outline a psychological theory based on research on the subject.

The phenomenon is known throughout the world where people inject illicit drugs and it is known by different names. In the USA, people with a needle fixation are known as 'needle freaks' and in Australia they refer to 'the feel for steel'. Other languages have phrases for it such as 'nadelgeilheit' in German, 'pica manie' in French, 'dipendenza di insulina o ago' in Italian, 'závislost na jehele' in Czech ('kručení v žíle' in Czech slang), Εμμονη με τις βελονες in Greek and 'fixação em injeção' in Portuguese (Brazilian).

Not all IDUs who claim to have a needle fixation do so, and some who do have it do not recognise it. Needle fixation appears to be not one single behaviour, but rather a collection of behaviours, each of which reinforces injecting and tends to become as or more important than the drug itself. In order to study the literature on the subject Pates *et al.* (2001) defined it as follows:

> Repetitive puncturing of the skin with or without the injection of psychoactive drugs via intravenous, subcutaneous or intramuscular routes, irrespective of the drug or drugs injected or the anticipated effects of the drug.

This appears to be the only attempted definition of the phenomenon. For most IDUs the process of injecting is merely the most efficient and cost effective way of introducing the drug to the body. However, for a minority, the process of injecting becomes more important either through secondary gains from injecting or because of the ritualistic nature of their injecting. For example, the process of flushing (pulling the blood repeatedly back into the syringe after a vein is found and reinjecting it) is more common with those with a needle fixation than those without it (Pates, 2004).

Pates *et al.* (2001) identified a number of behaviours that might contribute to needle fixation, such as: the injection of substances other than drugs (substitution); perseverance where the IDU will search for hours for a vein in which to inject despite alternative methods of drug administration; dividing the drug into smaller quantities to inject more frequently but with less effect; and flushing. They also identified a number of secondary gains to the injecting process such as sexual satisfaction, pain and the status of being a skilled injector.

The clinical importance of needle fixation is that when IDUs seek treatment to help stop using drugs, substitution of the drug of choice may not be sufficient to help stop injecting. During a time when blood borne disease spread by injecting is increasing, such an impediment to the effectiveness of treatment becomes a public health issue.

Evidence for needle fixation

Published information about needle fixation was scarce until the publication of papers by Pates *et al.* (2001) and McBride *et al.* (2001). Levine (1974) described two cases of compulsive injecting in women at the Lexington treatment centre. The first case was a 28 year old woman who injected opiates intravenously and who started injecting more and more frequently despite getting no effect from the drug. She said she felt relieved after an injection: 'I was shooting when I didn't need it and wasn't sick. I couldn't stop'. The second patient was a 27 year old nurse who injected intramuscularly. When her supplies of drugs became unavailable she would inject tap water intramuscularly. She pushed the needle in slowly to maximise the pain and repeated the process as often as every 5 minutes. Levine described both of these women as having psychiatric problems.

Other disparate pieces of evidence exist in the literature from the nineteenth century onwards. None of these describe needle fixation *per se*, but can be argued as describing those behaviours associated with needle fixation. For example, Allbutt (1870) describes patients who injected themselves daily or more often than daily over long periods of time. They did this to treat neuralgia. The injections did not effect a cure, but patients all found relief in the incessant use of the syringe. They said that without the syringe, life would be insupportable.

Substitution

Substitution was described by Light and Torrance (1929) who reported a study where they withdrew the supply of morphine to a group of opiate addicts and studied their physiological responses. The addicts were deprived of morphine for 36 hours despite their begging for their drug to be reinstated. In one case an injection of sterile water calmed one of the addicts and sent him to sleep. He did not know that this was not morphine. This seemed to be a placebo effect mediated by the use of the needle, whereby he anticipated that the result of the injection would be a morphine-like effect. In their commentary, Light and Torrance said that the addicts commonly spoke of 'the needle habit' in which a single prick of the needle brought relief. They also commented that it is not uncommon for an addict to give another an injection of sterile water and for the recipient to derive a 'kick' and become quiet. Substitution of substances other than water has been described, including bizarre substances such as chocolate and petrol (van Epen, 2001), shampoo (Pates, 2004) and vegemite (D. Burrows, personal communication).

Perseverence

Some IDUs will persevere in trying to find that elusive vein and will not accept that alternative methods of drug administration are acceptable. This may occur even to the extent of trying for several hours during which time the drug could have been taken by another method and the effect of the drug have been obtained. McBride *et al.* (2001) cited four examples of this. In one case, the subject described going from a situation of being able to inject without a tourniquet (to bring up the vein) to having the arm strapped with a friend holding it and poking at the arm trying to find a vein. The second case describes how after 3 years of injecting in the same place the subject was injecting into holes in his arm despite being disgusted with himself. The third subject described trying for hours to get a vein 'and whether I get speed into my body afterwards is just secondary'. The fourth described spending 5 hours trying to find a vein and using 80 needles because they kept getting blocked with blood clots. Stewart (1987) also describes perseverance, observing that addicts will try to get a works and endure being mildly ill for lack of heroin before they will capitulate and snort or smoke it.

Sexual associations

Levine (1974), in his discussion of the possible causes of needle fixation, suggested that continued and increased self-injection in the absence of continued reinforcement, as in his two patients, can be seen as an instance of secondary reward conditioning in which behaviour is directed towards a stimulus with no intrinsic utility that has been conditioned in the past by a biologically significant stimulus. Pates *et al.* (2001) identified a number of secondary rewards that may be gained from the process of injecting. These included sexual satisfaction, pain and the pleasure gained from acquisition of skills.

Pates (2004) described three ways in which some sexual connection with injecting may be seen. First, there is the symbolic representation of the penetration of the skin by the phallic shaped needle and the subsequent rush which some users have said is 'like' an orgasm. The French philosopher Jacques Lacan equated the whole process of injecting to sadomasochistic sex. He compared the two practices thus: 'It is a heavy clandestine affair, whose nearest cousin is hardcore sex. There are other similarities: the obvious sadomasochism, the sexual symbolism of penetration and the needle, the investment with fetishistic qualities of the equipment and the ritual present. Both groups eschew conventional bodily sites and practices of pleasure.' (Lacan quoted by Lemaire, 1977). In this case injecting is seen as analogous to sex.

Second, Pates (2004) described the situation where injecting becomes a substitute for sex. A number of studies have found this. For example Howard and Borges (1971) interviewed injectors in San Francisco in 1971 and stated that injecting seems to be a sexual substitute for men. 'Their own insecurity and paranoia can't let them become involved with anyone else. Thus they can't have sex and turn to the needle as a sexual substitute'. In an anthropological study, Connors (1988) interviewed 120 injectors in a therapeutic community about their practices and beliefs. She found that 40% of the sample felt that the needle was a substitute for sex, not necessarily like having sex, but in some way fulfilling the same need. She said that a decrease in sexual activity during periods of needle use may lend some support to the idea that sexual drive can find an outlet through injecting. An IDU interviewed in McBride *et al.* (2001) related, 'I know at least two occasions when a girl has come to me for a hit and its like in lieu of sex and everything is as though it was sex, but it was not'.

A third explanation may be that injecting actually produces sexual pleasure. A female IDU interviewed in McBride *et al.* (2001) said in a very direct way, 'You get a fanny-flash, that is what I call it, and it is a wicked feeling'. In an interview with one gay man, Pates (2001), found that sex had a strong relationship with his injecting. He had injected both into his anus (without the needle on the syringe) and his penis. He said he did this because they were both areas that gave him great pleasure. He also reported having an orgasmic experience after injecting, not a feeling like an orgasm but an actual orgasm. It was not an effect of the drug because it occurred before the drug had time to act. He also said that as he no longer injected, the sexual pleasure is what he missed most about not injecting. One of the IDUs interviewed by Howard and Borges (1971) said, 'There's no need to go into Freudian symbolism. Guys dig chicks hitting them and vice versa. One chick that hit me up would play around with the blood awhile before injecting it. I usually hit myself. It's a sexual thing to me to have a chick hit me'.

Pain

For some injectors there may be an element of liking the pain. Pain is associated with injecting because of the insertion of the needle through the skin and into the vein. For some injectors the pain may be a necessary product of injecting, but for others there may be pleasure or reward similar to that of self-injury. One of the IDUs interviewed by McBride *et al.* (2001) said that she thought that it could be associated with self-mutilation. She mentioned that she had previously cut her arms, that a lot of addicts take drugs because they like the pain, 'a lot of addicts self-mutilate and things like that so it could be connected to that, you know a form of causing pain to yourself'. Lockley (1995) suggested that the pain that often goes with injecting, 'could be a help to those internally aggressive or wanting to portray a macho image'.

One of Levine's (1974) subjects reported the injection of tap water. This was injected intramuscularly and slowly in order to maximise the pain. Howard and Borges (1971) reported that half of the males they interviewed and two-thirds of the females thought that the injecting experience was masochistic. They commented that many needle users enjoy the experience of self-inflicted pain, 'they talk as though self punishment were a pleasure'. Pates's (2001) interviewee said that he enjoyed the feeling of pain associated with injecting.

A patient of Hampl (2003) thought that there was an aspect of pain that contributed to his enjoyment of injecting. He described the process whereby he enjoyed the pain from the injecting which was then followed by the rush from the injection and then the removal of the pain because he was injecting opiates. Although pain is part of injecting for most injectors, the pain is probably something they have to endure to gain from their injecting, but for others the pain is part of the pleasure.

Skills and status

The skills associated with injecting may also reinforce injecting behaviour. Howard and Borges (1971) found that 39% of their sample of injectors felt that their track marks and bruises gave them some status as symbols of their injecting. Van Epen (2001) also confirms that at the beginning of the 1970s heroin epidemic in The Netherlands, injecting had status. Those who injected thought that they had a higher status than those who did not. He reported that they were also proud of their track marks. For some, because the act of drug taking is a rejection of societal values, injecting is seen as a really taboo behaviour and therefore has a greater status (McBride *et al.*, 2001). Another participant in this study said that the stigmata of injecting were evidence of group membership. In her study of injectors, Connors (1988) stated that it was needle use, not type or amount of the drug used, that was the criterion of membership.

Kohn (1987), in discussing habituated heroin injectors, described the skill of injecting where 'blood drawn into the syringe confirms that the user's anatomical skills are adequate and also makes the syringe part of the organism'. The skill of injecting is another thing that is celebrated (McBride *et al.*, 2001). To be able to inject well or to be able to inject others can have an effect on both the injector's self-esteem and, when they inject others, on their role and social standing. Friedman *et al.* (1999) describe how skill at injecting others can prevent a user from becoming 'sick' (withdrawing). This is because in exchange for injecting another user the injector may be given drugs in payment. This will prevent the injector withdrawing if he/she has no drugs.

Ritual

Ritual is known to be a strong component in habitual drug use. The process of preparing a drug for injection follows a sequence of events that lends itself to the development of ritual. The scoring (buying the drug), the preparation involving paraphernalia such as spoons and filters, adding the water to the drug (usually with a syringe to measure the quantity), heating the drug, the tying of the tourniquet, the finding of the vein and the process of injecting itself comprise a sequence of actions anticipating the pleasure of the hit. Agar (1977) describes a ritual as a sequence of psychomotor activities that is rigidly prescribed. He goes on to say that for an event to be a ritual, it must prescribe a sequence of psychomotor acts and that the prescribed psychomotor sequence must be invested with special meaning for the person performing the sequence. Agar argues that a percentage of the addict population are 'needle freaks', those to whom the process of injecting is more important than the effect of the heroin. He goes on to say that while some are obsessed with the ritual, others view injecting strictly as an instrumental act. Most of the addicts known to Agar place the event of injecting between these two extremes. Trebach (1982) has suggested that there is some evidence that much of the junkie culture and the very habit itself are centred around the injection ceremony – that the drug may hold less importance for some addicts than the needle itself.

Hampl (2002) has argued that insufficient notice is taken of ritual in the treatment of drug dependence. He suggests that when some treatment practitioners and researchers discuss the role of drug craving they mistake this for a conditioned response to the ritualistic aspects of drug use. Among a group of heroin addicts being treated with methadone, he observed that drug craving should not have been present because pharmacologically they were being adequately medicated, but that there was still a strong desire to inject. He identified a number of differences between the role of ritual and craving, including the dose, which may be much smaller than one would expect in a situation of craving (i.e. drug injectors would be satisfied with small doses of the drug if they were able to inject). Hampl (2002) also pointed out that although craving might be predicted to arise because of withdrawal symptoms, in reality the desire to inject can be unrelated to the withdrawal state. What Hampl has identified is clearly a conditioned state but one which is independent of drug withdrawal or craving.

A psychological theory of needle fixation

Pates (2004) has investigated the phenomenon of needle fixation using qualitative methods of research via semi-structured interviews and psychometric measures. Thirty-three IDUs were interviewed about their history of injecting and their injecting practices. They were allocated to a needle fixated group or non-needle fixated group on the basis of the interview and then completed questionnaires about their dependence, craving for injecting, a scale for obsessive–compulsive disorders and a scale developed for measuring needle fixation (the NEFPRO: unpublished, see Appendix). The NEFPRO confirmed the needle fixated status of the needle fixated group.

The results revealed that those in the needle fixated group showed significantly higher scores on the NEFPRO at the $p < 0.05$ level of significance on the sexually arousing possibilities of injecting or the substitution of injecting for sexual behaviour, and the role of injecting within the sexual behaviour between partners. The same level of significance was found with flushing, substitution and on the scale overall. This indicates a difference in the role of injecting between the two groups. The roles of ritual and pain approached significance, but were not significant at the $p < 0.05$ level.

The results also showed that there were significant differences between the two groups on measures of obsessive–compulsive behaviour. Using the Padua scale, there were significant differences on the washing and checking subscales at the $p < 0.05$ level and the overall scale was significant at $p < 0.1$ level. There were differences at the $p < 0.1$ level on the other scales of impulsivity, rumination and precision between the two groups.

There were no differences in levels of dependence on drugs or craving for injecting between the two groups.

Pates (2004) identified four groups of injectors from those who were interviewed. These were as follows:

(1)   Those injectors who have no needle fixation, and for whom injecting was part of their drug use, the aim of which was efficient delivery of the drug.
(2)   Those injectors for whom the rush was the most important aspect of injecting. These injectors were always searching for the initial sensation of the rush they experienced at the beginning of their drug use. Because the sensation of the rush tends to reduce in strength very rapidly, there is a belief that this can be regained. Because of the variable purity of street drugs there will always be a variation of quality of the rush.
(3)   Those injectors for whom there is a strong element of ritual or pride in the skills of injecting, a part of the definition of needle fixation remains. The rewarding aspects of injecting drug use will produce a strongly reinforced reaction, which will maintain their injecting and also produce the secondary reinforcement of the behaviours described by Pates *et al.* (2001).
(4)   A group of injectors who may be truly described as needle fixated who report the secondary gains from injecting and may show the behaviours associated with needle fixation (i.e. substitution of inert substances or prolonged flush of blood into their veins). These injectors may show signs of a greater degree of psychological problems such as obsessive–compulsive behaviour.

This would suggest that those who are truly needle fixated are a small group, and for others the role of injecting may have as great a significance as the delivery of the drug. All these groups may be differentiated, but the group for whom injecting is merely instrumental to their drug use are the largest group by far.

Evidence against needle fixation

There are those in the field who would deny the existence of the problem of needle fixation. For example, Al-Adwani (2001) described a group of drug injectors who were being prescribed injectable diamorphine or methadone. There was a threat to convert their prescriptions to oral medication. The drug injectors claimed to have needle fixation and Al-Adwani stated that they were using this as an excuse in the hope of getting their prescriptions of injectable drugs continued. Although it is known that some IDUs may claim to have needle fixation, in the absence of evidence it does not obviate the existence of needle fixation.

Fraser *et al.* (2004) argue via a Foucaultian analysis of the papers published by Pates *et al.* (2001) and McBride *et al.* (2001) that the label 'needle fixation' is inaccurate because of the psychological meanings of the term 'fixation'. They ignore the fact that the term 'needle fixation' has been around for many years and is not the product of the aforementioned papers; more importantly, they argue that this term appears to encompass a range of different behaviours and is therefore imprecise. Post-modernist thinking is clear that meanings are plural for all narratives, and both the papers by Pates *et al.* (2001) and McBride *et al.* (2001) propose that needle fixation can only be seen as an umbrella term for a number of behaviours which may have differing aetiologies and outcomes. Pates (2004) goes further and defines groups of injectors with differing patterns of behaviour, including those with needle fixation and others who have some compulsive aspects to their behaviour but are not needle fixated.

Fraser *et al.* (2004) also express the concern that using the phrase 'needle fixation' pathologises an aspect of injecting. We would argue, on the contrary, that the two papers represent exploratory work attempting to explain a behaviour which is widely recognised but for which there was virtually no literature. Criticisms of examples of behaviour used by Pates *et al.* (2001) and McBride *et al.* (2001) cited by Fraser *et al.* (2004) were not claimed to be examples of needle fixation, but cited as examples of the complexity of injecting behaviour. Some of the interviewees of Fraser *et al.* (2004) referred spontaneously to complex ideas about injecting for which they used the term 'needle fixation', supporting the notion that the term is widely used if little understood by drug users themselves. Clearly what is needed is greater research interest, not premature conclusions about the important questions raised.

Treatment

There are no current treatment modalities for needle fixation. As this is clearly a psychological problem, psychological solutions should be found. However, it is clear that if substitute prescribing is being planned as part of treatment, then an adequate level of substitute drug must be provided to ensure that the client feels comfortable. This was one of the aspects described by a patient of Hampl (2003) who described fear of withdrawal as one aspect of his continuing to inject. The use of cue exposure combined with systematic desensitisation is a possibility, but probably not sufficient on its own. Because the presentation of injecting equipment and injecting practice may be arousing, the mere presence of these will not help extinguish the response. If this were combined with cognitive behavioural therapy alongside a detailed behavioural analysis of the injecting behaviour, treatment effects might be optimised and the client would understand the nature of their own associations with injecting.

Conclusions

This chapter has sought to describe best current understanding of needle fixation. There are few people in the population who inject themselves regularly. One other group who have to do this are people with diabetes. They may have to inject several times per day and the question arises of whether they would also develop needle fixation. There seem to be no reports of this in the literature and a pilot study (Ryan *et al.*, in preparation) suggests that they view injecting very differently and consider it a necessary part of the maintenance of their health. It would appear therefore that needle fixation behaviour is peculiar to injectors of illicit drugs.

Another aspect that has been suggested is the connection with self-harm. It has been suggested that people who cut themselves get a similar feeling of relief when they see the blood as do injectors when they flush (R. Pates, unpublished observations); this may be a fruitful area of future research. Another area of research showing some promise is the similarities of effect between people with needle fixation and those who have multiple body piercings or tattoos. Christofides *et al.* (submitted for publication) interviewed 80 participants recruited from a body art convention and two body art studios who filled in a self-report questionnaire regarding their motivations and experiences of obtaining tattoos or piercings. Findings suggest that there are many motivations for obtaining body art, including some similar to those found in needle fixation; for example, pain, ritual, sexual gratification, physiological and compulsive feelings. This may indicate that certain practices other than injecting involving body modification may become compulsive for similar reasons in terms of reinforcement and maintenance of the behaviour.

Needle fixation is a part of the behaviour of a small number of IDUs which may need to be addressed during treatment if individuals wish to cease injecting drugs. This may have implications for the growing problem of the spread of blood borne diseases.

References

Agar, M. (1977) Into that whole ritual thing: ritualistic drug use among urban American heroin addicts. In B. Du Toit (ed.), *Drugs, Rituals and Altered States of Consciousness*, Rotterdam: A.A. Balkema.

Al-Adwani, A. (2001) The myth of needle fixation. *Addiction*, **96**(2) 334.

Allbutt, T.C. (1870) On the abuse of hypodermic injections of morphia. *Practitioner*, **5**, 327–331.

Connors, M.M. (1988) Anthropological investigations of the meaning and practices of needle sharing among intravenous drug users (IVDUs). *Paper presented at the 4th International Conference on AIDS*, Stockholm, Sweden.

Christofides, S., Pates, R.M. & McBride, A. (submitted for publication) Multiple motivations for acquiring a tattoo or piercing: are there similarities with needle fixation?

Fraser, S., Hopwood, M., Treloar, C. & Brener, L. (2004) Needle fictions: medical constructions of needle fixation and the injecting drug user. *Addiction Research and Theory*, **12**(1), 67–76.

Friedman, S.R., Curtis, R., Neaigus, A., Jose, B. & Des Jarlais, D.C. (1999) *Social Networks, Drug Injectors' Lives, and HIV/AIDS*, New York: Kluwer Academic/Plenum.

Hampl, K. (2002) Léčba závislosti na heroinu metadonem v zařízení AT bez lůžkového zázemí. *Čes. a Slov. Psychiat.*, **98**(2), 86–91.

Hampl, K. (2003) Notes of meeting beween Dr Karel Hampl and Richard Pates at the Ordinace AT Clinic, Mělník, Central Bohemia, Czech Republic. In R.M. Pates, (2004) *The development of a psychological theory of needle fixation*, unpublished dissertation, University of Wales.

Howard, J. & Borges, P. (1971) Needle sharing in the Haight: some social and psychological functions. *Journal of Psychedelic Drugs*, **4**(1), 71–80.

Kohn, M. (1987) *Narcomania, on Heroin*. London: Faber and Faber.

Lemaire, A. (1977) *Jacques Lacan*, p. 229. London: Routledge and Kegan Paul.

Levine, D.G. (1974) Needle freaks: compulsive self-injection by drug users. *American Journal of Psychiatry*, **131**(3), 297–300.

Light, A.B. & Torrance, E.G. (1929) Opiate addiction VI: the effects of abrupt withdrawal followed by readministration of morphine in human addicts with special reference to the composition of the blood, the circulation and the metabolism. *Archives of Internal Medicine*, **44**, 1–16.

Lockley, P. (1995) *Counselling Heroin and other Drug Users*. London: Free Association Books.

McBride, A.J., Pates, R.M., Arnold, K. & Ball, N. (2001) Needle fixation, the drug user's perspective: a qualitative study. *Addiction*, **96**(7), 1051–1060.

Pates, R.M. (2001) A case of needle fixation. *Journal of Substance Use*, **6**(3), 202–206.

Pates, R.M. (2004) *The development of a psychological theory of needle fixation*, unpublished dissertation, University of Wales.

Pates, R., McBride, A., Arnold, K. & Ball, N. (2001). Towards an holistic understanding of injecting drug use: an overview of needle fixation. *Addiction Research*, **9**(1), 3–17.

Ryan, S., Pates, R.M. & Alwyn, T. (in preparation) The views of people with diabetes about injecting.

Stewart, T. (1987) *The Heroin Users*. London: Pandora Press.

Trebach, A. (1982) *The Heroin Solution*, New Haven: Yale University Press.

van Epen, H. (2001) Interview with Hans van Epen by Richard Pates, June 2001, Ooltgensplaat, The Netherlands. In R.M. Pates, (2004) *The development of a psychological theory of needle fixation*, unpublished dissertation, University of Wales.

Appendix:
Questionnaire regarding needle fixation

(1) I inject water if I have no injectable drugs available.

Strongly Disagree	Disagree	Neither Agree nor Disagree	Agree	Strongly Agree
☐	☐	☐	☐	☐

(2) I enjoy the pain I experience when injecting myself or when injected by others.

Strongly Disagree	Disagree	Neither Agree nor Disagree	Agree	Strongly Agree
☐	☐	☐	☐	☐

(3) I think that I would find it more difficult to give up the act of injecting than to give up my preferred drug.

Strongly Disagree	Disagree	Neither Agree nor Disagree	Agree	Strongly Agree
☐	☐	☐	☐	☐

(4) I find the thought of injecting a partner sexually arousing.

Strongly Disagree	Disagree	Neither Agree nor Disagree	Agree	Strongly Agree
☐	☐	☐	☐	☐

(5) I am attracted to the needle because of the association with pain.

Strongly Disagree	Disagree	Neither Agree nor Disagree	Agree	Strongly Agree
☐	☐	☐	☐	☐

(6) If I could get the same rush without the hassle of using the needle I would give up injecting.

Strongly Disagree	Disagree	Neither Agree nor Disagree	Agree	Strongly Agree
☐	☐	☐	☐	☐

(7) **I find the thought of being injected by a partner sexually arousing.**
Strongly Disagree   Disagree   Neither Agree   Agree   Strongly Agree
                                                nor Disagree

☐   ☐   ☐   ☐   ☐

(8) **Injecting water has a calming effect on me.**   I have never injected water   ☐
Strongly Disagree   Disagree   Neither Agree   Agree   Strongly Agree
                                                nor Disagree

☐   ☐   ☐   ☐   ☐

(9) **I flush blood in and out of the syringe barrel before/after injecting the drug.**
Strongly Disagree   Disagree   Neither Agree   Agree   Strongly Agree
                                                nor Disagree

☐   ☐   ☐   ☐   ☐

(10) **I find injecting sexually arousing.**
Strongly Disagree   Disagree   Neither Agree   Agree   Strongly Agree
                                                nor Disagree

☐   ☐   ☐   ☐   ☐

(11) **If someone invented a method of taking drugs that gave me a better rush than the needle, I would give up injecting and use this.**
Strongly Disagree   Disagree   Neither Agree   Agree   Strongly Agree
                                                nor Disagree

☐   ☐   ☐   ☐   ☐

(12) **I continue to flush blood in and out of the syringe barrel even if there are blood clots.**
Strongly Disagree   Disagree   Neither Agree   Agree   Strongly Agree
                                                nor Disagree

☐   ☐   ☐   ☐   ☐

(13) **The act of injecting has become a substitute for sex for me.**
Strongly Disagree   Disagree   Neither Agree   Agree   Strongly Agree
                                                nor Disagree

☐   ☐   ☐   ☐   ☐

(14) **The preparation and process of the injection (the ritual) is more important to me than the drug rush.**
Strongly Disagree   Disagree   Neither Agree   Agree   Strongly Agree
                                                nor Disagree

☐   ☐   ☐   ☐   ☐

Chapter 5

Women and Injecting

Rossana Oretti and Pim Gregory

Introduction

The number of research studies that have looked specifically at female drug use, let alone female injecting drug use, are limited (Taylor, 1993). The issues surrounding female drug use were largely ignored until the late 1970s. In 1976 the National Institute on Drug Abuse in the USA became interested in this area and began to commission research (Rosenbaum & Murphy, 1990). The paucity of gender-specific research may be explained, in part, by early perceptions that female drug misuse was rare (Auld *et al.*, 1986; Ellinwood *et al.*, 1966) and that the experiences of female drug users were no different from those of male drug users (Christmas, 1978; Fuller, 1978; Ettore, 1985).

The misuse of drugs by women is not a new or surprising phenomenon. However, with the possible exception of over-the-counter and prescribed psychotropic medication misuse, male drug users are still significantly more common than women. There are approximately 180 million people using illicit drugs worldwide (UNODC, 2002), and approximately one-third of drug users are female (Hepburn, 2002). The difference in prevalence rates between men and women has rapidly diminished, especially in young females. Young men and women show the same frequency of experimentation with drugs (Hsu & du Gurny, 1995). It has been suggested that the difference in prevalence does not reflect a difference in the susceptibility of men and women to becoming addicted to drugs, but merely reflects a difference in the opportunity to use drugs (Van Etten & Anthony, 1999; NIDA, 1999). Indeed there is evidence from animal studies demonstrating that female rats, given the opportunity to self-administer heroin or cocaine intravenously, began self-administration sooner and administered higher doses of the drug than did male rats (NIDA, 1999; Hanson, 2002; Cicero *et al.*, 2003). In humans there is a growing body of evidence to suggest that gender is also an important factor in determining drug-using activities, help-seeking behaviour and service experience.

This chapter aims to detail gender differences in injecting drug use behaviours that have been identified within the current literature. It should be noted that few studies have directly compared male and female injecting populations. Most of the research identified focuses either on women's drug use as a whole, rather than specifically on injecting behaviour, or injecting drug using populations as a whole with little attention to possible gender differences. As a result, it is difficult to ascertain a consistent picture of female injecting drug use. This is perhaps compounded by the erroneous assumption that women injecting drug users represent a homogenous group. Clearly, other variables such as age, ethnicity, socioeconomic background and sexual orientation, amongst others, may be relevant confounding factors.

There are many methodological difficulties inherent to studying populations of injecting drug users. It is anticipated that these problems are exacerbated when studying female injecting drug users for a variety of reasons. Overall, women drug users are generally considered '*hard to reach*' by treatment services (Hunter & Judd, 1998) and as such, prevalence rates of injecting behaviour based on women who have accessed services may not be truly representative. If women drug users are harder to find, then there is no reason to believe that this will not apply equally in research settings.

This chapter will firstly detail what is known about the risk factors for initiation into injecting amongst women. It will then review the available literature on the injecting practices of females and the resultant associated risks.

Initiation into injecting

The transition from other modes of drug use to injecting drug use is seen as a crucial stage in the career of any drug user, both from the perspective of those working in the field of substance misuse and, most importantly, the users themselves (Rosenbaum, 1981). The use of a needle, '*has great symbolic import in all drug cultures, as it is seen as the divider between "hard" and "soft" drugs*' (Rosenbaum, 1981) and its initiation is seen as the moment when a person transcends from being a 'user' to an addict (Rosenbaum, 1981). It is crucial to understand the factors surrounding the transition into injecting drug use in order to provide successful preventative interventions. In particular, it is useful to consider what, if any, effect gender may have on this process.

There are a number of studies that have compared the age of onset of injecting drug behaviour between men and women. These studies have consistently reported no gender difference (Crofts *et al.*, 1996; Geoghegan *et al.*, 1999; Bennett *et al.*, 2000; Doherty *et al.*, 2000). However, research varies as to whether gender differences exist in the length of time that drugs are used by other routes before the transition to injecting. These studies have in the main focused on heroin use. Some have reported no gender difference in this respect (Crofts *et al.*, 1996; Doherty *et al.*, 2000). Crofts *et al.* (1996) suggest that 2.5 years is the average for both genders; Geoghegan *et al.* (1999) found that women had a shorter career smoking heroin before moving to injecting than men (130 vs 156 weeks ($p = 0.57$)), whereas another study has reported that women were less likely than men to move from smoking to injecting (Griffiths *et al.*, 1994).

In an Australian study by Crofts *et al.* (1996), amphetamine was reported to be the first drug injected in the majority of their sample (77%), usually after other routes had been tried (88%). Only 18% of this sample reported heroin as the first drug injected, but these individuals tended not to have used other routes prior to injecting (48%). Unfortunately, this study did not report on possible gender differences. Geoghegan *et al.* (1999), in a Dublin study, reported rates of 14% for individuals commencing drug use by the injecting route, although they did not differentiate drug type. They did not find any gender difference in those that commenced injecting as a first route.

There have been some studies looking at the environmental factors that may promote initiation into injecting drug use. Most of these have suggested that a person will be initiated into injecting by someone else (Crofts *et al.*, 1996; Darke *et al.*, 2001). This would seem intuitively correct given the complexity of the task. Crofts *et al.* (1996) found that only 12% of their study group had injected themselves on the first occasion and there was no gender difference. However, the person performing the injecting did vary according to the gender of the recipient. Crofts *et al.* (1996) found that women, as compared to men, were more frequently injected first by a heterosexual partner. This represented about a fifth of the female cohort, with the majority of females being first injected by friends. By contrast, another Australian study (Darke *et al.*, 2001) found a marked gender difference in the rates of first self-injecting. Males were significantly more likely to inject themselves on the first occasion than were females. This study also confirmed the finding that a proportion of women (a third) were first injected by a heterosexual partner. Other research has suggested that women are, in the main, first injected by female friends, whereas males are first injected by male friends (Doherty *et al.*, 2000). The initiation into injecting appears to be unplanned, albeit the idea of the person receiving the injection. The person assisting or administering the injection has usually obtained and paid for the drug (Crofts *et al.*, 1996). Gender differences in this respect have not been investigated. When looking at rates of sharing injecting equipment on the first injecting episode, Crofts *et al.* (1996) reported that only 50% of individuals did not share needles/syringes and only 30% did not share spoons. These figures are not surprising given the unplanned nature of the first injecting episode. Unfortunately, gender differences were not studied.

It has been established that women with a history of abuse have high rates of substance misuse when compared to women with no abuse history (Kilpatrick *et al.*, 1992; Swift *et al.*, 1996; Kendler *et al.*, 2000). Molitor *et al.* (2000) reported that women who had a history of sexual abuse were also more likely to have a higher incidence of sexually transmitted diseases and engage in more high risk sexual behaviour. There is empirical evidence to suggest that a history of sexual and/or physical abuse may predispose to injecting behaviour. Neaigus *et al.* (2001) found that 45% of injecting drug using women reported having been sexually abused, compared with 17% of injecting men.

Kilpatrick *et al.* (1992) reviewed the cases of 4008 women who had been raped. Sixty one per cent of the rapes occurred before the victim was aged 17 years; the rape victims were 10 times more likely to have a life time history of the use of drugs such as heroin and amphetamine. Of women in drug misuse treatment, 30–59% were found to be suffering from post traumatic stress disorder (PTSD); this rate of PTSD is 2–3 times higher than the rate seen in men (Najavits *et al.*, 1997).

Other apects of injecting

Some studies suggest gender differences in the frequency of injecting episodes. Women have been found to inject more frequently than men (Rosenbaum, 1973; Miller *et al.*, 2001) and to use more heroin per injection (Bretteville-Jensen, 2000). This is in contrast to the study of Geoghegan *et al.* (1999) who found no significant gender difference in the frequency of injecting. A paradox cited by Bretteville-Jensen (2000) is that although women in their study consumed more heroin and injected more frequently, women in general are less likely to die from an overdose of heroin.

One area of the literature that is relatively consistent is that of the gender differences between the sites used to inject, and the direct problems encountered due to injecting. By far the most common site for both men and women is the antecubital fossa. Compared with men, women find injecting more difficult and have increased health problems resulting from injecting (Geoghegan *et al.*, 1999; Darke *et al.*, 2001). Women injectors have been shown to be at high risk for deep vein thrombosis (DVT) (McColl *et al.*, 2001). Intravenous drug use is a risk factor in 21% of all cases of DVT found in women and 52% of cases found in women under the age of 40 (McColl *et al.*, 2001). Women are significantly more likely to report suffering from abscesses and other local complications of injecting (Geoghegan *et al.*, 1999). This phenomenon probably explains why women shift between injecting sites more frequently than men (Darke *et al.*, 2001). The use of more injection sites is, in itself, independently correlated with increased risk of health problems due to injecting (Darke *et al.*, 2001). It has been postulated that women have more difficulty injecting successfully because of differences in peripheral vasculature and the greater amount of subcutaneous fat, which result in less accessible veins (Morrison, 1999a). The finding that women are more likely to use tourniquets during injecting would support this hypothesis (Darke *et al.*, 2001). In addition, women have a greater propensity to engage in 'skin popping' (injecting subcutaneously) which can result in ulcers and low-grade infections (Morrison, 1999a).

There is some evidence for gender differences in the environments in which injecting takes place. Women are significantly less likely to report injecting themselves (Rosenbaum 1981; Taylor, 1993; Geoghegan *et al.*, 1999; Wood *et al.*, 2003). This may be associated with the difficulties women have in undertaking injecting, or they may not perceive themselves as being 'in control' of their injecting (Tortu *et al.*, 2003). Having difficulty injecting oneself may be a reason for others to carry out the injection, or, conversely, it could be that women have poorer injecting techinique because they do not rehearse their skills. By contrast, men are more likely to report injecting alone (Latkin *et al.*, 1998): 62% of men had injected alone half the time or more in the past 6 months, compared with 45% of women.

High risk behaviour

A number of studies have found that women are more likely to share injecting equipment than men (e.g. Barnard, 1993; Latkin *et al.*, 1998; Bennett *et al.*, 2000; Sherman *et al.*,

2001; Fernando *et al.*, 2003; Tortu *et al.*, 2003). The Public Health Laboratory Service (PHLS) Collaborative Survey of Salivary Antibodies to HIV and Hepatitis (Durante *et al.*, 1995) found that 26% of women, compared with 16% of men, reported sharing injecting equipment in the month prior to interview. This trend was again found by the Unlinked Anonymous Surveys Steering Group (Department of Health, 1998) which found that 23% of women, compared with 16% of men, reported sharing in the previous month. Women are more likely to have a heterosexual injecting partner (Rosenbaum, 1981; Gossop *et al.*, 1994; Geoghegan *et al.*, 1999) and are more likely to report sharing with that partner (Geoghegan *et al.*, 1999). Perhaps the most worrying finding is that women frequently fail to perceive any risk in sharing with a regular sexual partner (Barnard, 1993). The reason for this is that they expect that their partner will share only with them. This assumption has been shown to be naïve. Not only is it common for men to share works with other users, especially friends (Barnard, 1993), but research has also found that it is fairly common for men to have casual sexual partners as well as their regular partner (Davies *et al.*, 1996). Female injecting drug users have also been found not to practise safe sex with regular partners even when they are also injecting drug users (Houlding & Davidson, 2003). One review of women injectors found that 64% of those sexually active *never* used condoms (White *et al.*, 1993). These finding are perhaps counterintuitive, as women are generally deemed to be risk averse (Rosenbaum, 1981).

There has been an attitudinal change within drug using circles whereby sharing 'works' has become less acceptable (Bennett *et al.*, 2000). It is therefore quite possible that drug users have learnt to under-report sharing, so that prevalence data will increasingly underestimate the extent of high risk behaviour (Bennett *et al.*, 2000). It is not known whether there is any gender bias towards under- or over-reporting of sharing. Although sharing is now less acceptable, drug users still have considerable difficulty in refusing someone's requests to share injecting equipment (Barnard, 1993). The explanation given for this difficulty is that the act of sharing is one that carries social meaning. This could pose specific problems for women, given the fact that their primary injecting partners are often also their sexual partners. Clearly there is an emphasis on trust within a relationship that might make refusing to share equipment more difficult. It should be noted that most of the research on sharing has not distinguished between the acts of 'passing on' and 'receiving'. Bennett *et al.* (2000) have argued that this is a differentiation worth making, given that women seem to be particularly at risk from receiving works, whereas men tend to be more likely to pass works on.

There may be other factors that increase the likelihood of women sharing. It is argued that female injecting drug users do not access needle exchange and other treatment services as readily as men (e.g. Rosenbaum 1981; Ettore 1992). Female injecting drug users are seen by society as '*polluted women*' (Ettore, 1992). The stereotypical female drug user is a bad mother and irresponsible wife who neglects the needs of her children and husband (Ettore, 1992). Barnard (1993) found that, despite the presence of a local needle exchange service (NES), 60% of study individuals still reported sharing during the previous year; women made up a large proportion of this group. These women reported that they disliked or avoided having to buy or exchange works at NES. Only a minority of the men within the study held the same reservations. In a review of NES use in Oslo, women were found to inject more frequently than men but neither utilised the NES more frequently, nor acquired a greater number of syringes when they did (Miller *et al.*, 2001). The need to conceal their drug use prevents women presenting to NES (Hunter & Judd, 1998).

The propensity to share injecting equipment is influenced by the social networks of injecting drug users. Neaigus *et al.* (1994) found that individuals who have fewer drug injectors in their social network were themselves, considerably less likely to share. Gender differences with regard to social networks have been reported. Females have been found to share with a greater percentage of their networks when compared with men. This could be explained by the findings that women's sexual partners comprise a higher percentage of their social networks and women had daily contact with a much greater proportion of their social network (Sherman *et al.*, 2001). It is important to note that some research has shown no gender differences in rates of sharing (Geoghegan *et al.*, 1999).

The infrequent use of contraception amongst female injecting drug users, including those that inject, is in part representative of the belief that they cannot become pregnant. This belief is founded on the fact that drugs, in particular heroin, disrupt the menstrual cycle, causing irregular or absent periods (Cohen *et al.*, 1989). A quarter of opiate-dependent women report amenorrhoea (Morrison, 1999b). This has led to high rates of pregnancy amongst female injecting drug users (Deren, 1985; Dolan *et al.*, 1990; Weber *et al.*, 2003). Children of female injecting drug users are at high risk of contracting HIV and hepatitis. The European Collaborative Study (1991) found the vertical transmission rate for HIV infection to be 13%.

The risk of contracting HIV, hepatitis B (HBV), hepatitis C (HCV), and other blood borne diseases is theoretically increased in females who share injecting equipment. Over recent years, HIV in injecting drug users has exceeded that of any other risk group, particularly in ethnic minorities (Booth *et al.*, 1998). In a study in Glasgow, 54% of injecting drug users who were HIV positive were women, despite the fact that the majority of drug injectors were men (Barnard, 1993). A study in Vancouver showed that HIV in injecting drug users was 40% higher in women (Spittal *et al.*, 2002). A further study in Vancouver looked at young injectors, aged between 13 and 24 years. The baseline rate of HIV was 10% and was associated with female gender and injecting heroin daily (Miller *et al.*, 2002).

Although a number of studies have found female injectors to be at greater risk of contracting HIV (e.g. Barnard, 1993; Davies *et al.*, 1996; Miller *et al.*, 2002; Spittal *et al.*, 2002), there is some debate over whether this is due to risky injecting practices, and/or risky sexual practices (Freeman *et al.*, 1994). A 10-year study by Strathdee *et al.* (2001), whilst not differentiating by gender, concluded that it was high-risk sexual practice, and not high-risk injecting practice, that was the main causal factor in the increased prevalence of HIV seen in women who inject drugs. The difficulty in assessing this is the overlap between women's sexual and drug networks. Some drug using women will also be at an increased risk due to sex work. Miller & Neaigus (2002), found that 68% of the injecting women in their study had participated in sex work at some time. Rosenbaum (1981) quotes a similar figure of 60%. One study of US prostitutes found the rates of HIV infection to be 11% for injectors and 2% for non-injectors (Khabbaz *et al.*, 1990).

Conclusions

The literature on female injecting drug users is limited. A consistent finding is that women are typically at greater risk of all sorts when engaging in injecting than men. Women have more health-related problems resulting from injecting and tend to share injecting equipment more frequently, especially with male injecting partners. The prevalence of HIV is higher in female injectors than men. Women drug users have high rates of pregnancy due to poor contraception. There are numerous complications for the pregnancy and the newborn child. Despite these issues, existing treatment services may not attract or retain women. It is essential that further research should be directed specifically at female injecting drug use. If treatment services wish to provide effective interventions then it is necessary to first understand the processes underlying female injecting behaviour.

References

Auld, J., Dorn, N. & South, N. (1986) Irregular work, irregular pleasures: heroin in the 1980s. In R. Matthews & J. Young (eds), *Confronting Crime*. London: Sage.

Barnard, M.A. (1993) Needle sharing in context: patterns of sharing among men and women injectors and HIV risks. *Addiction*, 88, 805–812.

Bennett, G.A., Velleman, R.D., Barter, G. & Bradbury, C. (2000) Gender differences in sharing injecting equipment by drug users in England. *AIDS Care*, 12(1), 77–87.

Booth, R.E., Kwiatkowski, C.F. & Stephens, R.C. (1998) Effectiveness of HIV/AIDS interventions on drug use and needle risk behaviors for out-of-treatment injection drug users. *Journal of Psychoactive Drugs*, 30(3), 269–278.

Bretteville-Jensen, A.L. (2000) Sex differences concerning the habit patterns and health among intravenous heroin addicts in Oslo. *Tidsskrift for den Norske Laegeforening*, 120(2), 192–194.

Christmas, J.J. (1978) Women, alcohol and drugs: issues and implications. In A. Schecter (ed.), *Drug Abuse: Modern Trends, Issues and Perspectives*. New York: Dekker.

Cicero, T.J., Aylward, S.C. & Meyer, E.R. (2003) Gender differences in the intravenous self-administration of mu opiate agonists. *Pharmacology, Biochemistry and Behavior*, 74, 541–549.

Cohen, J.B., Hauer, L.B. & Wofsy, C.B. (1989) Women and IV drugs: parenteral and heterosexual transmission of human immunodeficiency virus. *Journal of Drug Issues*, 19, 39–56.

Crofts, N., Louie, R., Rosenthal, D. & Jolley, D. (1996) The first hit: circumstances surrounding initiation into injecting. *Addiction*, 91(8), 1187–1196.

Darke, S., Ross, J. & Kaye, S. (2001) Physical injecting sites among injecting drug users in Sydney, Australia, *Drug and Alcohol Dependence*, 62, 77–82.

Davies, A.G., Dominy, N.J., Peters, A.D. & Richardson, A.M. (1996) Gender differences in HIV risk behaviour of injecting drug users in Edinburgh. *AIDS Care*, 8(5), 517–527.

Department of Health (1998), *Unlinked Anonymous Surveys Steering Group: Prevalence of HIV in the United Kingdom*. London: Department of Health.

Deren, S. (1985) *Parents on methadone and their children*. Treatment Issue Report 50. New York: State Division of Substance Abuse Services.

Doherty, M.C., Garfein, R.S., Monterroso, E., Latkin, C. & Vlahov, D. (2000) Gender differences in the initiation of injection drug use amongst young adults. *Journal of Urban Health*, 77(3), 396–414.

Dolan, K.A., Donoghoe, M.C., Jones, S.J. & Stimson, G.V. (1990) *A cohort study of clients at four syringe exchange schemes and comparison groups of injectors*. London: Monitoring Research Group, Center for Research on Drugs and Health Behaviour, Charing Cross and Westminster Medical School.

Durante, A.J., Hart, G.J., Brady, A.R., Madden, P.B. & Noone, A. (1995) The Health of the Nation target on syringe sharing: a role for routine surveillance in assessing progress and targeting interventions. *Addiction*, **90**, 1389–1396.

Ellinwood, E.H., Smith, W.G. & Vaillant, G.E. (1966) Narcotic addiction in males and females: a comparison. *International Journal of the Addictions*, 1(2), 33–45.

Ettore, B. (1985) Psychotropics, passivity and the pharmaceutical industry. In A. Henman, R. Lewis & Malyon (eds) with B. Ettore & L. O'Bryan, *Big Deal: The Politics of the Illicit Drug Business*. London: Pluto.

Ettore, E. (1992) *Women and Substance Use*. London: Macmillan.

European Collaborative Study (1991) Children born to women with HIV-1 infection: natural history and risk of transmission. *Lancet*, **337**, 253–260.

Fernando, D., Schilling, R.F., Fontdevila, J., El-bassel, N. (2003) Predictors of sharing drugs among injection drug users in the Bronx: implications for HIV transmission. *Journal of Psychoactive Drugs*, **35**(2), 227–236.

Freeman, R.C., Rodriguez, G.M. & French, J.F. (1994) A comparison of male and female intravenous drug users' risk behaviors for HIV infection. *American Journal of Drug and Alcohol Abuse*, **20**(2), 129–157.

Fuller, M. (1978) Sex-role stereotyping and social science. In J. Chetwynd & O. Hartnett (eds), *The Sex-Role System*. London: Routledge and Kegan Paul.

Geoghegan, T., O'Shea, M. & Cox, G. (1999) Gender differences in characteristics of drug users presenting to a Dublin syringe exchange. *Irish Journal of Psychological Medicine*, **16**(4), 131–135.

Gossop, M., Griffiths, P. & Strang, J. (1994) Sex differences in patterns of drug taking behaviour – a study at a London community drug team. *British Journal of Psychiatry*, **164**(1), 101–104.

Griffiths, P., Gossop, M., Powis, B. & Strang, J. (1994) Transitions in patterns of heroin administration: a study of heroin chasers and heroin injectors. *Addiction*, **89**(3), 301–309.

Hanson, G.R. (2002) In drug abuse, gender matters. *NIDA Notes*, **17**(2), [electronic version]. Bethesda, MD: National Institute on Drug Abuse (http://www.drugabuse.gov/NIDA).

Hepburn, M. (2002) Drug use and women's reproductive health. In T. Petersen & A. McBride (eds), *Working with Substance Abusers*, pp. 285–295. London: Routledge.

Houlding, C. & Davidson, R. (2003) Beliefs as predictors of condom use by injecting drug users in treatment. *Health Education Research*, **18**(2), 145–155.

Hsu, L.-N. & du Gurny, J. (1995) *Towards a gender-sensitive approach to drug demand reduction: a process within the United Nations system.* Vienna: United Nations Office on Drugs and Crime.

Hunter, G.M. & Judd, A. (1998) Women injecting drug users in London: the extent and nature of their contact with drug and health services. *Drug and Alcohol Review*, 17, 267–276.

Kendler, K.S., Bulik, C.M., Silberg, J., Hettema, J.M., Myers, J. & Prescott, C.A. (2000) Childhood sexual abuse and adult psychiatric and substance use disorders in women: an epidemiological and co-twin control analysis. *Archives of General Psychiatry*, 57(10), 953–959.

Khabbaz, R.F., Darrow, W.W., Hartley, T.M., Witte, J., Cohen, J.B., French, J., Gill, P.S., Potterat, J., Sikes, R.K., Reich, R., *et al.* (1990) Seroprevalence and risk factors for HTLV-I/II infection among female prostitutes in the United States. *Journal of the American Medical Association*, 263(1), 60–64.

Kilpatrick, D.G., Edmunds, C.N. & Seymour, A.K. (1992) *Rape in America: A Report to the Nation.* Charleston, SC: Crime Victims' Research and Treatment Centre.

Latkin, C.A., Mandell, W., Knowlton, A.R., Doherty, M.C., Vlahov, D., Suh, T. & Celentano, D.D. (1998) Gender differences in injection-related behaviors among injection drug users in Baltimore, Maryland. *AIDS Education and Prevention*, 10(3), 257–263.

McColl, M.D., Tait, R.C., Greer, I.A. & Walker, I.D. (2001) Injecting drug use is a risk factors for deep vein thrombosis in women in Glasgow. *British Journal of Haematology*, 112(3), 641–643.

Miller, C.L., Spittal, P.M., LaLiberte, N., Li, K., Tyndall, M.W., O'Shaughnessy, M.V. & Schechter, M.T. (2002) Females experiencing sexual and drug vulnerabilities are at elevated risk for HIV infection among youth who use injection drugs. *Journal of Acquired Immune Deficiency Syndrome*, 30(3), 335–341.

Miller, M. & Neaigus, A. (2002) An economy of risk: resource acquisition strategies of inner city women who use drugs. *International Journal of Drug Policy*, 13, 409–418.

Miller, M., Eskild, A., Mella, I., Moi, H. & Magnuse, P. (2001) Gender differences in syringe exchange program use in Oslo, Norway. *Addiction*, 96, 1639–1651.

Molitor, F., Ruiz, J.D., Klausner, J.D. & McFarland, W. (2000) History of forced sex in association with drug use and sexual HIV risk behaviors, infection with STDs, and diagnostic medical care: results from the Young Women Survey. *Journal of Interpersonal Violence*, 15(3), 262–278.

Morrison, C.L. (1999a) Medical problems of illicit drug misuse in pregnancy and harm minimisation. In C. Siney (ed.), *Pregnancy and Drug Misuse*, pp. 43–53. Edinburgh: Books for Midwives.

Morrison, C.L. (1999b) Medical problems of illicit drug misuse in pregnancy and harm minimisation. In C. Siney (ed.), *Pregnancy and Drug Misuse*, pp. 107–114. Edinburgh: Books for Midwives.

Najavits, L.M., Weiss, R.D. & Shaw, S.R. (1997) The link between substance abuse and posttraumatic stress disorder in women: a research review. *American Journal on Addictions*, 6(4), 273–283.

Neaigus, A., Friedman, S.R., Curtis, R., Des Jarlais, D.C., Furst, R.T., Jose, B. *et al.* (1994) The relevance of drug injectors social and risk networks for understanding and preventing HIV infection. *Social Science and Medicine*, 38(1), 67–78.

Neaigus, A., Miller, M., Friedman, S.R., Hagen, D.L., Sifaneck, S.J., Ildefonso, G. & Des Jarlais, D.C. (2001) Potential risk factors for the transition to injecting among non-injecting heroin users: a comparison of former injectors and never injectors. *Addiction*, **96**, 847–860.

NIDA (1999) Gender differences in drug abuse risks and treatment. *NIDA Notes*, **15**(4) [electronic version]. Bethesda, MD: National Institute on Drug Abuse (http://www.drugabuse.gov/NIDA).

Rosenbaum, M. (1973) *The World and Career of the Woman Heroin Addict*. San Francisco: Institute for Scientific Analysis.

Rosenbaum, M. (1981) *Women on Heroin*. New Brunswick: Rutgers University Press.

Rosenbaum, M. & Murphy, S. (1990) Women and addiction: process, treatment and outcome. *NIDA Research Monograph*, **98**, 120–127.

Sherman, S.G., Latkin, C.A. & Gielen, A.C. (2001) Social factors related to syringe sharing among injecting partners: a focus on gender. *Substance Use and Misuse*, **36**(14), 2113–2136.

Spittal, P.M., Craib, K.J., Wood, E., LaLiberte, N., Li, K., Tyndall, M.W., O'Shaughnessy, M.V. & Schechter, M.T. (2002) Risk factors for elevated HIV incidence rates among female injection drug users in Vancouver. *Canadian Medical Association Journal*, **166**(7), 894–899.

Strathdee, S.A., Galai, N., Safaiean, M., Celentano, D.D., Vlahov, D., Johnson, L. & Nelson, K.E. (2001) Sex differences in risk factors for HIV seroconversion among injection drug users: a 10 year perspective. *Archives of Internal Medicine*, **161**, 1281–1288.

Swift, W., Copeland, J. & Hall, W. (1996) Characteristics of women with alcohol and other drug problems: findings of an Australian national survey. *Addiction*, **91**(8), 1141–1150.

Taylor, A. (1993) *Women Drug Users – An Ethnography of a Female Injecting Community*. New York: Oxford University Press.

Tortu, S., McMahon, J.M., Hamid, R. & Neaigus, A. (2003) Women's drug injection practices in East Harlem: an event analysis in a high-risk community. *AIDS and Behavior*, **7**(3), 317–328.

UNODC (2002) *World Drug Report 2000*. Vienna: United Nations Office on Drugs and Crime.

Van Etten, M.L. & Anthony, J.C. (1999) Comparative epidemiology of initial drug opportunities and transitions to first use: marijuana, cocaine, hallucinogens and heroin. *Drug and Alcohol Dependence*, **54**, 117–125.

Weber, A.E., Tyndall, M.W., Spittal P.M., Li, K., Coulter, S., O'Shaughnessy, M.V. & Schechter, M.T. (2003) High pregnancy rates and reproductive health indicators amongst female injection-drug users in Vancouver, Canada. *European Journal of Contraception and Reproductive Health Care*, **8**(1), 52–58.

White, D., Phillips, K., Mulleady, G. & Cupitt, C. (1993) Sexual issues and condom use among injecting drug users. *AIDS Care*, **5**(4), 427–437.

Wood, E., Spittal, P.M., Kerr, T., Small, T., Tyndall, M.W., O'Shaughnessy, M.V. & Schechter, M.T. (2003) Requiring help injecting as a risk factor for HIV infection in the Vancouver epidemic: implications for HIV prevention. *Canadian Journal of Public Health*, **94**(5), 355–359.

Chapter 6

Injecting in Prisons

David Shewan, Heino Stöver and Kate Dolan

Introduction

Across different countries, prisons differ, as do prisoner populations. Prison regimes vary in terms of punitiveness, human rights, and basic conditions such as sanitation and food. Prisoner populations differ with regard to reasons for having been sent to jail, typicality of background, age and gender. But within prisoner populations, there are some common themes that can be identified. One of these is that most prisoner populations will include a high quotient of people with a background of mental health problems, one of which is addiction. One behavioural aspect strongly associated with addiction to certain drugs in particular, such as opiates, is injecting. There is a range of health risks associated with injecting and with sharing of injecting equipment. In many countries, therefore, injecting and sharing in prison will be of major public health concern. One focus of this chapter will be on these concerns.

Another focus of this chapter will be on *why* people should inject in prison. Attempted explanations for this apparently insensible behaviour will be discussed, not least as the authors would argue that an understanding of such risk behaviours is crucial to informed public health, and criminal justice, policy and practice. Also, injecting in prison will be looked at closely because it is interesting – and researchers into human behaviour who lose sight of this motivation for their work run the risk of making their work become predictable, without originality, and not informative. This focus of the chapter, we would argue, is curiously under-researched, and the possible reasons for this will be discussed. But first, how common is drug injecting in prison?

What prisons might inherit

There are different factors that might indicate the extent of drug injecting in prison. On one hand, there are data acquired from prevalence studies that look broadly at the level of drug use and drug problems in prisons, including injecting while in prison. An advantage of such studies is the degree to which they look at specific prisons. Due to the heterogeneity of prisoner populations from one prison to another, between regions, and across countries, there is value in identifying differences in trends that match these differences in population. On the other hand, the disadvantage of local studies is that by themselves they cannot be taken as representative of the situation as a whole. For example, as well as cultural differences, there may be differences between male and female prisoner populations, and there may be differences between adult prisoner populations and young people held in juvenile penal institutions. But by subsuming local studies within broader studies we can estimate what are general trends.

Substantial proportions of drug *users* in prisoner populations have been noted in many countries. Hiller *et al.* (1999) report that in the United States 68% of all new admissions test positive for an illegal drug in urine screening, and similar findings have been reported across Europe, North America and Australia. The European Network of Drug and HIV/AIDS Services in Prison (ENDHASP, 1997) estimated that 46.5% of prisoners across Europe would be users of illegal drugs before imprisonment. According to the European Monitoring Centre for Drugs and Drug Addiction (EMCDDA) Annual Reports for 1999 and 2000 see (http://www.emcdda.org/infopoint/publications/annrepstat _00_law.shtml), between 15 and 50% of prisoners in the European Union have, or have had, problems with illicit drug use. In the United States this figure has been calculated to be as high as 70% (US Department of Justice, 2000). In Australia, Butler (1997) reported that 73% of female prisoners and 64% of male prisoners had used an illegal drug at some point, with 23% of females and 18% of males having used heroin (see also Dolan & Crofts, 2000). In continents such as South America and Africa the situation is less clear, not least because of the lack of systematic research in these regions (Dunn *et al.*, 2000; Ohaeri, 2000).

A number of factors will likely contribute to this trend. In EU countries, for example, the number of drug law offences has been steadily rising in most countries over the past 15 years, as shown by EMCDDA figures from 1985 to 1998 see (http://www.emcdda.org/ infopoint/publications/annrepstat_00_law.shtml). At the same time, the overall numbers of people sent to prison have also been steadily rising, and although an increase in drug law offences is likely to be a contributor to this trend, it does not provide a full explanation. Indeed, this assumes that a rise in drug law offences reflects an increase in the number of illegal drug users, and the relationship between these figures remains unclear. For example, O'Mahony (1997) found in a study of a male prisoner population in Ireland that while 66% of the total sample had a history of heroin use, only 7% were in prison as a result of a conviction for an offence against the *Misuse of Drugs Act*. Similarly, in Denmark and Italy, it has been reported that half of the drug users in prison in 1998 were imprisoned for 'general offences', i.e. offences other than violations of the drug laws (Focal Point Denmark, 1998; Focal Point Italy, 1999). While there remains considerable debate concerning the relationship between drug use and general crime, the two are clearly associated (Bean, 2002). It remains unclear exactly why the number of prisoners is increasing in so many countries, but it is fairly safe to assume that as overall prison numbers increase, so will the numbers of problematic drug users held in custody. Furthermore, a significant proportion of the problematic drug users in prison will have co-existing psychiatric and mental health problems (Singleton *et al.*, 1999).

Paradoxically, in Scotland, the overall rates for crime, including crimes of theft, are going down, yet in Scotland the prisoner population is actually increasing *while* the crime rate is going down. Why is this? Is it because there is a disproportionately increasing number of drug users in Scotland who remain one of the main sources of crime in that country? No. The number of opiate addicts, for example, is actually relatively stable. So if we use Scotland as an example, the focus on public health, which is a laudable focus, has to take into account the role of the criminal justice system. Public health systems should therefore be questioning why there is such pressure being placed on prison systems, not just in terms of numbers, but also in terms of the range of health problems, including drug dependence, that prison staff are expected to deal with.

Within this general context, it is worth noting the potential for 'filters' that can be applied to try and reduce the number of drug users being sent to prison, often for relatively petty offences. As Alem *et al.* (1999) pointed out: 'These filters are based on the legal rules and phases as well as priority setting by law enforcement agencies. In a great number of countries police and prosecution are formally obliged to bring to court any crime that is detected (*legality principle*). In others the *expediency principle* (or *opportunity principle*) is applied which allows discretionary powers to the police and the prosecution'. Apart from these basic factors, which of course influence the overall numbers of prisoners as well as the number of arrested drug users, it is important to mention other factors specific to drug users.

One of these is the existence and utilisation of alternatives to imprisonment. These can be identified as developed at the stage of the court (where the court can have the power to review the offender's progress since being charged for the original offence); before imprisonment (where the court has the power to suspend sentence in order that the culprit can undergo treatment either in parallel with another community order or as a sentence in its own right); and during incarceration where the culprit can effectively serve their sentence in a community-based therapeutic community or institutions. More specifically to do with drug users, another 'filter' is the direct link between police arrest and referral to counselling agencies (e.g. 'arrest referral' in the UK, 'early intervention' in Germany and The Netherlands).

Within the specific context of this chapter, these filters can determine the number of drug users that finally end up in prison. And given that this group will predominantly be characterised as socioeconomically deprived, with a long history of times spent in secure institutions, several treatment attempts, high rates of relapse and severe health damages (including irreversible infectious diseases), there are many factors that could, perhaps should, mitigate against such damaged people being sent to prison. Any arguments, therefore, in relation to health policy as it affects drug users has to be seen in that context: a focus on drug use and addiction in the prisoner population is naïve if it does not take overall penal policy as the benchmark. In fact, the first, and perhaps the main point we would make in this chapter is, why are we continuing to send so many people, *including* high numbers of problematic drug users, to prison?

There are a lot of people in prison

Imprisonment, in most major regions of the world, remains the standard response to crime at various levels, from theft to extreme violence. Based on figures provided by the International Centre For Prison Studies (http://www.prisonstudies.org), the rates for prisoner populations vary across countries. The United States currently has the highest ratio of prisoners to the general population in the world, this being 714 per 100 000 inhabitants. The comparable figure for the Russian Federation is 548 per 100 000. In Europe, figures vary across countries: in England and Wales the figure is 142 per 100 000; Scotland 130 per 100 000; Germany 96 per 100 000; France, 95 per 100 000. In Australia, this figure is 117 per 100 000 and in China, the figure is similar at 118 per 100 000.

Here we enter the complex area of the use of prison as a final, or even penultimate, deterrence to crime or the attempted containment of crime. But can it be the case that in all these countries the prisoner population is directly related to a relative proportion of drug users in the general population, even problematic drug users, even drug users who are involved in general crime? It can be argued that within levels and increases in overall prison numbers, it is clearly the case that the *number* of drug users in prisons in *some countries* has also risen, but probably not all. And, returning to the specific focus of this chapter, do we know how much injecting there is actually *in* American prisons compared to prisons in Ukraine? Or India? No, we don't: such research has not been carried out within the vast majority of prisoner populations across the world. Indeed in most countries, the paucity of such in-depth research is comparable.

Injecting *in* prison

So, at one level, the evidence through research outcomes can at least be estimated. Within industrialised countries, certainly, the prison environment is one within which a majority of prisoners will already have some involvement, frequently a major involvement, with illegal drugs. This situation creates potential problems and challenges for prison systems, and for those who live and work in prisons, especially as there is a rising trend for sending people to prison, arguably regardless of whether this increase is characterised by an increase in the number of problematic drug users incarcerated. This is the broader context. We will now look at a more specific public health concern: that of infectious viruses and diseases for which prison serves as a dangerous environmental setting.

It can be seen, that in Europe certainly, one of the best ways to find a high representation of drug injectors in a single defined space is to go to a prison. Furthermore, many prisoners will have a history of injecting. This has obvious and serious potential implications for the transmission of viruses, and the potential for the prison setting to act as a conduit for viral transmission within the prisoner population and thence into the community. This has been, and remains, a major concern of public health researchers and policymakers (Advisory Council on the Misuse of Drugs, 1988; Farrell & Strang,

1991; Harding, 1987, 1990; Power *et al.*, 1992; World Health Organization, 1992) who wisely faced up to the worst case scenario where drug users in prison were unable or unwilling to reduce their risk taking behaviour while incarcerated and also after release. It is what Harding (1990) described as the [potential] epidemiological bridge for the transmission of HIV from prisons into the wider community. This could be broadly described as a medical epidemiological approach, and also as a very pragmatic one. But was it based on incorrect assumptions about people's behaviour?

Research in Scottish prisons has paid particular attention to patterns of injecting and sharing of injecting equipment in jail (Gore & Bird, 1995; Power *et al.*, 1992; Shewan *et al.*, 1994, 1995; Taylor *et al.*, 1995). These studies indicate that while drug use, and risky drug use, is a worrying feature of prison life in Scotland, drug use in prisons is generally characterised by a reduction in levels of use, and for the majority of prisoners with a history of injecting, a reduction in behaviours that could be described as high risk for the transmission of viral infections. Most drug injectors in Scotland stop injecting while they are in prison. These were welcome findings in the light of concern over the potential of prison to act as the setting for high levels of HIV transmission. This should not lead to any feelings of complacency, however. High risk behaviour does occur in Scottish prisons with serious repercussions, as evidenced by the outbreak of HIV transmission in HMP Glenochil (Taylor *et al.*, 1995). However, as the potential of the prison environ-ment to act as a modifier of drug using behaviour has been recognised, behavioural change in the prison environment should not simply be seen as representing an increase in high risk behaviour. Prisons have the potential to decrease, as well as potentially maintain, increase or reintroduce, high-risk drug using behaviour. This is a crucial point: we should not make assumptions that are based on the notion of prisons being the setting for the worst case scenario among drug using prisoners. In actual fact, some drug using prisoners, including injectors, are actually physically and behaviourally healthier while in prison than when in the community. But obviously there is no sustainability of this health status; the high number of relapses (or taking up the old usage patterns) and overdoses after this period of abstinence show that this health status typically only lasts for the time in prison. We should therefore be making considerably more effort to study the mechanisms of how and why the drug use is continued immediately after release by many, if not most, recently released prisoners with a history of problematic drug use.

The prison context

Prison is, generally, a rather bleak, sometimes hostile, sometimes even dangerous environ-ment. This is not intended as a criticism of those who work in and around the prison system. Nor does it make assumptions about the overall characteristics of the prisoner population (all types of people go to jail for all sorts of reasons). It is simply a fact. Official statistics with regard to mental health and violence back up this statement. Of course, one could also argue that in most countries prisons could be even worse places to be than they actually are, given the antiquated conditions in which people are housed, and the prevalence of mental health problems – including addiction – and violent behaviour that characterise the prisoner population. So which of these conclusions should be most predictive of drug injecting and sharing in prisons? Should we expect these behaviours to be at their worst in prison? Or, do injecting and sharing follow the recognition of their being a degree at least of self-control and environmental influence that reduces the worst case scenario of prison life? To try and answer this question we have to consider the predictive utility of different models of addiction.

A short bit of time for theory

There are two main overarching models of addiction, namely the medical model, and its alternative, that of drug, set and setting. The former, given its emphasis on loss of control, immediately suggests that prisons are inheriting a huge problem, and that treatment intervention is essential to at least try and reduce levels of risk. Injecting represents an extreme of addictive behaviour. Those who engage in it are clearly highly problematic drug users, very likely chaotic in their everyday lives and pessimistic in their outlook on the future. Add in the likelihood of reduced drug supply and availability in prisons, thereby increasing the potential effect of aspects such as craving and withdrawal, and the starting prognosis is very bleak. Within this model, one would expect a high proportion of drug injectors to continue to inject in prison, with the obligations of their addiction overriding behavioural modification in the light of perceived risk. And, of course, as injecting equipment is relatively scarce in prison, the likelihood of sharing equipment is greatly increased. So within this deterministic, disease model of addiction, the overriding *assumption* would be that drug use in prison would be at its most destructive and would be dangerously high-risk. And that can indeed be the case, sometimes with disturbing consequences in terms of health outcomes (e.g. Taylor *et al.*, 1995).

Alternatively, within prison, the drug, set and setting model can be used to systematically test the assumption that prison represents the environment where drug use will *likely* be at its most florid. The most negative prediction of the model would be similar to that of the medical model. For prisoners with a history of heavy, problematic, high-risk behaviour, the testable hypothesis is that each component will be negative when applied to this population. Drug use will be at best a negative reinforcer, set will be based on escapism or an attempt to reduce distress or psychological pain, and that prison setting is by definition unpleasant and disturbing. Again, the assumption here would be that levels of risk among drug using prisoners will be very high. Theoretically, it can be argued, therefore, that the concerns shown by the medically orientated organisations described above are based on a model which assumes an addicted population resistant to, and seriously challenged by, behavioural change. Again, as a pragmatic response to what potentially could still be a crisis for public health, this position can only be described as sensible, and in the embracing of harm reduction principles for services and interventions in prisons, radical. All of the authors of this chapter would support this overall policy and practice response to potential high risk behaviour among prisoner populations.

This would perhaps be the easiest point at which to finish this chapter. The fact remains, however, that drug research in prison presents us with a much more complex situation than that described through the above interpretations. Put simply, not all, perhaps the majority of prisoners do not behave as predicted by either of these models. The strictest application of the medical model is seriously challenged by the finding that high numbers of people stop injecting when they go to prison, often without intervention or treatment. Within the more flexible drug, set and setting model, we are perhaps better placed to analyse the complexities of drug using behaviour in prisons. Here, a number of key questions can be asked concerning the capacity of certain drugs and of the prevalence of addiction to lead to high risk behaviour, or, alternatively, the capability of drug users to modify their behaviour to reduce the risk to themselves and to others. Specifically, this model allows us to look systematically at findings of there being, among many prisoners, a generally lower level of risk taking behaviour in prisons. Within this framework, prisons can be seen to act as a setting in which drug using behaviour is reducing, maintaining *or* increasing risks. A crucial factor here would appear to be the role of *set*. In prison, with increased knowledge of risk factors among prisoners, the expectation of drug-related risk through transmission of HIV has become prominent. For the group with a history of drug injecting prior to, or even previously in, prison, it is likely that particular patterns of drug use, namely injecting and sharing, are associated with negative consequences. For the group who do not engage in risk behaviour in prison, therefore, rather than conform to stereotypical drug addict behaviour, their response to perceived risk is a rational one. This group do not engage in high risk behaviours such as injecting and sharing because they *choose* not to.

And the profile of drug injectors and drug injecting in prison becomes more complex when we explore the different patterns of behaviour that may apply to this group. Indeed, the need for further intensive, in-depth research becomes even more apparent when we examine the possibility of there being a typology for drug injecting and prisons. The following 'types' are all possible:

(1)   The group who inject on the outside but not in prison. This would be the group who most clearly make a definite decision not to engage in high risk behaviour while incarcerated.

(2)   The group who first inject in prison, who have no previous history of injecting in the community. If this group (as is common among most in-prison injectors) share injecting equipment, then they would provide the clearest evidence of prison being a high risk environment. We can really only speculate about the characteristics of this group. Prison may be a particularly depressing and/or threatening experience for them, and they may perceive extreme drug using behaviour as a means of escape. Or they may simply be more impressionable, and more susceptible to the influence of those already involved in injecting in jail.

(3)   An in some ways similar group are those who smoked drugs such as heroin in the community, but who inject in prison, perhaps for reasons of economy, which could be described as being a more efficient drug user. This group are interesting because

while they have crossed a particular boundary in terms of their using 'harder' drugs, they now move on to a more 'extreme' method of using their main drug. (Could somebody explain – to the first author at least – why injecting heroin, if done sensibly, is a more extreme way of using drugs than smoking cigarettes?)

(4) The group who have prior history of injecting in prison but no longer do so. This group could comprise individuals who have stopped injecting completely, but also those who continue to inject while in the community where there is availability of clean injecting equipment, but not in prison, where there is typically no such availability. Like group (1), they have identified and resisted high risk behaviour.

(5) The 'occasional' in-prison injectors. For this group, injecting may be an opportunistic, impulsive behaviour. If so, one would speculate that this outlook would also apply to sharing of injecting equipment.

(6) The independent injectors. These individuals are disciplined about their injecting in terms of risk, have their own injecting equipment, which they will not share or lend.

(7) The closed circle injectors. This group will share, but only within their own group. One can speculate that the rationale behind this is reduced risk, but this argument fails if there are members of the group who have viral infection. An alternative explanation could be that the 'closed circle' ensures that the injecting behaviour is more covert, more controllable, and less likely to be identified and acted upon by staff.

(8) The 'renters'. This group will basically 'hire' injecting equipment, either for money, drugs or favours.

(9) The 'hirers'. The group who rent out injecting equipment.

There are obvious differences between these groups or types in terms of potential risk, especially in terms of infection through contaminated equipment. The 'renters', for example, are clearly more at risk than the independent injectors. While it is definitely the case that one of the few consistencies among sharers in prison is that they will attempt to clean equipment before using it, there are degrees of likely effectiveness associated with different methods. Examples of more risky methods include licking the needle before injecting, pumping air through it, simply flushing with water, or making rules about who is injecting last. These examples, on the one hand, retain high elements of risk for viral infection and could potentially include 'fatal errors', but at the same time indicate that prisoners do take precautionary measures which, given the unavailability of community resources such as sterile injecting equipment, could be described as 'second best solutions', or 'better that nothing strategies', which are intended to at least reduce risk.

Cleaning with available disinfectant is likely to be more effective than the above methods, although this raises the issue of availability of cleansing agents, and also the deteriorating effect of strong cleaning agents (such as bleach) on injecting equipment. And while there is evidence of high levels of knowledge regarding risk behaviour among drug injectors, there is also evidence of prevailing mistaken beliefs which could have serious effects on health (for example, the belief among some injectors that one can not get re-infected with HCV; see Long et al., 2004, for an overview).

One final point when discussing this 'typology' is that, allowing for obvious logical qualifications (one can inject for the first time only once, for example), it can be entirely feasible that individuals can move from one category to the other. Here we have a dynamic typology that in terms of explanation is beyond the medical model, and which poses a set of challenges to the predictive utility of the drug, set and setting model.

It is hoped that further research that builds on theoretical principles and confirms or refutes them, will lead to more sophisticated drug theory and to explanations of behaviour that recognise the complexities and dynamics of drug use. The complexities of drug use are realities that researchers are required to identify and try and explain. Look again at the above guessed typology and think of some of the possibly predictive variables that should be included in the test analyses of this 'model': self-harm; depression, perhaps; schizophrenia; psychopathy? New diagnoses of viral infections such as HIV and hepatitis B or C? Indeed, being told for the first time that one is infected with a potentially fatal virus such as HIV has unpredictable implications for behaviour, in that the degree of risk the individual decides to take after such a diagnosis could go up, could reduce, could even just stay the same. And of course there are the obvious underlying factors such as childhood abuse. A professional statistician would be looking for a very big sample at this point, and would certainly not be making assumptions about addiction leading to risk behaviour in a noxious environment.

Theory is all very well and clever, but. . .

Drug researchers should also seek to identify the applied value of their results. Applied research in the area focused on here should have as its primary aim to inform and help further develop drug policy and practice in prisons. At the risk of being repetitive, the authors would not wish to underestimate the potential of prison to act as a setting for high risk drug use, nor against a response to this that seeks to minimise the personal and general harm that could result. But nor could we argue with the evidence that indicates huge levels among staff (and indeed many prisoners) of direct opposition to injecting (e.g. Shewan *et al.*, 1994). It is very difficult to produce an argument in defence of injecting in prison, particularly within a framework that this behaviour is one that is done *on purpose*. Ideally, there would be no injecting in prisons. It is potentially risky in terms of personal and public health. It is potentially disruptive in terms of prison security and the interaction between staff and prisoners. As such, it may fall outside the standard and pragmatic harm reduction maxim of minimising dangers and negative outcomes in a health context. Injecting, and sharing, in prisons may *essentially* be problematic. However, it does go on. So, what is an effective and justifiable response?

One intervention, the introduction of which has been rigorously debated, is that of syringe exchange programmes in prisons. Such programmes are currently in place, still predominantly as pilot projects in Switzerland (for more than 12 years), Germany, Spain and Moldova. These programmes have been evaluated in eleven prisons, where results did not support fears that commonly arise in the start-up of implementation of exchange projects: syringe distribution was not followed by an increase in drug use or injecting drug use. Syringes were not misused, and disposal of used syringes was uncomplicated. Sharing of syringes among drug users disappeared almost completely or was rarely reported. In five prisons, blood tests were performed for HIV or hepatitis infection and no seroconversion was observed. Based on these experiences, it can be concluded that in these settings harm reduction measures, including syringe exchange, were not only feasible but also efficient. Despite these positive results, promising in public health terms, there continues to be widespread opposition to their introduction in most prison systems. This highlights a basic factor regarding drug interventions in prisons: they must be agreed to and accepted by not only those who live and work in prisons, but also at various levels of involvement within the criminal justice system.

An interesting recent (June 2001) development in Spain (Lines *et al.*, 2004) involved a government decree that sterile syringes should be provided to drug users in all Spanish prisons, this being highly influenced by concerns and added pressure on prisons of high HIV infections among drug-dependent prisoners. Whether this is paralleled in other countries remains to be seen. But what requires to be carefully monitored is the extent to which infectious diseases among drug injectors in prisons are spreading in the absence of preventive interventions such as syringe exchange. It has been established that prisons are required to provide levels of healthcare comparable to those available in the community, and it could be argued that syringe exchange programmes should be assessed within this context. (See *UN Basic Principles for the Treatment of Prisoners*: Principle 9 requires that: 'Prisoners shall have access to the health care services available in the country without discrimination on the grounds of their legal situation'. See also *Standard Minimum Rules for the Treatment of Prisoners* (Art. 22), Council of Europe, Committee of Ministers, Recommendation no. R(98) 7 of the Committee of Ministers to member states concerning the ethical and organisational aspects of healthcare in prison.) The Council of Europe has (2003) recommended that: 'Member States should . . . consider making available to drug abusers in prison access to services similar to those provided to drug abusers not in prison, in a way that does not compromise the continuous and overall efforts of keeping drugs out of prison'. This can only be described as a marvellously ambiguous policy statement!

But more harm reduction initiatives *are* being discussed, and some are being introduced in prison health care services in some countries. It is also possible, necessary perhaps, to show some imagination when introducing harm reduction measures. In Scotland, for example, while there are no syringe exchange schemes and no formal provision of suitable cleansing agents for syringes in use in the prison, such fluids are made available for sterilising cups and cutlery. And it so happens that instruction leaflets are available in Scottish prisons for using suitable disinfectants for cleaning injecting equipment. This might appear somewhat bizarre, perhaps absurd, but it does highlight that prisons are highly complex places, requiring adaptive outlooks from those who live and work there, and subject to vicarious involvement from a range of health, criminal justice and political interests.

This is a book about injecting, and this chapter has to provide, or try to provide, a description of what it is *like* to inject in prison. Firstly, this is a very secretive behaviour.

The likelihood of there being a 'blind eye' turned to current injecting and sharing is very much lower than, for example, smoking cannabis. While those from a medical perspective might argue that there is huge pressure *on* addicts to inject in prison, there can surely be little debate concerning there being huge pressure on people *while* they inject in prison. Is this indicative of the desperation inherent in this behaviour? Alternatively, are we in danger of accepting this explanation at the risk of ignoring an alternative: that it is *exciting* to inject in prison. Prisons, indeed, may be bleak and dangerous places, but they can also be very boring. Add in the element of an ambition to break prison rules, and we have a challenging argument to that of the medical model. *Risk* can be seen in a different light here. Among some groups of prisoners, the main risk could be defined as that of being caught by the prison authorities and being identified for transgression of not only security rules, but also the general disapproval, even hostility, among staff and some other prisoners towards injecting. Even when sharing – and it should be borne in mind that most but not all in-prison injectors will share equipment – there is typically some attempt among sharers to clean equipment, indicating at least an attempt to reduce health risk. But overall, in prison, as elsewhere, most people who do not inject do not like injecting.

But surely anyone who has any viewing experience of the equipment typically used to inject in prison must doubt the validity that we are talking about a group of people taking measured risk on purpose? Many prisons will have a 'black museum', within which one of the chief sets of exhibits will involve injecting equipment. This can involve dirty syringes, dirtier and blunt needles, and even somewhat bizarre examples of adapting everyday objects, such as biro pens, into vehicles for injecting drugs. Evidence of desperation? Alternatively, are the rather worn sets of injecting equipment more likely to be found by prison staff, perhaps even with prisoner assistance, because they have been replaced by newer sets of equipment which are better to use. And is the creation of a syringe from a ballpoint pen an example of last resort, or better viewed as a representation of ingenuity? An interesting analogy can be made here with the other main set of exhibits in most prison 'black museums': weapons. As well as standard weapons such as knives, here there are also examples of adaptation of everyday objects for use in unusual ways. It should not, for example, take the reader very long to work out how to create a weapon from the necessary parts of a pencil sharpener and a toothbrush, and a match. To explain *these* exhibits, we must move into theories of violence. And within this theoretical domain, while there is much debate concerning culpability, there is no discussion of ongoing helplessness, nor of non-volitional behaviour.

In conclusion

And now we are back to a similar debate as that discussed earlier. To summarise, are people who inject and share equipment in prison doing these things because they somehow *have to*, or because they *want to*. We are also back to the same principle as outlined at the beginning of this chapter: to predict and respond to behaviours that concern us, we have to understand them. And, it must be admitted, as yet we don't completely.

Where we are reasonably well-informed is on what happens with regard to drug use and injecting in prison. Many prisoners stay abstinent or drastically reduce their drug use; certainly, a majority cease injecting while in prison. This is likely to be for a variety of reasons, such as reduced access to amounts and the range of drugs available, trepidation of losing remission, or it may simply be that these prisoners *choose* to reduce their drug intake and *choose* to avoid high risk behaviours. What is perhaps more difficult to understand is why some prisoners maintain or even increase their risk taking behaviour. Here we return to one of the main themes of this chapter: the contrast, contradiction even, between explaining such behaviours from the perspective of the medical model, or the drug, set and setting model, and the highlighting of the curious lack of knowledge as to the *why* of the variations in drug using behaviours in prison. This is a crucial area for designing and implementing drug services in prison, and also for consulting, informing and training staff. It is also important in terms of how we respond to the prisoner population. One should not rely overly on assumptions about people because it so happens they are drug users who are in prison.

References

Advisory Council on the Misuse of Drugs (1988) *AIDS and Drug Misuse, Part 1*. London: HMSO.

Alem, van V.C.M., Wisselink, D.J. & Groen, H. (1999) *Drug use in prison: Patterns of Change in The Netherlands*. Duivendrecht: Herausgeber: IVZ – Stiching Informatievoorziening Zorg.

Bean, P. (2002) *Drugs and Crime*. Devon: Willan Publishing.

Butler, T. (1997) *Preliminary findings from the inmate health survey of the inmate population in the New South Wales correctional system*. Sydney: NSW Department of Corrective Services.

Council of Europe (2003) Recommendation of 18th June, 2003. On the prevention and reduction of health-related harm associated with drug dependence (2003/488/EC).

Dolan, K. & Crofts, N. (2000) A review of risk behaviours, transmissions and prevention of blood-borne viral infections in Australian prisons. In D. Shewan & J.B. Davies (eds), *Drug Use and Prisons: An International Perspective*, pp. 215–232. Chur: Harwood.

Dunn, J., Laranjeira, R. & Marins, J. (2000) HIV, drug use, crime, and the penal system: competing priorities in a developing country – the case of Brazil. In D. Shewan & J.B. Davies (eds), *Drug Use and Prisons: An International Perspective*, pp. 45–56, 117–142. Chur: Harwood.

ENDHASP (1997) Report of the 3rd European Conference on Drug and HIV/AIDS Services in Prison. Amsterdam: European Network of Drug and HIV/AIDS Services in Prisons.

Farrell, M. & Strang, J. (1991) Drugs, HIV, and prisons. *British Medical Journal*, **302**, 1477–1479.

Focal Point Denmark (1998) *Annual report on the drug situation in Denmark*. Copenhagen: Focal Point.

Focal Point Italy (1999) *Annual report on the drug situation in Italy*. Rome: Focal Point.

Gore, S.M. & Bird, A.G. (1995) Cross-sectional willing anonymous HIV salivary (WASH) surveillance studies and self-completion risk factor questionnaire in establishments of the Scottish Prison Service. *Answer*, 29th September, 1–4.

Harding, T. (1987) *AIDS in Prison*. Geneva: University Institute of Legal Medicine.

Harding, T. (1990) HIV infection and AIDS in the prison environment: a test case for the respect of human rights. In J. Strang & G.V. Stimson (eds), *AIDS and Drug Misuse*, pp. 197–210. London: Routledge.

Hiller, M.L., Knight, K. & Simpson, D. (1999) Prison-based substance abuse treatment, residential aftercare and recidivism. *Addiction*, **94**(6), 833–842.

Lines, R., Jürgens, R., Stöver, H., Laticevschi D. & Nelles, J. (2004) *Prison Needle Exchange: A Review of International Evidence and Experience*. Montreal: Canadian HIV/AIDS Legal Network (in press) (see also http://www.aidslaw.ca/Maincontent/issues/prisons.htm).

Long, J., Allwright, S. & Begley, C. (2004) Prisoners' views of injecting drug use and harm reduction in Irish prisons. *International Journal of Drug Policy*, **15**(2), 139–149.

Ohaeri, J.U. (2000) Drug use and HIV/AIDS in sub-Saharan African prisons. In D. Shewan & J.B. Davies (eds), *Drug Use and Prisons: An International Perspective*, pp. 117–140. Chur: Harwood.

O'Mahony, P. (1997) *Mountjoy prisoners: a sociological and criminological profile*. Dublin: Department of Justice.

Power, K.G., Markova, A., Rowlands, A., McKee, K.J., Anslow, P. J. & Kilfedder, C. (1992) Intravenous drug use and HIV transmission amongst inmates in Scottish prisons. *British Journal of Addiction*, **87**, 35–45.

Shewan, D., Gemmell, M. & Davies, J.B. (1994) Prison as a modifier of drug using behaviour. *Addiction Research*, **2**, 203–216.

Shewan, D., Macpherson, A., Reid, M.M. & Davies, J.B. (1995) Patterns of injecting and sharing in a Scottish prison. *Drug and Alcohol Dependence*, **39**, 237–243.

Singleton, N., Meltzer, H., Gatward, R., Coid, J. & Deasy, D. (1999) *Psychiatric morbidity among prisoners*. London: Office for National Statistics.

Taylor, A., Goldberg, D., Emslie, J., Wrench, J., Gruer, L., Cameron, S. *et al.* (1995) Outbreak of HIV infection in a Scottish prison. *British Medical Journal*, **310**, 293–296.

US Department of Justice (2000) *Drug use, testing and treatment in jails*. Washington DC: Bureau of Justice Studies.

World Health Organization (1992) *Drug abusers in prisons: managing their health problems*. Copenhagen: WHO Regional Publications, European Series, No. 27.

Chapter 7

Hepatitis C associated with Injecting Drug Use

Nick Crofts

Introduction

The act of injecting releases blood to the outside world, potentially exposing others to blood borne viruses. People who inject illicit drugs (injecting drug users, IDUs) are especially at risk, because of the frequency, social nature and 'bloodiness' of their injecting. Behaviours common to IDUs, such as the sharing of needles, syringes and other injecting paraphernalia, handling bloody equipment, injecting in public places, and the use of 'professional injectors' and 'shooting galleries', all create multiple opportunities for transmission of these viruses. As a result, infection with various viruses is endemic among IDUs globally – most commonly the blood borne hepatitis viruses, hepatitis B, C and D (HBV, HCV, HDV), and the human T-leukaemic viruses (HTLV-I, HTLV-II).

HCV is the most common of these infections, and has been spreading globally among IDUs as the practice of injecting drug use has grown and spread worldwide since the 1960s. High proportions of all IDUs, wherever they are, have been and continue to be exposed to HCV; high proportions of these are chronically infected with HCV, and are therefore at risk of long term HCV-associated disease, especially cirrhosis, liver failure and liver cancer. Conversely, a history of IDU is the most common risk factor among sexually transmitted disease (STD) clinic patients, prison inmates or general populations such as blood donors. In fact, the HCV epidemic among IDUs is not one epidemic, but recurring waves of transmission of HCV, as different genotypes appear in different populations, and for unknown reasons tend to displace the genotypes already present (Hocking *et al.*, 2001).

Prevalence and associations of prevalence with HBV and HCV among injecting drug users

Every population of IDUs studied to date shows variably high prevalences of exposure to HCV. Among over 45 000 IDUs surveyed in 162 studies in 33 countries, 70% had antibodies to HCV (Hocking *et al.*, 2001). The highest prevalences, up to 90% or more, were recorded in North America and in Asia. In this same analysis, the average prevalence of HBV markers was highest among IDUs in North America (71%) and lowest among IDUs in Australia (44%) and the Middle East (26%). Prevalence of antibodies to HBV is generally lower than that of antibodies to HCV, and both are generally higher than prevalence of antibodies to HIV. However, there is no relationship between HBV/HCV prevalences and HIV prevalences, generally reflecting the more recent introduction of HIV into these populations.

HCV antibodies were detected in sera of Air Force recruits in Wyoming, USA, as early as 1950; retrospective testing of stored sera in two studies conducted in Australia found that HCV was present at high prevalences among people with histories of IDU at least as early as 1971 (Moaven *et al.*, 1993; Freeman *et al.*, 2000), and in Sweden in the late 1960s (Blackberg *et al.*, 2000). HCV and HBV were well established among IDU populations before the appearance of HIV from the late 1970s, and before the implementation and expansion of HIV prevention strategies.

Exposure to HBV is strongly associated with past exposure to HCV (Bolumar *et al.*, 1996; Hickman *et al.*, 1998; Chang *et al.*, 1999). IDUs who have been exposed to both are more commonly exposed to HCV before their contact with HBV (Rodriguez *et al.*, 1992; Coppola *et al.*, 1994; Crofts *et al.*, 1994; Lamden *et al.*, 1998). At any one time, greater numbers of IDUs in any injecting network will be more infectious for HCV than for HBV, because infection with HCV leads to chronic infection and infectiousness in 50–80% of cases, whereas for HBV this proportion is much lower, perhaps less than 5%.

Associations with HCV seropositivity, and to a lesser extent HBV seropositivity, among IDUs include *duration* of injecting, *age*, *type of drug* injected, *frequency* of injecting, *sharing* of needles and syringes, and *sharing of injecting equipment other than needles and syringes*. HBV differs from HCV in being sexually and vertically (from pregnant or parturient mother to child) transmitted with reasonable efficiency.

Duration of injecting

The number of years since the person first began injecting is the commonest and strongest association found with HBV and HCV seropositivity among IDUs. In broad sweep, risk of HCV infection remains with the IDU throughout their injecting career, beginning with their first injection (MacDonald *et al.*, 2000; Taylor *et al.*, 2000); the issue of superinfection with a different HCV genotype is dealt with below. *Age* is also positively associated with HCV exposure – the older the IDU the more likely he or she is to have been exposed to HCV – but simply because duration of injecting is associated with age (Crofts *et al.*, 1993; MacDonald *et al.*, 2000).

This general association with duration of injecting hides much variation. In some places at some times, prevalence of HCV rises rapidly after initiation into injecting, implying very rapid spread among novice populations: for instance, in one study in Manipur in northeast India, HCV prevalence reached 90% within the first year of injecting (Eicher *et al.*, 2000). Elsewhere, spread can be much slower: studies in London have shown prevalences of 30% or less even after several years' injecting. One attempt to standardise across these different regions found the extrapolated number of years from initial injection to 50% HCV seroprevalence varied widely, from a few months to many years. This period bore some general relationship with the degree to which countries had adopted harm reduction measures. An alternative explanation which requires investigation is that there is less social mixing across age groups in those IDU populations where transmission is slower.

Frequency of injecting

HCV seropositivity is strongly associated with the frequency of injecting, suggesting that every act of injection poses a risk of HCV transmission; and/or that those who inject more frequently are also riskier in their injecting behaviours (Garfein *et al.*, 1996; Smyth *et al.*, 1998). Frequency of injecting, together with differences in social organisation of IDU networks, explains most of the observed association of HCV exposure with the type(s) of drug most commonly injected. Those who regularly inject heroin or other opiates have higher prevalences of HCV, adjusted for age and duration of injecting, than do those regularly injecting amphetamines or other stimulants (van Beek *et al.*, 1994; Hickman *et al.*, 1998; Abraham *et al.*, 1999; Hagan *et al.*, 1999; MacDonald *et al.*, 2000). Those who inject cocaine as their major drug have higher prevalences yet (Garfein *et al.*, 1996; Rezza *et al.*, 1996; Garfein *et al.*, 1998; Ford *et al.*, 2000); cocaine injectors have higher risk injecting practices (Greenfield *et al.*, 1992) and sexual practices (Hudgins *et al.*, 1995).

Sharing of equipment and contamination

As with HIV transmission among IDUs, after duration of injecting it is the frequency of *sharing of needles and syringes* which is the strongest determinant of HCV exposure (e.g. Garfein *et al.*, 1998; Lamden *et al.*, 1998), along with other behavioural markers such as the reuse of needles and syringes (Garfein *et al.*, 1998; Kemp *et al.*, 1998) and the number of different people to whom injecting equipment has been lent (Chetwynd *et al.*, 1995). However, unlike HIV, there is mounting and convincing evidence that HCV is transmitted between IDUs by the sharing of other equipment involved in injecting – water, spoon/ cookers, filters, tourniquets – or by environmental contamination ('*indirect sharing*') (Hagan *et al.*, 2001). This higher 'infectiousness' of HCV (and HBV) – which means that smaller amounts of blood (even inapparent amounts) are likely to carry an infectious dose of the virus (Crofts *et al.*, 1999) – may be one of the elements that explains the continuing high incidence of HCV among IDU populations where HIV is not spreading.

Many of these factors come into play in prison and other incarcerated settings, where a history of injecting drug use is common among inmates, and injecting continues while inside – generally less frequently, but far less safely. Few items of injecting equipment are shared between many users over time, with little access to sterile equipment or the means to disinfect used equipment. HCV is highly prevalent amongst prison populations, especially among those prisoners with histories of IDU. A history of *imprisonment* is a common association of HCV exposure among IDUs (Crofts *et al.*, 1995; Butler *et al.*, 1999; Ford *et al.*, 2000; Weild *et al.*, 2000; Macalino *et al.*, 2004).

Rates of HCV transmission among IDUs

There is little evidence to suggest that the rates of transmission of HCV between IDUs are declining, or have stabilised in most populations of IDUs, since it apparently entered these populations in the 1960s. Several major cohort studies in very different settings since the early 1990s have recorded incidences of HCV of between 10 and 40 cases per 100 person-years (py), with little evidence of decline since those times (van den Hoek *et al.*, 1990; Chamot *et al.*, 1992; Crofts *et al.*, 1993; Crofts & Aitken 1997; Stark *et al.*, 1997; Miller *et al.*, 2002). In all cases where HIV transmission was studied in the same cohort, HIV incidence was far lower and in some circumstances did show evidence of decline.

In Vancouver, for example, Patrick *et al.* (2001) found that while HIV incidence declined from 19 to 5 cases per 100 (py) from 1994 to 1999, HCV incidence remained stable above 16 cases per 100 py. In Glasgow between 1993 and 1997, HIV prevalence fell from 40% to 3.6%, but over the same period HCV prevalence remained around 65% (McIntyre *et al.*, 2001). In Sweden in 1999, HIV incidence among attenders at a needle and syringe programme remained at zero cases per 100 py, but HCV incidence was 26.3 cases per 100 py (Mansson *et al.*, 2000).

Variation in these HCV incidence rates is at least in part due to sampling characteristics and sample size, but there may be some associations with group and individual behaviours. Discovering which particular behaviours – aside from the obvious sharing of needles and syringes – are key intervention points to prevent transmission has proven difficult.

Relevant studies have found a variety of factors associated with an increased risk of HIV seroconversion, in general confirming the findings of prevalence association studies. These include predictable risks for blood exposure, such as recent injecting, frequent drug use, sharing of needles, attending a 'shooting gallery', not always using their own needles, the number of other IDUs shared with (Villano *et al.*, 1997), polydrug use, needle sharing during the study period and a history of imprisonment (van Beek *et al.*, 1998). Other studies have found variable, sometimes high, rates of seroconversion among IDUs who do not report these risk behaviours – notably the sharing of needles and syringes. For instance, in an English study Green *et al.* (2001) found that among HCV-seroconverter IDUs interviewed, 10% had shared other equipment but not needles and syringes.

This has led researchers to seek other ways in which blood might pass from one IDU to another. A range of vectors has been indentified – generally equipment other than needles and syringes used and shared in the injecting process. These vectors include the sharing of 'cookers' or spoons for mixing and heating drug solutions (in Seattle: Hagan *et al.*, 2001; in Chicago: Thorpe *et al.*, 2000); the sharing of filters or cotton wool (in Belgium: Denis *et al.*, 2000; in Seattle: Hagan *et al.*, 2001; in New York: Diaz *et al.*, 2001; and in Chicago: Thorpe *et al.*, 2000); the sharing, mixing and/or rinsing used in drug preparation (in Chicago: Thorpe *et al.*, 2000). A biological basis for this method of transfer of HCV between injectors was demonstrated when the presence of HCV was demonstrated on equipment and in water which had been used in injecting settings where there was at least one known HCV PCR-positive person (Crofts *et al.*, 2000).

There are indications that social factors such as the social organisation of IDUs, and the structure of their injecting networks, are also important determinants of transmission risks and rates. For example, some studies have found that younger age, and younger age at initiation into injecting, are predictive of HCV infection (e.g. Crofts *et al.*, 1995; van Beek *et al.*, 1998) while others find older age predictive (e.g. Crofts *et al.*, 1993; Stark *et al.*, 1997).

There are recent findings of continuous genotype change amongst some IDUs infected with HCV who continue to practise risk behaviours (Aitken *et al.*, 2004). This may imply that there is a constant 'current' of HCV transmission going on among IDUs, with frequent infection and reinfection with different genotypes.

Control of HCV transmission among IDUs

Given the evidence of continuing high rates of transmission of HCV among IDUs, even where HIV prevention strategies are in place and apparently working well – many years of control of the HIV epidemic among IDUs in some places, and declining HIV prevalences in others – the question must be raised as to how these epidemics might be defeated. The evidence already discussed supports the idea that transmission of HCV is associated with the sharing of injecting equipment other than (as well as) needles and syringes, and perhaps simply by environmental contamination. An analysis of the factors involved in the different epidemiologies of the two viruses suggests that the critical factor is prevalence. HCV had reached high prevalences among IDUs before it was discovered, indeed, before harm reduction programmes began to be instituted. The degree of sterility and quantity of intervention necessary for control of HCV is very high (Crofts *et al.*, 1999).

There is some evidence that the introduction of HIV prevention programmes among IDUs has had a positive but less dramatic impact on HCV. An ecological study of the differences in HCV prevalence between those countries which had introduced harm reduction programmes for control of the HIV epidemic among IDUs and those which had not, to any degree, found a general relationship between the presence of harm reduction programmes and lower HCV prevalence (Hocking *et al.*, 2001). A more specific ecological study of the relationship of the presence and introduction of needle and syringe programmes (NSPs) at city level found a stronger relationship: the median HCV prevalence in cities without NSPs was 75%, compared with 60% in those with NSPs, a significant difference (Health Outcomes, 2002). This same study found that following the introduction of NSPs to a city which previously had not had such programmes, there was an overall decline in the prevalence of HCV among IDUs of 1.5–2% p.a. thereafter.

This ecological modelling is supported to some degree by field studies. Examples include one of the cohort studies reported above, which found a decrease in HCV incidence between 1990 and 1995 from 16.1 to 8.1 cases per 100 py, associated with a decline in sharing of needles and syringes (Crofts & Aitken, 1997). This was mirrored by the finding that among first time methadone clients in Australia, HCV prevalence declined from over 70% to around 50% during the same time period (Crofts et al., 1997). A similar reduction was found among IDUs attending NSPs, from 63% to 50% between 1995 and 1997 (MacDonald et al., 2000). Goldberg et al., (1998) found a similar trend in Glasgow, showing that between 1990 and 1995 HCV prevalence fell significantly among IDUs of all ages from around 90% to around 75%, which suggests a fall in incidence with the introduction of NSPs in the late 1980s. Similar findings have been reported from Madrid (Delgado-Iribarren et al., 1993, 2000), Baltimore, USA (Villano et al., 1997), and in Switzerland (Broers et al., 1998).

These declines tend to be small and slow, and there are many parts of the world in which there is no evidence of a decline in the incidence of HCV among often growing populations of IDUs. The degree of behaviour change necessary to control the spread of HCV among populations of IDUs is probably not achievable in all circumstances, especially where there is repressive drug policy and little commitment on the part of government (Edlin, 2004). Some strategies that have proven effective against transmission of HIV among IDUs still await proof of their effectiveness against HCV transmission, such as methadone maintenance therapy (Crofts et al., 1997; Sorensen & Copeland, 2000). Others, such as treatment of HCV-infected IDUs, are yet to be attempted on any meaningful scale.

As Hagan and des Jarlais (2000) point out, a reduction in transmission of HIV among IDUs may only require the risk to be reduced, especially by reducing sharing of needles and syringes; but the control of HCV may need injecting practices which guarantee elimination of exposure to equipment contaminated with even small amounts of blood. This will require far greater efforts, as evidenced by the high incidence of HCV among IDU populations already in touch with harm reduction measures such as NSPs and methadone maintenance (Crofts et al., 1999).

The case for prevention of HCV transmission among IDUs is well made, and strategies for its implementation well worked out (Edlin, 2004). What remains lacking is the will to implement them.

References

Abraham, H.D., Degli-Esposti, S. & Marino, L. (1999) Seroprevalence of hepatitis C in a sample of middle class substance abusers. *Journal of Addictive Diseases*, **18**, 77–87.

Aitken, C.K., McCaw, R., Jardine, D., Bowden, D.S., Higgs, P., Nguyen, O., Crofts, N. & Hellard, M. (2004) Change in hepatitis C virus genotype in injecting drug users. *Journal of Medical Virology*, **74**, 543–545.

Blackberg, J., Braconier, J.H., Widell, A. & Kidd-Ljunggren, K. (2000) Long-term outcome of acute hepatitis B and C in an outbreak of hepatitis in 1969–1972. *European Journal of Clinical Microbiology and Infectious Diseases*, **19**, 21–26.

Bolumar, F., Hernandez-Aguado, I., Ferrer, L., Ruiz, I., Avino, M.J. & Rebagliato, M. (1996) Prevalence of antibodies to hepatitis C in a population of intravenous drug users in Valencia, Spain, 1990–1992. *International Journal of Epidemiology*, **25**, 204–209.

Broers, B., Junet, C., Bourquin, M., Deglon, J., Perrin, L. & Hirschel, B. (1998) Prevalence and incidence rate of HIV, hepatitis B and C among drug users on methadone maintenance treatment in Geneva between 1988 and 1995. *AIDS*, **12**, 2059–2066.

Butler, T., Spencer, J., Cui, J., Vickery, K., Zou, J. & Kaldor, J. (1999) Seroprevalence of markers for hepatitis B, C and G in male and female prisoners – NSW, 1996. *Australia and New Zealand Journal of Public Health*, **23**, 377–384.

Chamot, E., de Saussure, B., Hirschel, B., Deglon, I.J. & Perrin, L.H. (1992) Incidence of hepatitis C, hepatitis B and HIV infections among drug users in a methadone maintenance programme. *AIDS*, **6**, 430–431.

Chang, C.-J., Lin, C.-H., Lee, C.-T., Chang, S.-J., Ko, Y.-C. & Liu, H.-W. (1999) Hepatitis C virus infection among short-term intravenous drug users in southern Taiwan. *European Journal of Epidemiology*, **15**, 597–601.

Chetwynd, J., Brunton, C., Blank, M., Plumridge, E. & Baldwin, D. (1995) Hepatitis C seroprevalence amongst injecting drug users attending a methadone programme. *New Zealand Medical Journal*, **108**, 364–366.

Coppola, R.C., Manconi, P.E., Piro, R., DiMartino, M.L. & Masia, G. (1994) HCV, HIV, HBV and HDV infections in intravenous drug addicts. *European Journal of Epidemiology*, **10**, 279–283.

Crofts, N. & Aitken, C.K. (1997) Incidence of bloodborne virus infection and risk behaviours in a cohort of injecting drug users in Victoria, 1990–1995. *Medical Journal of Australia*, **167**, 17–20.

Crofts, N., Hopper, J.L., Bowden, D.S., Breschkin, A.M., Milner, R. & Locarnini, S.A. (1993) Hepatitis C virus infection among a cohort of Victorian injecting drug users. *Medical Journal of Australia*, **159**, 237–241.

Crofts, N., Hopper, J.L., Milner, R., Breschkin, A.M., Bowden, D.S. & Locarnini, S.A. (1994) Blood-borne virus infections among Australian injecting drug users: implications for spread of HIV. *European Journal of Epidemiology*, **10**, 687–694.

Crofts, N., Stewart, T., Hearne, P., Ping, X.Y., Breschkin, A.M. & Locarnini, S.A. (1995) Spread of bloodborne viruses among Australian prison entrants. *British Medical Journal*, **310**, 285–288.

Crofts, N., Nigro, L., Oman, K., Stevenson, E. & Sherman, J. (1997) Methadone maintenance and hepatitis C virus infection among injecting drug users. *Addiction*, **92**, 999–1005.

Crofts, N., Aitken, C.K. & Kaldor, J. (1999) The force of numbers: why hepatitis C is spreading among Australian injecting drug users while HIV is not. *Medical Journal of Australia*, **170**, 220–221.

Crofts, N., Caruana, S., Bowden, S. & Kerger, M. (2000) Minimising harm from hepatitis C virus needs better strategies (letter). *British Medical Journal*, **321**, 899.

Delgado-Iribarren, A., Wilhelmi, I., Padilla, B., Canedo, T., Gomez, J. & Elviro, J. (1993) Infection by HIV and the hepatitis B, C and D viruses in intravenous drug addicts. Seroprevalence at 1 year and its follow up. *Enfermedades Infecciosas y Microbiologia Clinica*, **11**, 8–13.

Delgado-Iribarren, A., Calvo, M., Perez, A., del Alamo, M. & Cercenado, S. (2000) Intra-venous drug users serologic control: what may be prevented? *Enfermedades Infecciosas y Microbiologia Clinica*, **18**, 2–5.

Denis, B., Dedobbeleer, M., Collet, T., Petit, J., Jamoulle, M. & Hayani, A. (2000) High prevalence of hepatitis virus infection in Belgian intravenous drug users and potential role of the 'cotton filter' in transmission: the GEMT Study, *Acta Gastroenterologica Belgica*, **63**, 147–153.

Diaz, T., Des Jarlais, D.C., Vlahov, D., Perlis, T.E., Edwards, V., Friedman, S.R., Rockwell, R., Hoove, D., Williams, I.T. & Monterroso, E.R. (2001) Factors associated with prevalent hepatitis C: differences among young injection drug users in lower and upper Manhattan, New York City. *American Journal of Public Health*, **91**, 23–30.

Edlin, B. (2004) Hepatitis C prevention and treatment for substance users in the United States: acknowledging the elephant in the living room. *International Journal of Drug Policy*, **15**, 81–91.

Eicher, A.D., Crofts, N., Benjamin, S., Deutschmann, P. & Rodger, A.J. (2000) A certain fate: spread of HIV among young injecting drug users in Manipur, North-East India. *AIDS Care*, **12**, 497–504.

Ford, P.M., Pearson, M., Sankar-Mistry, P., Stevenson, T., Bell, D. & Austin, J. (2000) HIV, hepatitis C and risk behaviour in a Canadian medium-security federal penitentiary. *Ottawa Journal of Medicine*, **93**, 113–119.

Freeman, A.J., Zekry, A., Whybin, L.R., Harvey, C.E., van Beek, I.A., de Kantzow, S.L., Rawlinson, W.D., Boughton, C.R., Robertson, P.W., Marinos, G. & Lloyd, A.R. (2000) Hepatitis C prevalence among Australian injecting drug users in the 1970s and profiles of virus genotypes in the 1970s and 1990s. *Medical Journal of Australia*, **172**, 588–591.

Garfein, R.S., Vlahov, D., Galai, N., Doherty, M.C. & Nelson, K.E. (1996) Viral infections in short-term injection drug users: the prevalence of the hepatitis C, hepatitis B, human immunodeficiency and human T-lymphocyte viruses. *American Journal of Public Health*, **86**, 655–661.

Garfein, R.S., Doherty, M.C., Monterroso, E.R., Thomas, D.L., Nelson, K.E. & Vlahov, D. (1998) Prevalence and incidence of hepatitis C virus infection among young adult injection drug users. *Journal of AIDS*, **18**, S11–S19.

Goldberg, D., Cameron, S. & McMenamin, J. (1998) Hepatitis C virus antibody prevalence among injecting drug users in Glasgow has fallen but remains high. *Communicable Diseases and Public Health*, **1**, 95–97.

Green, S.T., Mohsen, A.H., McKendrick, M.W., Dawes, Y., Prakasam, S.F., Walberg, R. & Schmid, M.L. (2001) Potential for hepatitis C transmission among non-needle/syringe sharing Sheffield drug injectors through the sharing of drug preparation paraphernalia. *Communicable Diseases and Public Health*, **4**, 38–41.

Greenfield, L., Bigelow, G.E. & Brooner, R.K. (1992) HIV risk behaviour in drug users: increased blood 'booting' during cocaine injection. *AIDS Education and Prevention*, **4**, 95–107.

Hagan, H. & des Jarlais, D.C. (2000) HIV and HCV infection among injecting drug users. *Mt Sinai Medical Journal*, **67**, 423–428.

Hagan, H., McGough, J.P., Thiede, H., Weiss, N.S., Hopkins, S. & Alexander, E.R. (1999) Syringe exchange and risk of infection with hepatitis B and C viruses. *American Journal of Epidemiology*, **149**, 203–213.

Hagan, H., Thiede, H., Weiss, N.S., Hopkins, S.G., Duchin, J.S. & Alexander, E.R. (2001) Sharing of drug preparation equipment as a risk factor for hepatitis C. *American Journal of Public Health*, **91**, 42–46.

Health Outcomes (2002) *Report to Commonwealth Department of Health and Ageing: returns on investment in needle and syringe programs in Australia*. Sydney: National Centre in HIV Epidemiology and Clinical Research.

Hickman, M., Judd, A., Stimson, G.V., Hunter, G., Jones, S. & Parry, J. (1998) Prevalence of HIV, hepatitis B virus (HBV) and hepatitis C virus (HCV) among injecting drug users (IDU) in England, 1997–8. 12th World AIDS Conference, Geneva. Abstract no. 23214.

Hocking, J., Crofts, N., Aitken, C.K. & MacDonald, M. (2001) Epidemiology of HCV among injecting drug users. In N. Crofts, G. Dore & S. Locarnini (eds), *Hepatitis C: An Australian Perspective*, pp. 260–298. Melbourne: IP Communications.

Hudgins, R., McCusker, J. & Stoddard, A. (1995) Cocaine use and risky injection and sexual behaviours. *Drug and Alcohol Dependency*, **37**, 7–14.

Kemp, R., Miller, J., Lungley, S. & Baker, M. (1998) Injecting behaviours and prevalence of hepatitis B, C and D markers in New Zealand injecting drug user populations. *New Zealand Medical Journal*, **111**, 50–53.

Lamden, K.H., Kennedy, N., Beeching, N.J., Lowe, D., Morrison, C.L., Mallinson, H., Mutton, K.J. & Syed, Q. (1998) Hepatitis B and hepatitis C virus infections: risk factors among drug users in northwest England. *Journal of Infection*, **37**, 260–269.

MacDonald, M.A., Wodak, A.D., Dolan, K.A., van Beek, I., Cunningham, P.H. & Kaldor, J.M. (2000) For the Collaboration of Australian NSPs. Hepatitis C virus antibody prevalence among injecting drug users at selected needle and syringe programs in Australia, 1995–1997. *Medical Journal of Australia*, **172**, 57–61.

Macalino, G.E., Hou, J.C., Kumar, M.S., Taylor, L.E., Sumantera, I.G. & Rich, J.D. (2004) Hepatitis C infection and incarcerated populations. *International Journal of Drug Policy*, **15**, 103–114.

Mansson, A.S., Moestrup, T., Nordenfelt, E. & Widell, A. (2000) Continued transmission of hepatitis B and C viruses, but no transmission of human immunodeficiency virus among intravenous drug users participating in a syringe/needle exchange programme. *Scandinavian Journal of Infectious Diseases*, **32**, 253–258.

McIntyre, P.G., Hill, D.A., Appleyard, K., Taylor, A., Hutchinson, S. & Goldberg, D.J. (2001) Prevalence of antibodies to hepatitis C. virus, HIV and human T-cell leukaemia/lymphoma viruses in injecting drug users in Tayside, Scotland 1993–7. *Epidemiology and Infection*, **126**, 97–101.

Miller, C.L., Johnston, C., Spittal, P.M., Li, K., LaLiberte, N., Montaner, J.S.G. & Schecter, M.T. (2002) Opportunities for prevention: hepatitis C prevalence and incidence in a cohort of young injection drug users. *Hepatology*, **36**, 737–742.

Moaven, L.D., Crofts, N. & Locarnini, S.A. (1993) Hepatitis C virus in Victorian injecting drug users in 1971 (letter). *Medical Journal of Australia*, **158**, 574.

Patrick, D.M., Tyndall, M.W., Cornelisse, P.G., Li, K., Sherlock, C.H. & Rekart, M.L.K. (2001) Incidence of hepatitis C virus infection among injection drug users during an outbreak of HIV infection. *Canadian Medical Association Journal*, **165**, 889–895.

Rezza, G., Sagliocca, L., Zaccarelli, M., Nespoli, M., Siconolfi, M. & Baldassarre, C. (1996) Incidence rates and risk factors for HCV seroconversion among injecting drug users in an area with low HIV seroprevalence. *Scandinavian Journal of Infectious Diseases*, **28**, 27–29.

Rodriguez, M., Navascues, C.A., Martinez, A., Suarez, A., Sotorrio, N.G., Cimadevilla, R., Linares, A., Perez, R. & Rodrigo, L. (1992) Hepatitis C virus infection in patients with acute hepatitis B. *Infection*, **20**, 316–319.

Smyth, B.P., Keenan, E. & O'Connor, J.J. (1998) Bloodborne viral infection in Irish injecting drug users. *Addiction*, **93**, 1649–1656.

Sorensen, J.L. & Copeland, A.L. (2000) Drug abuse treatment as an HIV prevention strategy: a review. *Drug and Alcohol Dependence*, **59**, 17–31.

Stark, K., Bienzle, U., Vonk, R. & Guggenmoos-Holzmann, I. (1997) History of syringe sharing in prison and risk of hepatitis B virus, hepatitis C virus and human immunodeficiency virus infection among injecting drug users in Berlin. *International Journal of Epidemiology*, **26**, 1359–1366.

Taylor, A., Goldberg, D., Hutchinson, S., Cameron, S., Gore, S.M., McMenamin, J., Green, S., Pithie, A. & Fox, R. (2000) Prevalence of hepatitis C virus infection among injecting drug users in Glasgow 1990–1996: are current harm reduction strategies working? *Journal of Infection*, **40**, 176–183.

Thorpe, L.E., Ouellet, L.J., Levy, J.R., Williams, I.T. & Monterroso, E.R. (2000) Hepatitis C virus infection: prevalence, risk factors, and prevention opportunities among young injection drug users in Chicago, 1997–1999. *Journal of Infectious Diseases*, **182**, 1588–1594.

van Beek, I., Buckley, R., Stewart, M., MacDonald, M. & Kaldor, J. (1994) Risk factors for hepatitis C virus infection among injecting drug users in Sydney. *Genitourinary Medicine*, **70**, 321–324.

van Beek, I., Dwyer, R., Dore, G.J., Luo, K. & Kaldor, J.M. (1998) Infection with HIV and hepatitis C virus among injecting drug users in a prevention setting: retrospective cohort study. *British Medical Journal*, **317**, 433–437.

van den Hoek, J.A.R., van Haastrecht, H.J.A., Goudsmit, J., de Wolf, F. & Coutinho, R.A. (1990) Prevalence, incidence and risk factors of hepatitis C virus infection among drug users in Amsterdam. *Journal of Infectious Diseases*, **162**, 823–826.

Villano, S.A., Vlahov, D., Nelson, K.E., Lyles, C.M., Cohn, S. & Thomas, D.L. (1997) Incidence and risk factors for hepatitis C among injection drug users in Baltimore, Maryland. *Journal of Clinical Microbiology*, **35**, 3274–3277.

Weild, A.R., Gill, O.N., Bennett, D., Livingstone, S.J.M., Parry, J.V. & Curran, L. (2000) Prevalence of HIV, hepatitis B and hepatitis C antibodies in prisoners in England and Wales: a national survey. *Communicable Diseases and Public Health*, **3**, 121–126.

Chapter 8

HIV and Injecting Drug Use

Robert Heimer

Introduction

The purpose of this book is to provide perspectives from diverse sources on the widespread and persistent injection of illegal psychotropic and addictive drugs. Even a skimming of the previous chapters should have convinced readers that illegal drug injection is a worldwide phenomenon. This seems irrefutable. No nation can claim to be immune from the practice and no nation can safely ignore the negative consequences of illegal drug injection among its citizens. A second irrefutable fact is that a most significant negative consequence is a global epidemic of HIV-1 disease among injecting drug users (IDUs).

Although injectors in every country are becoming infected with and dying from HIV-1, there is no single epidemic. Instead, locally developed injection practices and the social responses to illegal injection influence HIV-1 transmission and shape the nature and course of local epidemics. In this chapter, I will describe the transmission dynamics and epidemiology of HIV-1 among injectors. The purpose of the chapter is to encourage its readers to devise plans to take action against their epidemic. Therefore, I will not provide a detailed review of transmission dynamics and global epidemiology. Rather, I will present examples in which behavioural and structural factors influence the extent to which HIV is transmitted. I believe that it is more useful, at this point in the global epidemic, to focus on similar populations with different levels of HIV-1 infection and attempt to understand how these differences have come about and why the differences have remained. In other words, why have some places experienced severe epidemics when others have been spared. For those wishing a more traditional approach, one that identifies similarities in responses among localities that have kept HIV-1 prevalences under control, I refer readers to articles by Des Jarlais and colleagues (Des Jarlais *et al.*, 1995; Des Jarlais, 1998).

In the developed world, shifts in the available choice of illicit drugs injected keep total drug use fairly constant. In the developing world, in contrast, injection of illicit drugs seems to be increasing (Observatoire Géopolitique des Drogues, 2000; UNODCCP, 2000). Throughout the world, the extent to which HIV-1 infects injectors varies as result of injection practices, social norms, and societal influences.

Biology, behaviour and social policy

The first of these factors is directly related to the nature of the virus itself. Under most circumstances, HIV-1 does not remain infectious for long after it has left the body of an infected individual. For example, in dried blood HIV-1 generally is inactivated within a day or two (Resnick *et al.*, 1986; Tjøtta *et al.*, 1991). The exceptions to this general rule have enormous consequences. First, the high prevalence of HIV-1 infection among haemophiliacs treated with dried blood products during the late 1970s and early 1980s resulted from the survival of the virus during the careful freeze-drying practices used in the products' manufacture. Second, blood in syringes used by injectors does not rapidly dry out; this protects the virus from the inactivating consequences of dehydration. We have demonstrated that HIV-1 routinely remains viable in the closed milieu of needle lumens and syringe barrels far longer than if the HIV-1 infected blood had been left to dry on an open surface (Abdala *et al.*, 1999).

Three factors influence survival in syringes. The first is the volume of blood in syringes. We compared 1 ml syringes with fixed needles (like the disposable insulin syringes most commonly used in the United States) to equal volume syringes with detachable needles of equal gauge (Figure 8.1). When the syringes were handled as they might be by injectors, after the plunger was fully depressed as at the end of the injection, the detachable pair retained ten times more liquid – 16–20 µl – than did the fixed syringe (Abdala *et al.*, 1999). Syringes with larger volumes have been found to retain even more liquid; for example, 2 ml syringes with detachable needles retained 35 µl (Hoffman *et al.*, 1989). HIV-1 from contaminated blood survived longer in the syringes that retained more volume. We could recover viable HIV-1 from almost 40% of syringes containing 20 µl blood that had been stored at room temperature for 6 weeks, whereas less than 10% of syringes containing 2 µl blood yielded viable virus after storage for just 3 weeks (Abdala *et al.*, 1999).

The second factor influencing HIV-1 survival in syringes is storage temperature. Cooler temperatures promote prolonged survival. Regardless of volume, the viability of HIV-1 in syringes was reduced to only a day or two if syringes were stored at 37°C. On the other hand, viable HIV-1 can be recovered from syringes containing only 2 µl of blood after 6 weeks of storage when the storage temperature was decreased from room temperature to 4°C (Abdala *et al.*, 2000).

The third factor is the titre of HIV-1 in the blood remaining in the syringe. It appears that the loss of viability is a simple stochastic process and that more virus translates into longer duration of potential infectivity. This factor may play a role in the observations that epidemics among injectors seem to blossom rapidly in many locations, with well documented examples coming from New York, Sao Paulo, Edinburgh, Milan, northeastern India, Bangkok, and most recently, cities in the former Soviet Union (Robertson *et al.*, 1986; Marmor *et al.*, 1987; Naik *et al.*, 1991; Nicolosi *et al.*, 1992; Lima *et al.*, 1994; Mashkilleyson & Leinikki, 1999; Nabatov *et al.*, 2002; Nguyen *et al.*, 2002; Rhodes *et al.*, 2002). Periods of rapidly rising prevalence are characterised by large numbers of injectors with acute HIV-1 infection. During acute infection, HIV-1 titres are frequently 10–100

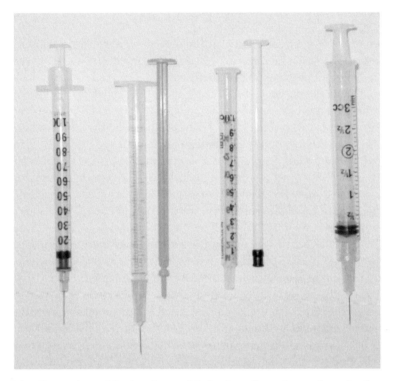

Figure 8.1   Comparison of 1 ml syringes with fixed needle syringes of equal volume compared with detachable needles of equal gauge.

times higher than during the clinical latency that follows acute infection (Clark & Shaw, 1993), and higher viral loads are associated with an increased likelihood of transmission (Pedraza *et al.*, 1999). With many injectors especially infectious, the syringes they contaminate, and which then are shared with the uninfected, pose great risks for spreading the infection.

HIV-1 is not an easy virus to transmit. Hospital needlestick data on transmission rates following known exposure suggest that HIV-1 is about ten times less likely to be transmitted than hepatitis C virus and one hundred times less likely to be transmitted than hepatitis B virus (Short & Bell, 1993). HIV-1 appears to be transmitted in about 0.3% of incidents. Shared syringes among injectors are somewhat more likely to transmit the virus, but transmission has been calculated to occur in less than 1% of exposures. Two estimates for the transmission rate have been published. The first, based on mathematical modelling of data from a US city, estimated a transmission rate of 0.67% (Kaplan & Heimer, 1992). The second estimate, based on data from Thailand, was 0.8% (Hudgens *et al.*, 2001). These estimates make it seem that transmission of HIV-1 is unlikely, but it must be remembered that heroin addicted injectors inject on average three times a day and that cocaine-addicted injectors may inject much more frequently during binges. The

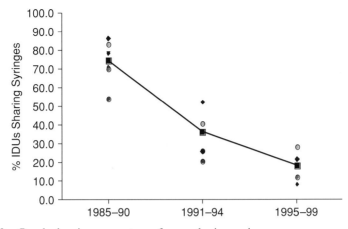

Figure 8.2   Graph showing percentage of users sharing syringes.

laws of probability suggest that an IDU has a 50–50 chance of being infected by the time he has shared 100 syringes with an infected IDU.

There are behavioural and structural factors that increase the likelihood that syringes will be shared. Many studies have found that syringe sharing was common at the outset of the HIV-1 epidemics. This appears to have been the case in western Europe in the early 1980s, southern and southeast Asia in the early 1990s, and Russia and the Ukraine in more recent years (Donoghoe *et al.*, 1989; Hartgers *et al.*, 1989; Celentano *et al.*, 1998; Des Jarlais *et al.*, 2002; Rhodes *et al.*, 2002). It was also the case in the US during the mid-to-late 1980s (Friedland *et al.*, 1985; Chaisson *et al.*, 1987; Marmor *et al.*, 1987; Vlahov *et al.*, 1990; Battjes *et al.*, 1991; Booth *et al.*, 1991; Watters *et al.*, 1991). Analysis of several studies revealed that 70% of the injectors reported that they shared syringes (Figure 8.2). As educational campaigns and bleach-and-teach programmes took to the streets in the late 1980s (Wiebel, 1988; Watters, 1994), sharing frequencies reported by injectors were cut in half (Battjes *et al.*, 1995; Chitwood *et al.*, 1995; Koester *et al.*, 1996; McCoy *et al.*, 1998; Needle *et al.*, 1998; Beardsley *et al.*, 1999). More recently, in the era of expanding syringe exchange services, these frequencies have again been halved (Vlahov *et al.*, 1997; Bluthenthal *et al.*, 1998; Des Jarlais *et al.*, 1998; Paone *et al.*, 1998; Bluthenthal *et al.*, 2000; Monterroso *et al.*, 2000; Heimer *et al.*, 2002a; Thorpe *et al.*, 2002; Buchanan *et al.*, 2004).

Structural interventions to reduce HIV-related injection risk require changes at the levels of social norms, laws and policy (Tawil *et al.*, 1995; Blankenship *et al.*, 2000; Rhodes *et al.*, 2001). An example from my home state of Connecticut in the northeastern United States is illustrative. In 1992, the law making possession or purchase of syringes without a prescription was repealed (Bray *et al.*, 2001). Injectors purchased syringes in increasing numbers (Groseclose *et al.*, 1995; Heimer *et al.*, 1996). But in some jurisdictions, police continued to harass injectors, using another law on drug paraphernalia, to argue that the contents of used syringes was admissible evidence of injecting drug use.

The resultant ambiguity – repealed possession law, newly enforced paraphernalia law – proved confusing to injectors. Syringes were rarely carried, and syringe sharing remained widespread (Grund *et al.*, 1995). Further relaxation of syringe possession did little to increase syringe availability (Heimer *et al.*, 2002b). Standard police practice in some locations continued to influence behaviours negatively.

The ambiguity was resolved in favour of injectors by judicial action. A federal court ruled that the state legislature, by consciously acting to permit the purchase and possession of clean syringes and to establish syringe exchange for the purposes of returning used syringes, must have expected that syringes, new or used, could be legally carried. In 2002, the court enjoined a local police department from arresting or harassing those possessing used syringes. This ruling has not yet ended harassment and further court action is anticipated.

In the next sections, I will discuss how virology, behaviour and policy interact to create divergent HIV-1 epidemics among injectors. Each section will cover a region of the world and will identify the major difference between locales within the region that have witnessed serious epidemics and those that seem to have kept the epidemic within limits. What appears most interesting, in comparing the different regions, is that the reasons for the differences are not consistent.

North America

Some of the most striking and dramatic differences in HIV prevalence among injectors can be observed when one compares the northeastern and western United States. Throughout the AIDS epidemic, prevalence among injectors in the New York region has been higher than elsewhere. HIV was introduced and spread rapidly among the region's injectors in the late 1970s, reaching levels of 50% or more in New York City, Newark, New Jersey, and directly connected urban areas like San Juan, Puerto Rico (Hahn *et al.*, 1989; Des Jarlais *et al.*, 1994). These high prevalence levels remained constant throughout the 1980s and began to decline only when HIV prevention outreach and education became widespread, and syringe exchange became institutionalised and widespread. In contrast, prevalence has remained much lower west of the Mississippi River in cities such as Houston, Denver, Los Angeles and Seattle. Here, HIV prevalence has remained below 10% and is probably closer to 5% (Kral *et al.*, 1998).

What can account for this difference? It is not a result of delayed introduction of HIV into the IDU communities in the west. HIV appeared among injectors and its prevalence among men having sex with men increased at the same time out west as it did in New York. It is not a result of safer syringe hygiene in the west. The prevalence of hepatitis C, which is overwhelmingly blood borne, exceeds 90% throughout the west, a level equivalent to or exceeding that found in the east (Hagan *et al.*, 1999; Lorvick *et al.*, 2001; Murrill *et al.*, 2002). Some have argued that the difference might be the result of a reduced availability of sterile syringes in the New York area, and there are some data to support an association between lack of legal availability and higher HIV prevalence (Taussig *et al.*, 2000; Friedman *et al.*, 2001). However, such an argument is moot because throughout the period of high incidence among drug injectors in the 1980s, syringes were equally unavailable without a prescription in New York, Illinois, California and Texas (Gostin *et al.*, 1997), jurisdictions with widely disparate HIV prevalences among injectors. Nor does the difference in prevalence appear to be the result of drug choice, for in all these cities, heroin or speedball (mixtures of heroin and cocaine) use is the predominant choice among injectors (Kral *et al.*, 1998). One possible explanation for the difference in prevalence may be related to the different forms of heroin available in New York compared to its western counterparts (Ciccarone & Bourgois, 2003). White powder heroin, easily dissolved in water without heat, has been the norm in New York for many years, whereas a dark resinous form of heroin, requiring heat to dissolve it, predominates out west. The typical heating required to dissolve the heroin is sufficient to inactivate HIV-1 if introduced from an infected syringe or water source (Clatts *et al.*, 1999). This might explain the observation that where easily dissolved heroin is found, HIV prevalence among injectors is high.

While drug form may explain differences in prevalence among injectors in the United States, drug choice has played a large role in the epidemic of HIV north of the border in Vancouver, Canada. HIV prevalence among injectors was low throughout the 1980s and appeared to be stable, with the city's injectors protected by one of the largest syringe exchange programmes in North America (Bardsley *et al.*, 1990). Most injectors injected brown heroin an average of twice daily. Beginning in about 1993, heroin was supplanted by cocaine as the drug of choice. With this switch came more frequent injection, especially among the unstably housed injectors congregating in the downtown eastside of Vancouver (Tyndall *et al.*, 2003). This combination led to an outbreak of HIV with incidence rates exceeding 18% per year, among the highest observed among injectors in the developed world (Strathdee *et al.*, 1997). The syringe exchange programme, hampered by restrictions on the number of syringes it could get into the hands of those most at risk, proved ineffectual, playing no role in preventing the outbreak (Strathdee *et al.*, 1997). Subsequent changes in exchange policies and practices increased syringe availability and may have checked further explosive growth of the epidemic, but not until HIV prevalence had passed 30%.

Even within small areas of the United States, there are variations in the prevalence of HIV among injectors. Such patterns have been examined in greatest detail in the San Francisco Bay area. In the early 1990s, HIV prevalence varied from a low of 14% of injectors in the city of San Francisco to a high of 32% in East Palo Alto (Watters *et al.*, 1995). The difference in prevalence could not be explained by the usual demographic and drug use variables (race/ethnicity, age, cocaine use, frequency of injection, shooting gallery use, prior drug treatment, etc.). Watters *et al.* (1995) found that prevalence was higher in small, poor communities and was strongly associated with the number and range of services targeting injectors. These data argue strongly that municipalities without ample resources to develop and implement IDU-targeted HIV prevention programmes are likely to bear the brunt of the ongoing epidemic (Watters, 1996). This pattern may be continuing today as the epidemic appears to be gaining strength in the impoverished smaller cities of the southern United States (Davis *et al.*, 1998; Karon *et al.*, 2001).

Latin America

Despite the fact that Latin America is home to the major coca and poppy growing regions and transportation routes for the heroin and cocaine used throughout the Americas, two factors have slowed the epidemics of HIV infection in injectors in this area. First, injecting drug use itself is not common in the region; second, high concentrations of injectors, often a prerequisite for epidemic spread, can be found in only a few locations. In some of these locations the epidemic is extensive and growing; in others, the epidemic appears to be stable, and incidence may even be slowing to the point where the spread among and from injectors may be of little importance in perpetuating the epidemic.

In Argentina, where the major metropolitan areas have large communities of injectors, the epidemic has been growing continuously since 1987 (Diaz Lestrem *et al.*, 1989). Injectors accounted for 10% of the total number of AIDS cases in 1987, 23% in 1989, 40% in 1991 and 44% in 1993. By the end of the twentieth century, the pattern of the HIV epidemic in Argentina was similar to that seen in southern European countries and in the northeastern United States, two locations where injecting drug use is the most important exposure category.

HIV infection among injectors in Brazil displays distinct regional differences, much like the United States, but its roots are different. In the less industrialised areas of the north, injectors have thus far had a negligible role in the AIDS epidemic, whereas they have played a central role in the HIV epidemic in the industrialised southeast, especially in São Paulo State and the southern coast. From the beginnings of the Brazilian epidemic it was noted that injectors were concentrated in the richest socioeconomic regions of Brazil, but belonged to the poorer, less educated strata of Brazilian society, living mainly in the impoverished belts surrounding Brazil's richest cities. While the IDU-driven epidemic of HIV seems to be of lesser importance in the rest of Latin America, two trends appear to be taking place: the spread of crack cocaine injection and the emergence of heroin as a new crop cultivated by drug cartels (Miguez *et al.*, 1997). While prevalence among injectors remains low, the pattern of drug use – polydrug injection, injection among commercial sex workers and injecting while incarcerated – suggests that rapid increases in prevalence might occur in the absence of targeted interventions.

Western Europe

HIV prevalence among injectors varies widely across Europe. It does not seem likely that a geographical difference in the scarcity of syringes can explain much of the pattern. Europeans, with rare exceptions, did not respond to the spread of illicit drug injection by banning or restricting access to syringes. One exception does show the power of such a foolhardy policy. In Scotland, Edinburgh and Glasgow are separated by 75 kilometres and by demography. Edinburgh is an historically prosperous capital city and Glasgow a poorer industrial city. Based on what we know of the opportunistic spread of HIV, we might suppose that the HIV epidemic would manifest itself first among the injectors of

Glasgow. But such was not the case. In response to reports of increasing heroin use in Edinburgh, pharmacists decided, in late 1982, to stop selling syringes to those suspected of being heroin injectors (Burns *et al.*, 1996). The police further increased scarcity by routinely searching for and destroying syringes. Over the next 3 years, more than 1000 HIV infections resulted. Among injectors attending one general practice, prevalence reached 50% (Robertson *et al.*, 1986; Brettle, 1990). Edinburgh achieved the dubious distinction of having the greatest density of HIV in the United Kingdom. When syringes are generally regulated and scarce, the Edinburgh experience demonstrated the results of forced scarcity.

As in the United States, there is a gradient in the prevalence of HIV among injectors, but it seems to run north–south. Prevalences are highest among injectors in Italy and Spain, and generally lower as one moves northward (Hamers *et al.*, 1997; European Monitoring Centre for Drugs and Drug Addiction, 2003). The reasons for this gradient are obscure, but appear to be rooted in the early history of the epidemic. National Focal Point sentinel surveillance studies from the mid 1990s suggest that prevalence is declining in France, Italy and Spain. Thus, there is reason for guarded optimism regarding the control of HIV among western European injectors.

Eastern Europe

There is less reason for optimism in eastern Europe, where HIV transmission among injectors in Russia, Belarus and Ukraine has made this region the scene of one of the most explosive HIV epidemics on record. As of the end of 2003, it was estimated that more than two million people had been infected with HIV and that the vast majority of these cases were among injectors (UNAIDS, 2003). This region is the first one in which it is anticipated that a generalised HIV epidemic (2% of the population infected) will have been driven by transmission among injectors (Grassly *et al.*, 2003). This begs the question, then, of whether there are special factors that created such an epidemic. As with the rapid spread of HIV among injectors in New York in the 1970s, Edinburgh in the 1980s and Vancouver in 1990s, there has been a concomitant increase in drug use and frequency of injection with the first introduction of the virus into the IDU community. But other former Warsaw Pact countries have experienced a similar increase in injection alongside the introduction of HIV without an explosive increase in prevalence (Dehne *et al.*, 1999a). Several possible explanations can be put forward to explain why the countries of the former Soviet Union differ from their more westerly neighbours. These include heightened disorder following the abrupt end of 75 years of Communist Party rule, a highly dysfunctional public health infrastructure, increasing feelings of hopelessness and worthlessness among youth, and the widespread use of homemade liquid drugs contaminated with HIV (Dehne *et al.*, 1999b). Little work has been done to investigate these possibilities.

We have begun to investigate the role of homemade drugs in the HIV-1 epidemic in the countries of the former Soviet Union. There have been reports that blood is occasionally used during the preparation of homemade heroin (chorine, hanka, khimiya) from poppy heads, poppy straw, or opium gum (Broadhead *et al.*, 1997; Grund, 2001; Selimova *et al.*, 2002). We have used reports from ethnographers and from our own field observations to simulate such manufacturing practices in our laboratory. We have added HIV-1-contaminated blood at various stages of the manufacture and filled contaminated syringes with the liquid drug preparations. We then attempted to recover viable virus from syringes using the same culture techniques we used to demonstrate the prolonged viability of HIV-1 in stored syringes. Simply put, HIV-1 does not survive the rigours of the manu-facturing process that includes repeated evaporative heating and harsh chemicals such as sulphuric acid and sodium anhydride. When syringes contaminated with infected blood were used to store the liquid drug preparations, the HIV-1 in most syringes was rapidly inactivated, suggesting that liquid drugs were not contributing to the spread of HIV-1 in the region. Instead, the rapid and widespread HIV-1 epidemic among injectors may be related to the social norms of those using homemade drugs. The typical pattern for such drug use is their communal preparation followed by communal consumption, which may lead to high rates of syringe sharing among users of liquid drugs. At least one study has linked the injection of liquid drugs to higher HIV-1 prevalence (Rhodes *et al.*, 2002). Even when each IDU has his own syringe, the division of the liquid is with a single syringe. If that syringe is contaminated, everyone is at risk (Koester *et al.*, 2003). These findings should convince authorities that the standard harm reduction measures which have proven effective elsewhere will prove effective if implemented on a sufficient scale in the region.

Epidemiological data are beginning to support the belief that harm reduction will work in eastern Europe. The HIV-1 epidemic appears to be limited to some of the countries of the former Soviet Union. Countries such as Poland, Lithuania, Hungary and the Czech Republic, which more quickly adopted the harm reduction practices and policies of western Europe, seem to have been spared the HIV-1 epidemic which struck Russia and the Ukraine beginning in 1996 (Hamers & Downs, 2003). In Russia, cities such as Kazan, which instituted a large, government-supported harm reduction programme, have kept HIV-1 prevalence among injectors low. By contrast, cities such as Moscow (where syringe exchange has been suppressed) and St Petersburg (where the syringe exchange bus was firebombed, probably by the police) appear to have uncontrolled epidemics among IDUs. In St Petersburg, for instance, prevalence among cross-sectional samples of injectors has seen the prevalence rise from 2% in 1998 to 12–18% in 2000 and to 30% or more in 2002 (Ostrovsky, 2000; Ostrovski, 2002; Abdala *et al.*, 2003; Kozlov *et al.*, 2003). Perhaps the major difference between Kazan and St Petersburg has been the active participation of local health authorities in spearheading harm reduction.

Central Asia

One of the more tumultuous regions of the world of late has been central Asia. The war in Afghanistan has dislocated poppy cultivation and heroin production northward into the five central Asian republics that were formerly part of the Soviet Union. Given these changes, both the use of heroin and the medical sequelae might also be expected to increase (Reid & Costigan, 2002). Renewed poppy cultivation in Afghanistan following the collapse of the Taliban has increased the movement of heroin along the trade routes that run through Pakistan and Iran. Both of these countries are experiencing rapid increases in heroin use and injection-related HIV transmission. Common features in promoting these trends are the youthfulness of these populations and the replacement of traditional opium smoking by heroin injection. Half the population are less than 18 years old and another sixth are between 19 and 25. Estimates of the number of injectors vary, but are believed to be at least half a million in Pakistan and at least 1.2 million in Iran (UNODCCP, 2002). Informal estimates of the number of drug dependent persons exceeds three million each in Pakistan (2% of the adult population) and Iran (15% of the adult population). In Pakistan, the sharing of contaminated syringes has been reported as the main risk factor fuelling the epidemic, and at least 60% of all HIV infections are among injectors (Reid & Costigan, 2002; Ahmed et al., 2003). In Iran, injecting drug use is perhaps most problematic among the prison population, especially because more than 70% of Iran's prison population is behind bars for drug related offences. Injecting drug use is spreading with particular rapidity among women, youth, and in rural areas. HIV infection is on the rise, with 15 000 people already infected (United Nations Development Programme, 2003). Iran may soon follow Russia and the Ukraine in becoming a nation in which a large HIV epidemic is led by a vanguard of injectors.

The explosive new HIV epidemics among injectors in Pakistan and in Iran appear to have quite different underlying causes. In Pakistan, the epidemic is concentrated among the poor, especially the virtual orphans created by large families and increasing urban migration. In Iran, social disaffection of restive youth, weary of years of oppressive Islamic law, may be driving heroin use.

Concluding remarks

The explanations for local epidemics make it hard to design, a priori, a single approach that will reduce HIV-1 transmission among injectors. On the other hand, the range of reasons is not so large that it is impossible to develop simple approaches to collect relevant data and to devise and implement successful prevention interventions. The development of rapid assessment techniques to identify the problems, potential interventions, and the likely impediments to their implementation have already sped responses to injection-driven epidemics in eastern Europe and Asia (Burrows et al., 2000; Fitch et al., 2000; Reid & Crofts, 2000).

This brief synopsis of the global epidemiology of HIV infection among drug users is designed to be neither comprehensive nor tabular. Rather than try to use reports of varying accuracy and currency to create a picture of the epidemic, I have tried to place the international *epidemics* of HIV-1 in context. I use the plural deliberately since the introduction and spread of HIV-1 among injectors and between injectors and their sex partners differ by location. These differences have been highlighted in the preceding paragraphs. Certain consistent features across epidemics also need to be emphasised.

First, syringe sharing – whether through ignorance of risk or imposed through laws, policies, or practices that keep syringes scarce – is at the root of these epidemics.

Second, shared injections also pose significant risks for transmission (Koester *et al.*, 2003). Injectors can believe that they are protected because they inject with their own syringe, oblivious to the risks posed when other injectors use dirty syringes to prepare or divide drugs.

Third, when syringe sharing and shared injections are combined with the high viral titres found during acute HIV-1 infection (and for some weeks thereafter), the incidence of HIV-1 can increase rapidly in populations of injectors.

One after another, countries which at first declared themselves immune from an HIV-1 epidemic among injectors, have had to confront the nasty reality of skyrocketing HIV-1 prevalence. As a result, the epidemic has repeatedly taken root in drug using communities and become endemic before effective prevention measures could be implemented.

This leads to the fourth consideration. Prevention measures need to be implemented early, before reality demands reaction. Places that have done so have generally been spared massive epidemics (Des Jarlais *et al.*, 1995). Prevention programmes need to evolve in order to maintain their integrity and effectiveness. Failure to do so has been at the root of epidemics in Vancouver, Canada, and Kathmandu, Nepal, where prevention programmes did not adjust to changing conditions. In Vancouver, the change from on average thrice daily heroin injection to more frequent cocaine injection and a concentration of injectors in certain neighbourhoods was coupled with the failure to provide injectors in these locations with increased access to syringes (Tyndall *et al.*, 2003; Wood *et al.*, 2003). In Kathmandu, prevention programmes served the expatriate Westerners but were not prepared for a massive increase in the number of indigenous injectors. A rapidly expanding epidemic from just a few seed cases has resulted (Oelrichs *et al.*, 2000).

Fifth, as prevention programmes take hold and decrease injection-related HIV-1 transmission, sexual transmission may become a more pressing problem (Kral *et al.*, 2001; Strathdee *et al.*, 2001). Capturing these trends and responding to them requires resources, sentinel surveillance systems, and an understanding of the complex behaviour patterns of injectors.

Sixth, we should not overlook the potential to reduce transmission through pharmacology. This takes two forms. Successful treatment of the addiction that accompanies injection drug use is possible. Opioid substitution therapy has proven effective in reducing HIV-1 transmission (Novick *et al.*, 1990; Blix & Grönbladh, 1991; Metzger *et al.*, 1993; Broers *et al.*, 1998; Langendam *et al.*, 1999; Mansson *et al.*, 2000). Pharmacological treatment for cocaine and amphetamine addiction is more problematic since there are no drugs with proven efficacy. But data suggest that heroin users who also use cocaine can diminish their cocaine use once stabilised on methadone or heroin-based treatment (Condelli *et al.*, 1992; Rehm *et al.*, 2001; Magura *et al.*, 2002).

Antiretroviral treatment also has a role in reducing transmission. Data from studies of HIV-1 transmission from mother to child and in discordant couples demonstrates a tight link between viral titre and transmission probability (Sperling *et al.*, 1996; Quinn *et al.*, 2002). Our laboratory has also found an association between viral titre and the probability of recovering viable HIV-1 from syringes (Abdala *et al.*, 1999). Taken together, it seems logical that lowering viral load through treatment would reduce the probability of syringe-mediated transmission. While there are no data that allow us to directly test this supposition, the provision of antiretroviral therapy to injectors may reduce subsequent transmission and help prevent the epidemic spread of HIV-1, as well as benefitting the infected injector.

Finally, while HIV-1 infection has drawn the attention of public health professionals and providers to problems of injection drug use, preventing HIV-1 infection is rarely the injectors' primary concern. Rather than worrying about HIV-1 infection, a health problem that may devastate in 10 years, many injectors focus on their immediate medical problem: withdrawal. In avoiding withdrawal, injectors may forsake safe injection: for fear of arrest or persecution they may refuse to carry their own syringes, and they may avoid visible prevention programmes that would reveal their status as injectors. Thus, the global epidemiology is shaped by the interplay of individual behaviours and social forces. Prevention programmes will need to take stock of local social circumstances if they are to succeed.

References

Abdala, N., Stephens, P.C., Griffith, B.P. & Heimer, R. (1999) Survival of human immunodeficiency virus type 1 in syringes. *Journal of Acquired Immune Deficiency Syndrome and Human Retroviruses*, **20**, 73–80.

Abdala, N., Reyes, R., Carney, J.M. & Heimer, R. (2000) Survival of HIV-1 in syringes: effects of temperature during storage. *Substance Use and Misuse*, **35**, 1–19.

Abdala, N., Carney, J.M., Durante, A.J., Klimov, N., Ostrovski, D., Somlai, A.M., Kozlov, A.P. & Heimer, R. (2003) Estimating the prevalence of syringe-borne and sexually transmitted diseases among injection drug users in St. Petersburg, Russia. *International Journal of STD & AIDS*, **14**, 697–703.

Ahmed, M.A., Zahar, T., Brahmbhatt, H., Imam, G., ul Hassan, S., Bareta, J.C. & Strathdee, S.A. (2003) HIV/AIDS risk behaviors and correlates of injection drug use among drug users in Pakistan. *Journal of Urban Health*, **80**, 232–239.

Bardsley, J., Turvey, J. & Blatherwick, J. (1990) Vancouver's needle exchange program. *Canadian Journal of Public Health*, **81**(1), 39–45.

Battjes, R.J., Pickens, R.W. & Amsel, Z. (1991) HIV infection and AIDS risk behaviors among intravenous drug users entering methadone treatment in selected US cities. *Journal of Acquired Immune Deficiency Syndrome*, **4**, 1148–1154.

Battjes, R.J., Pickens, R.W. & Brown, L.S.J. (1995) vHIV infection and AIDS risk behaviors among injecting drug users entering methadone treatment: an update. *Journal of Acquired Immune Deficiency Syndrome*, **10**, 90–96.

Beardsley, M., Deren, S., Tortu, S., Goldstein, M.F., Ziek, K. & Hamid, R. (1999) Trends in injection risk behaviors in a sample of New York City injection drug users: 1992–1995. *Journal of Acquired Immune Deficiency Syndrome*, **20**, 283–289.

Blankenship, K.M., Bray, S.J. & Merson, M.H. (2000) Structural interventions in public health. *AIDS*, **14**(Suppl 1), S11–S21.

Blix, O. & Grönbladh, L. (1991) The impact of methadone maintenance treatment on the spread of HIV among heroin addicts in Sweden. In N. Loimer, R. Schmid & A. Springer (eds), *Drug Addiction and AIDS*, pp. 200–205. Vienna: Springer-Verlag.

Bluthenthal, R.N., Kral, A.H., Erringer, E.A. & Edlin, B.R. (1998) Use of an illegal syringe exchange and injection-related risk behaviors among street-recruited injection drug users in Oakland, California, 1992–1995. *Journal of Acquired Immune Deficiency Syndrome*, **18**, 505–511.

Bluthenthal, R.N., Kral, A.H., Gee, L., Erringer, E.A. & Edlin, B.R. (2000) The effect of syringe exchange use on high-risk injection drug users: a cohort study. *AIDS*, **14**, 605–611.

Booth, R., Koester, S., Brewster, J.T., Weibel, W.W. & Fritz, R.B. (1991) Intravenous drug users and AIDS: risk behaviors. *American Journal of Drug and Alcohol Abuse*, **17**, 337–353.

Bray, S., Lawson, J. & Heimer, R. (2001) Doffing the cap: increasing syringe availability in law but not in practice, Connecticut 1999. *International Journal of Drug Policy*, **12**, 221–235.

Brettle, R.P. (1990) Implications of the Edinburgh AIDS epidemic for the United Kingdom. *Journal of Infection*, **20**, 215–217.

Broadhead, R.S., Sergeyev, B. & Oparina, T. (1997) *Jeff Preparation*. Russia: Yaroslavl.

Broers, B., Junet, C., Bourquin, M., Deglon, J.J., Perrin, L. & Hirschel, B. (1998) Prevalence and incidence rate of HIV, hepatitis B and C among drug users on methadone maintenance treatment in Geneva between 1988 and 1995. *AIDS*, **12**, 2059–2066.

Buchanan, D., Singer, M., Shaw, S., Teng, W., Stopka, T.J., Khoshnood, K. & Heimer, R. (2004) Syringe access, HIV risk, and AIDS in Massachusetts and Connecticut: the health implications of public policy. In A. Castro & M. Singer (eds), *Unhealthy Health Policy: A Critical Anthropological Examination*, pp. 275–285. Walnut Creek, CA: Altamira Press.

Burns, S.M., Brettle, R.P., Gore, S.M., Peutherer, J.F. & Robertson, J.R. (1996) The epidemiology of HIV infection in Edinburgh related to the injecting of drugs. *Journal of Infection*, **32**, 53–62.

Burrows, D., Trautmann, F., Frost, L., Bijl, M., Sarankov, Y., Sarang, A. & Chernenko, O. (2000) Processes and outcomes of training on rapid assessment and response methods on injecting drug use and related HIV infection in the Russian Federation. *International Journal of Drug Policy*, **11**, 151–167.

Celentano, D.D., Jittiwutikorn, J., Hodge, M.J., Beyrer, C. & Nelson, K.E. (1998) Epidemiology of HIV-1 infection in opiate users in Northern Thailand. *Journal of Acquired Immune Deficiency Syndrome*, **17**, 73–78.

Chaisson, R., Moss, A., Onishi, R., Osmond, D. & Carlson, J. (1987) Human immunodeficiency virus infection in heterosexual intravenous drug users in San Francisco. *American Journal of Public Health*, **77**(2), 169–172.

Chitwood, D.D., Griffin, D.K., Comerford, M., Page, J.B., Trapido, E.J., Lai, S. & McCoy, C.B. (1995) Risk factors for HIV-1 seroconversion among drug injectors: a case–control study. *American Journal of Public Health*, **85**, 1538–1542.

Ciccarone, D. & Bourgois, P. (2003) Explaining the geographical variation of HIV among injection drug users in the United States. *Substance Use and Misuse*, **38**, 2049–2063.

Clark, S.J. & Shaw, G.M. (1993) The acute retroviral syndrome and the pathogenesis of HIV-1 infection. *Seminars in Immunology*, **5**, 149–155.

Clatts, M.C., Heimer, R., Abdala, N., Sotheran, J.L., Goldsamt, L.A., Anderson, K.T., Gallo, T.M., Hoffer, L.D., Luciano, P.A. & Kyriakides, T. (1999) Illicit drug injection and HIV-1 transmission: heating drug solutions may inactive HIV-1. *Journal of Aquired Immune Deficiency Syndrome*, **22**, 194–199.

Condelli, W.S., Fairbank, J.A. & Dennis, M.L. (1992) Cocaine use by clients in methadone programs: significance, scope, and behavioral interventions. *Journal of Substance Abuse and Treatment*, **8**, 203–212.

Davis, S., Rosen, D.H., Steinberg, S., Wortley, P.M., Karon, J.M. & Gwinn, M. (1998) Trends in HIV prevalence among childbearing women in the United States, 1989–1994. *Journal of Acquired Immune Deficiency Syndrome*, **19**, 158–164.

Dehne, K.L., Khodakevich, L., Hamers, F.F. & Schwärtländer, B. (1999a) The HIV/AIDS epidemic in eastern Europe: recent patterns and trends and their implication for policy making. *AIDS*, **13**, 741–749.

Dehne, K.L., Grund, J.-P.C., Khodakevich, L. & Kobyshcha, Y. (1999b) The HIV/AIDS epidemic among drug injectors in eastern Europe: patterns, trends, and determinants. *Journal of Drug Issues*, **29**, 729–776.

Des Jarlais, D.C. (1998) Understanding the long-term course of HIV epidemics. *AIDS*, **12**, 669–670.

Des Jarlais, D.C., Friedman, S.R., Sotheran, J.L., Wenston, J., Marmor, M., Yancovitz, S.R., Frank, B., Beatrice, S. & Mildvan, D. (1994) Continuity and change within an HIV epidemic. *Journal of the American Medical Association*, **271**(2), 121–127.

Des Jarlais, D.C., Hagan, H., Friedman, S.R., Friedmannm, P., Goldberg, D., Frischer, M., Green, S., Tunving, K., Ljungberg, B., Wodak, A., Ross, M., Purchase, D., Millson, M.E. & Myers, T. (1995) Maintaining low HIV seroprevalence in populations of injecting drug users. *Journal of the American Medical Association*, **274**, 1226–1231.

Des Jarlais, D.C., Perlis, T., Friedman, S.R., Deren, S., Chapman, T., Sotheran, J.L., Tortu, S., Beatrice, S.T., DeBernardo, E., Monterosso, E. & Marmor, M. (1998) Declining seroprevalence in a very large HIV epidemic: injecting drug users in New York City, 1991 to 1996. *American Journal of Public Health*, **88**, 1801–1806.

Des Jarlais, D.C., Grund, J.P., Zadoretzky, C., Milliken, J., Friedmann, P., Titus, S., Perlis, T., Bodrova, V. & Zemlianova, E. (2002) HIV risk behavior among participants of syringe exchange programmes in central/eastern Europe and Russia. *International Journal of Drug Policy*, **13**, 165–174.

Diaz Lestrem, M., Fainboim, H., Mendez, N., Boxaca, M., Libonatti, O., Calello, M.A., Astarloa, L. & Weissenbacher, M. (1989) HIV-1 infection in intravenous drug abusers with clinical manifestations of hepatitis in the city of Buenos Aires. *Bulletin of the Pan American Health Organization*, **23**, 35–41.

Donoghoe, M., Stimson, G., Dolan, K. & Alldritt, L. (1989) Changes in HIV risk behaviour in clients of syringe-exchange schemes in England and Scotland. *AIDS*, **3**, 267–272.

European Monitoring Centre for Drugs and Drug Addiction (2003) The state of the drugs problem in the European Union and Norway. In *Annual Report*, pp. 24–26. Lisbon, Portugal: European Monitoring Centre for Drugs and Drug Addiction.

Fitch, C., Rhodes, T. & Stimson, G.V. (2000) Origins of an epidemic: the methodological and political emergence of rapid assessment. *International Journal of Drug Policy*, **11**, 63–82.

Friedland, G.H., Harris, C., Butkus-Small, C., Shine, D., Moll, B., Darrow, W. & Klein, R.S. (1985) Intravenous drug abusers and the acquired immunodeficiency syndrome (AIDS). Demographic, drug use, and needle-sharing patterns. *Archives of Internal Medicine*, **145**, 1413–1417.

Friedman, S.R., Perlis, T. & Des Jarlais, D.C. (2001) Laws prohibiting over-the-counter syringe sales to injection drug users: relations to population density, HIV prevalence, and HIV incidence. *American Journal of Public Health*, **91**, 791–793.

Gostin, L.O., Lazzarini, Z., Jones, T.S. & Flaherty, K. (1997) Prevention of HIV/AIDS among injection drug users: a national survey on the regulation of syringes and needles. *Journal of the American Medical Association*, **277**, 53–62.

Grassly, N.C., Lowndes, C.M., Rhodes, T., Judd, A., Renton, A. & Garnett, G. (2003) Modelling emerging HIV epidemics: the role of injecting drug use and sexual transmission in the Russian Federation, China, and India. *International Journal of Drug Policy*, **14**, 25–43.

Groseclose, S.L., Weinstein, B., Jones, T.S., Valleroy, L.A., Fehrs, L.J. & Kassler, W.J. (1995) Impact of increased legal access to needles and syringes on practices of injecting-drug users and police officers – Connecticut, 1992–1993. *Journal of Acquired Immune Deficiency Syndrome and Human Retrovirology*, **10**, 82–89.

Grund, J.-P.C. (2001) A candle lit from both sides: the epidemic of HIV infection in central and eastern Europe. In K. McElrath (ed.), *HIV and AIDS: A World View*, pp. 41–67. Westport, CT: Greenwood Press.

Grund, J.P., Heckathorn, D.D., Broadhead, R.S. & Anthony, D.L. (1995) In eastern Connecticut, IDUs purchase syringes from pharmacies but don't carry syringes [letter]. *Journal of Acquired Immune Deficiency Syndrome*, **10**, 104–105.

Hagan, H., McGough, J.P., Thiede, H., Weiss, N.S., Hopkins, S. & Alexander, E.R. (1999) Syringe exchange and risk of infection with hepatitis B and C viruses. *American Journal of Epidemiology*, **149**, 203–213.

Hahn, R.A., Onorato, I.M., Jones, S. & Dougherty, J. (1989) Prevalence of HIV infection among intravenous drug users in the United States. *Journal of the American Medical Association*, **261**(18), 2677–2684.

Hamers, F.F., Batter, V., Downs, A.M., Alix, J., Cazein, F. & Brunet, J.B. (1997) The HIV epidemic associated with injecting drug use in Europe: geographic and time trends. *AIDS*, **11**, 1365–1374.

Hamers, F.F. & Downs, A.M. (2003) HIV in central and eastern Europe. *Lancet*, **361**, 1035–1044.

Hartgers, C., Buning, E., van Santen, G., Verster, A. & Coutinho, R. (1989) The impact of the needle and syringe-exchange programme in Amsterdam on injecting risk behaviour. *AIDS*, **3**, 571–576.

Heimer, R., Bluthenthal, R.N., Singer, M. & Khoshnood, K. (1996) Structural impediments to operational syringe exchange programs. *AIDS and Public Policy Journal*, **11**, 169–184.

Heimer, R., Clair, S., Grau, L.E., Bluthenthal, R.N., Marshall, P.A. & Singer, M. (2002a) Hepatitis-associated knowledge is low and risks are high among HIV-aware injection drug users in three US cities. *Addiction*, **97**, 1277–1287.

Heimer, R., Clair, S., Teng, W., Grau, L.E., Khoshnood, K. & Singer, M. (2002b) Effects of increasing syringe availability on syringe exchange use and HIV risk: Connecticut 1990–2001. *Journal Urban Health*, **79**, 556–569.

Hoffman, P.N., Larkin, D.P. & Samuel, D. (1989) Needlestick and needleshare – the difference. *Journal of Infectious Diseases*, **160**, 545.

Hudgens, M.G., Longini, I.M., Halloran, M.E., Choopanya, K., Vanichseni, S., Kitayaporn, D., Mastro, T.D. & Mock, P.A. (2001) Estimating the transmission probability of human immunodeficiency virus in injecting drug users in Thailand. *Journal of the Royal Statistical Society, Applied Statistics*, **50**, 1–14.

Kaplan, E. & Heimer, R. (1992) A model-based estimate of HIV infectivity via needle sharing. *Journal of Acquired Immune Deficiency Syndrome*, **5**, 1116–1118.

Karon, J.M., Fleming, P.L., Steketee, R.W. & De Cock, K.M. (2001) HIV in the United States at the turn of the century: an epidemic in transition. *American Journal of Public Health*, **91**, 1060–1068.

Koester, S., Heimer, R., Baron, A., Glanz, J. & Teng, W. (2003) Re: Risk of hepatitis C virus among young adult injection drug users who share injection equipment [comment]. *American Journal of Epidemiology*, **157**, 376.

Koester, S.K., Booth, R.E. & Zhang, E. (1996) The prevalence of additional injection-relation HIV risk behaviors among injection drug users. *Journal of Acquired Immune Deficiency Syndrome and Human Retrovirology*, **12**, 202–207.

Kozlov, A.P., Shaboltas, A.V., Hoffman, I. & Ryder, R.W. (2003) *Preliminary results from the St. Petersburg site of the HPTN033 protocol.* HIV Prevention Trials Network Annual Meeting, Washington, DC.

Kral, A.H., Bluthenthal, R.N., Booth, R.E. & Watters, J.K. (1998) HIV seroprevalence among street-recruited injection drug and crack cocaine users in 16 US municipalities. *American Journal of Public Health*, **88**, 108–113.

Kral, A.H., Bluthenthal, R.N., Lorvick, J., Gee, L., Bacchetti, P. & Edlin, B.R. (2001) Sexual transmission of HIV-1 among injection drug users in San Francisco, USA: risk-factor analysis. *Lancet*, **357**, 1397–1401.

Langendam, M.W., van Brussel, G.H., Coutinho, R.A. & van Ameijden, E.J. (1999) Methadone maintenance treatment modalities in relation to incidence of HIV: results of the Amsterdam cohort study. *AIDS*, **13**, 1711–1716.

Lima, E.S., Friedman, S.R., Bastos, F.I., Telles, P.R., Friedmann, P., Ward, T.P. & Des Jarlais, D.C. (1994) Risk factors for HIV-1 seroprevalence among drug injectors in the cocaine-using environment of Rio de Janeiro. *Addiction*, **89**, 689–698.

Lorvick, J., Kral, A.H., Seal, K.H., Gee, L. & Edlin, B.R. (2001) Prevalence and duration of hepatitis C among injection drug users in San Francisco, CA. *American Journal of Public Health*, **91**, 46–47.

Magura, S., Rosenblum, A., Fong, C., Villano, C. & Richman, B. (2002) Treating cocaine-using methadone patients: predictors of outcomes in a psychosocial clinical trial. *Substance Use and Misuse*, **37**, 1927–1955.

Mansson, A.S., Moestrup, T., Nordenfelt, E. & Widell, A. (2000) Continued transmission of hepatitis B and C viruses, but no transmission of human immunodeficiency virus among intravenous drug users participating in a syringe/needle exchange program. *Scandinavian Journal of Infectious Diseases*, **32**, 253–258.

Marmor, M., Des Jarlais, D.C., Cohen, H., Friedman, S.R., Beatrice, S.T., Dubin, N., el-Sadr, W., Mildvan, D., Yancovitz, S. & Mathur, U. (1987) Risk factors for infection with human immunodeficiency virus among intravenous drug abusers in New York City. *AIDS*, **1**, 39–44.

Mashkilleyson, N. & Leinikki, P. (1999) Evolution of HIV epidemic in Kaliningrad, Russia. *Journal of Clinical Virology*, **12**, 37–42.

McCoy, B., Metsch, L.R., Chitwood, D.D., Shapshak, P. & Comerford, S.T. (1998) Parenteral transmission of HIV among injection drug users: assessing the frequency of multiperson use of needles, syringes, cookers, cotton, and water. *Journal of Acquired Immune Deficiency Syndrome and Human Retrovirology*, **18**(Suppl 1), S25–S29.

Metzger, D.S., Woody, G.E., McLellan, A.T., O'Brien, C.P., Druley, P., Navaline, H., DePhilippis, D., Stolley, P. & Abrutyn, E. (1993) Human immunodeficiency virus seroconversion among intravenous drug users in- and out-of-treatment: an 18-month prospective follow-up. *Journal of Acquired Immune Deficiency Syndrome*, **6**, 1049–1056.

Miguez, M.J., Page, B. & Baum, M.K. (1997) Illegal drug use and HIV-1 infection in Columbia. *Lancet*, **350**, 1635.

Monterroso, E.R., Hamburger, M.E., Vlahov, D., Des Jarlais, D.C., Ouellet, L.J., Altice, F.L., Byers, R.H., Kerndt, P.R., Watters, J.K., Bowser, B.P., Fernando, M.D. & Holmberg, S.D. (2000) Prevention of HIV infection in street-recruited injection drug users. The Collaborative Injection Drug User Study (CIDUS). *Journal of Acquired Immune Deficiency Syndrome*, **25**, 63–70.

Murrill, C.S., Weeks, H., Castrucci, B.C., Weinstock, H.S., Bell, B.P., Spruill, C. & Gwinn, M. (2002) Age-specific seroprevalence of HIV, hepatitis B virus, and hepatitis C virus among injection drug users admitted to treatment in 6 US cities. *American Journal of Public Health*, **92**, 395–398.

Nabatov, A.A., Kravchenko, O.N., Lyulchuk, M.G., Shcherbinskaya, A.M. & Lukashov, V.V. (2002) Simultaneous introduction of HIV type 1 subtype A and B viruses into injecting drug users in southern Ukraine at the beginning of the epidemic in the former Soviet Union. *AIDS, Research and Human Retroviruses*, **18**, 891–895.

Naik, T., Sarkar, S., Singh, H., Bhunia, S., Singh, Y., Singh, P. & Pal, S. (1991) Intravenous drug users – a new high-risk group for HIV infection in India. *AIDS*, **5**, 116–117.

Needle, R.N., Coyle, H., Cesari, H., Trotter, R., Clatts, M.C., Koester, S., Price, L., McLellan, E., Finlinson, A., Bluthenthal, R.N., Pierce, T., Johnson, J., Jones, T.S. & Williams, M. (1998) HIV risk behaviors associated with the injection process: multiperson use of drug injection equipment and paraphernalia in injection drug user networks. *Substance Use and Misuse*, **33**, 2403–2423.

Nguyen, L., Hu, D.J., Choopanya, K., Vanichseni, S., Kitayaporn, D., van Griensven, F., Mock, P.A., Kittikraisak, W., Young, N.L., Mastro, T.D. & Subbarao, S. (2002) Genetic analysis of incident HIV-1 strains among injection drug users in Bangkok: evidence for multiple transmission clusters during a period of high incidence. *Journal of Acquired Immune Deficiency Syndrome*, **30**, 248–256.

Nicolosi, A., Leite, M.L., Molinari, S., Musicco, M., Saracco, A. & Lazzarini, A. (1992) Incidence and prevalence trends of HIV infection in intravenous drug users attending treatment centers in Milan and northern Italy, 1986–1990. *Journal of Acquired Immune Deficiency Syndrome*, **5**, 365–373.

Novick, D.M., Joseph, H., Croxson, T.S., Salsitz, E.A., Wang, G., Richman, B.L., Poretsky, L., Keefe, J.B. & Whimbey, E. (1990) Absence of antibody to human immunodeficiency virus in long-term, socially rehabilitated methadone maintenance patients. *Archives of Internal Medicine*, **150**, 97–99.

Observatoire Géopolitique des Drogues (2000) *The World Geopolitics of Drugs 1998/1999*. Paris: Observatoire Géopolitique des Drogues.

Oelrichs, R.B., Shrestha, I.L., Anderson, D.A. & Deacon, N.J. (2000) The explosive human immunodeficiency virus type 1 epidemic among injecting drug users of Kathmandu, Nepal, is caused by a subtype C virus of restricted genetic diversity. *Journal of Virology*, **74**, 1149–1157.

Ostrovski, D.V. (2002) *WHO drug injecting study in S-Petersburg. Phase two*. 14th International AIDS Conference, Barcelona, Spain.

Ostrovsky, D. (2000) *Injection drug use, HIV, hepatitis, and overdose in St. Petersburg.* 8th International Conference on AIDS, Cancer, and Related Problems, St. Petersburg, Russia.

Paone, D., Des Jarlais, D.C. & Shi, Q. (1998) Syringe exchange use and HIV risk reduction over time. *AIDS*, **12**, 121–123.

Pedraza, M.A., del Romero, J., Roldan, F., Garcia, S., Ayerbe, M.C., Noriega, A.R. & Alcami, J. (1999) Heterosexual transmission of HIV-1 is associated with high plasma viral load levels and a positive viral isolation in the infected partner. *Journal of Acquired Immune Deficiency Syndrome*, **21**, 120–125.

Quinn, T.C., Wawer, M.J., Sewankambo, N., Serwadda, D., Li, C., Wabwire-Mangen, F., Meehan, M.O., Lutalo, T. & Gray, R.H. (2002) Viral load and heterosexual transmission of human immunodeficiency virus type 1. *New England Journal of Medicine*, **342**, 921–929.

Rehm, J., Gschwend, P., Steffen, T., Gutzwiller, F., Dobler-Mikola, A. & Uchtenhagen, A. (2001) Feasibility, safety, and efficacy of injectable heroin prescription for refractory opioid addicts: a follow-up study. *Lancet*, **358**, 1417–1423.

Reid, G. & Costigan, G. (2002) Revisiting 'The Hidden Epidemic': A situation assessment of drug use in Asia in the context of HIV/AIDS. Fairfield, Victoria, Australia: Centre for Harm Reduction, Burnet Institute.

Reid, G. & Crofts, N. (2000) Rapid assessment of drug use and HIV vulnerability in southeast and east Asia. *International Journal of Drug Policy*, **11**, 113–124.

Resnick, L., Veren, K., Salahuddin, Z., Tondreau, S. & Markhman, P.D. (1986) Stability and inactivation of HTLV-III/LAV under clinical and experimental environments. *Journal of the American Medical Association*, **255**, 1887–1891.

Rhodes, T., Judd, A., Craine, N. & Walker, M. (2001) Harm reduction: less ideology than praxis. *Addiction*, **96**, 1674–1676.

Rhodes, T., Lowndes, C., Judd, A., Mikhailova, L., Sarang, A., Rylkov, A., Tichonov, M., Lewis, K., Ulyanova, N., Alpatova, T., Karavashkin, V., Khutorskoy, M., Hickman, M. & Parry, J.V. (2002) Explosive spread and high prevalence of HIV infection among injecting drug users in Togliatti City, Russia. *AIDS*, **16**, F25–F31.

Robertson, J., Bucknall, A., Welsby, P., Roberts, J., Inglis, J., Peutherer, J. & Brettle, R. (1986) Epidemic of AIDS related virus (HTLV-III/LAV) infection among intravenous drug abusers. *British Medical Journal*, **292**, 527–529.

Selimova, L.M., Khanina, T.A., Kazennova, E.V., Zverev, S., Pokrovskii, V.V. & Bobkov, A.F. (2002) Effect of heroin-containing substances on the infectivity of the human immunodeficiency virus type 1 in vitro [in Russian]. *Voprosy Virusologii*, **47**(5), 16–20.

Short, L.J. & Bell, D.M. (1993) Risk of occupational infection with blood-borne pathogens in operating and delivery room settings. *American Journal of Infection Control*, **21**, 343–350.

Sperling, R.S., Shapiro, D.E., Coombs, R.W., Todd, J.A., Herman, S.A., McSherry, G.D., O'Sullivan, M.J., Van Dyke, R.B., Jimenez, E., Rouzioux, C., Flynn, P.M. & Sullivan, J.L. (1996) Maternal viral load, zidovudine treatment, and the risk of transmission of human immunodeficiency virus type 1 from mother to infant. *New England Journal of Medicine*, **335**, 1621–1629.

Strathdee, S.A., Patrick, D.M., Currie, S.L., Cornelisse, P.G.A., Rekart, M.L., Montaner, J.S.G., Schechter, M.T. & O'Shaughnessy, M.V. (1997) Needle exchange is not enough: lessons from the Vancouver injecting drug use study. *AIDS*, **11**, F59–F65.

Strathdee, S.A., Galai, N., Safaiean, M., Celentano, D.D., Vlahov, D., Johnson, L. & Nelson, K.E. (2001) Sex differences in risk factors for HIV seroconversion among injection drug users: a 10-year perspective. *Archives of Internal Medicine*, **161**, 1281–1288.

Taussig, J.A., Weinstein, B., Burris, S. & Jones, T.S. (2000) Syringe laws and pharmacy regulations are structural constraints on HIV prevention in the US. *AIDS*, **14**(Suppl 1), S47–S51.

Tawil, O., Verster, A. & O'Reilly, K.R. (1995) Enabling approaches for HIV/AIDS prevention: can we modify the environment and minimize the risk? *AIDS*, **9**, 1299–1306.

Thorpe, L.E., Ouellet, L.J., Hershow, R., Bailey, S.L., Williams, I.T., Williamson, J., Monterosso, E.R. & Garfein, R.S. (2002) Risk of hepatitis C virus infection among young adult injection drug users who share injection equipment. *American Journal of Epidemiology*, **155**, 645–653.

Tjøtta, E., Hungnes, O. & Grinde, B. (1991) Survival of HIV-1 activity after disinfection, temperature and pH changes, or drying. *Journal of Medical Virology*, **35**, 223–227.

Tyndall, M.W., Currie, S., Spittal, P., Li, K., Wood, E., O'Shaughnessy, M.V., & Schechter, M.T. (2003) Intensive injection cocaine use as the primary risk factor in the Vancouver HIV-1 epidemic. *AIDS*, **17**, 887–893.

UNAIDS (2003) *Ukraine Epidemiological Fact Sheet: 2003 Update*. Geneva: WHO/UNAIDS.

United Nations Development Programme (2003) HIV/AIDS and Development in South Asia 2003. *Regional Human Development Report*. New Delhi: New Concept Information Systems.

UNODCCP (2000) *Global Illicit Drug Trends, 2000*. Vienna: United Nations Office for Drug Control and Crime Prevention.

UNODCCP (2002) *Global Illicit Drug Trends, 2002*. New York: United Nations Office for Drug Control and Crime Prevention.

Vlahov, D., Munoz, A., Anthony, J.C., Cohn, S., Celentano, D.D. & Nelson, K.E. (1990) Association of drug injection patterns with antibody to human immunodeficiency virus type 1 among intravenous drug users in Baltimore, Maryland. *American Journal of Epidemiology*, **132**, 847–856.

Vlahov, D., Junge, B., Brookmeyer, R., Cohn, S., Riley, E., Armenian, H. & Beilenson, P. (1997) Reductions in high-risk drug use behaviors among participants in the Baltimore Needle Exchange Program. *Journal of Acquired Immune Deficiency Syndrome*, **16**, 400–406.

Watters, J.K. (1994) Historical perspective on the use of bleach in HIV/AIDS prevention. *Journal of Acquired Immune Deficiency Syndrome*, **7**, 743–746.

Watters, J.K. (1996) Impact of HIV risk and infection and the role of prevention services. *Journal of Substance Abuse and Treatment*, **15**, 375–385.

Watters, J.K., Bluthenthal, R.N. & Kral, A.H. (1995) HIV seroprevalence in injection drug users. *Journal of the American Medical Association*, **273**, 1178.

Watters, J.K., Cheng, Y.-T. & Lorvick, J.J. (1991) Drug-use profiles, race, age, and risk of HIV infection among intravenous drug users in San Francisco. *International Journal of Addictions*, **26**, 1247–1261.

Wiebel, W.W. (1988) Combining ethnographic and epidemiologic methods in targeted AIDS interventions: the Chicago model. *NIDA Research Monograph*, **80**, 137–150.

Wood, E., Kerr, T., Small, W., Jones, J., Schechter, M.T. & Tyndall, M.W. (2003) The impact of a police presence on access to needle exchange programs. *Journal of Acquired Immune Deficiency Syndrome*, **34**, 116–118.

Chapter 9

*Odde Commotions**: Some Other Health Consequences of Injecting

Andrew McBride and Jan Wichter

Introduction

This chapter provides a brief overview of some of some of the health complications of injecting that are not dealt with specifically in other chapters (drug contaminants, HIV, hepatitis, overdose and psychological consequences).

Early history

Charles Hunter (1858) was the first to report a patient developing a 'considerable-sized abscess' during his treatment with repeated injections of morphine. Howard-Jones (1947) noted that in most of the earlier writings there is a remarkable absence of references to septic complications. A German physician, Eulenburg (1865), announced that although the mere accumulation of injections in one area did not contribute to the danger of an abscess, irritating injection fluids could cause them (as opposed to injected water or non-acidic morphia injections). Eulenburg was probably also the first person to refer to the possibility of infectious diseases such as syphilis, infections of wounds, etc. being caused through injections.

In the early days an alarming range of 'therapeutic' substances were injected: Derricott *et al.* (1999) reported the use of cinnamon, oil of sulphur and arsenic; Howard-Jones (1947) reported injections of creosote; one of Wood's (1858) first hypodermic injections was of sherry! Wood described his reason for doing so: 'I thought it would not irritate and smart so much as alcohol, and it would not rust the instrument as a water solution of opium would do'.

These early accounts show great enthusiasm (or should that be recklessness?) among the medical profession for experimentation with new injectable substances and only limited awareness of the need for hygiene. These two factors remain at the centre of

---

* Transactions of The Royal Society (1665).

high-risk behaviour. It is terrible to realise that health professionals in much of the world still frequently give unnecessary injections with unsterile injecting equipment. In the Eastern Mediterranean and South East Asian regions there are an estimated three non-sterile injections per person per year (Hutin *et al.*, 2003).

Disease transmission

Infectious organisms may enter the picture during the growth and harvest, or manufacture of the drug, its transportation and storage, preparation for injection, or at the time of injection. Almost any form of infectious agent may be implicated, including those that are usually harmless unless introduced through the skin. These include the smallest possible agents, such as prions, which are responsible for diseases such as variant Creutzfeldt–Jakob disease (vCJD), viruses such as hepatitis C and a very wide range of single cell organisms.

The most common route of transmission for blood borne diseases is by the shared use of injection equipment. Faget (1933) first described sharing as an important behaviour pattern for transmission of infection among addicts during the malaria outbreaks of the 1930s. Crane (1991), with a focus on the United States, observed that 'needle and syringe sharing are now commonplace among drug addicts, particularly with friends or relatives'. Even before the advent of HIV, Howard and Borges (1971) showed that 92% of drug users in a sample questioned in San Francisco knew about the possibilities of hepatitis transmission via shared syringes and needles. It was the spread of HIV infection via shared injecting equipment in the 1980s that reawakened concern in public health circles. HIV and hepatitis have overshadowed all other infectious complications of injecting and are dealt with in detail in other chapters. Some other infectious diseases and complications are briefly discussed here.

Needlestick injuries

As Bartley (1991) observed, needlestick injuries have long been a concern among health-care workers, and before hepatitis and HIV, 'syphilis and gonorrhoea have historically been of concern'. The accidental event of needlestick injury among injecting drug users has not been well recognised. Hunt (1995) and Hunt *et al.* (1996) questioned 179 drug injectors of whom 30.2% had experienced a needlestick injury at some time. Over half of those injured did nothing about it, while some used an alcohol swab, or their tongue to clean the site. Just one person went for testing for possible infection.

Tetanus

One of the first reported infectious complications of injecting was a case of tetanus in a British addict reported in an editorial in the *Lancet* (Anon., 1876). Cherubin *et al.* (1968)

describe tetanus as an 'occupational' disease of addicts. Tetanus is known to occur more commonly among IDUs than the general population (King & Cave, 1991) and occurs more with 'skin poppers' than intravenous injectors (Cherubin et al., 1968). Cherubin et al. (1968) also noted that in the Harlem district of New York City, skin popping (subcutaneous injection) and tetanus were most common among older women of African-American origin. They suspected this difference might be due to the fact that older women more often have to resort to subcutaneous injection because of inflammatory changes and their smaller and less prominent veins. It has also been pointed out (MMWR, 1998) that 'Drug injection provides several potential sources for infection with Clostridium tetani, including the drug, its adulterants, injection equipment, and unwashed skin'. Even though tetanus has become a rare disease, the mortality rate in drug addicts is much higher than in the general population, and case reports confirm the dangerous role of skin popping (e.g. King & Cave, 1991).

Malaria

Brettle (1992) has stated that malaria was 'the first blood-borne organism to be associated with equipment sharing'. Biggam (1929) first reported malaria to be transmitted as a result of intravenous drug abuse and sharing of injecting equipment among a group of Egyptian heroin addicts.

In 1934, Helpern reported cases of malaria among addicts in New York City: 'The disease was directly transmitted from addict to addict as a result of the common practice of sharing the use of unsterilized hypodermic syringes for intravenous injection of heroin'. Some addicts considered the diagnosis to be a joke, because the locality and climate of New York City made the presence of malaria transmitting mosquitoes impossible and the role of needle sharing in disease transmission was unrecognised.

More recent studies of malaria transmission by needle sharing derive from cases reported in Italy (Senaldi et al., 1985) or Spain, where five drug addicts in Madrid, who had never travelled to endemic areas, were admitted to hospital (Gonzalez Garcia et al., 1986): 'All had shared contaminated injection equipment' the source of infection being a young drug addict 'who had often travelled to Equatorial Guinea'.

Dover (1971) made an interesting suggestion as to why the 1930s malaria epidemic in the United States came to an end. During the course of the epidemic, crime laboratories detected quinine as 'a common diluent or adulterant of confiscated heroin'. Quinine tastes bitter, like heroin, and may have been used 'to disguise the true amount of heroin present'. Quinine, which in Europe is most commonly known now as a constituent of tonic water, is an antimalarial agent. Dover found that, in laboratory tests, quinine was capable of rendering ineffective the malarial parasites in contaminated syringes. Whether or not this was a contributory factor, the New York epidemic was over by 1943.

Interest in quinine rose again in the US due to an epidemic of heroin-related deaths in the late 1970s and early 1980s. A study by Ruttenber and Luke (1984) revealed that during the initial stage of the epidemic, there had been a significant increase in the concentration of quinine in street heroin. The use of quinine may prevent the spread of malaria, but its use as an adulterant can also lead to medical complications. Ruttenber and Luke (1984) stated that the toxic effects of quinine include hypersensitivity and alterations in cardiac conduction and rhythm; they concluded that the epidemic of heroin-related deaths started because of the increase in the casual use of heroin in combination with ethanol and quinine. 'Analyses of the composition of street-level preparations of heroin and quarterly mortality indicate that the quantity of heroin in packages sold on the street, the price of heroin in these packages, and the quinine weight per package each predict deaths equally. An increase in combination with ethanol and quinine is the probable cause of this epidemic.' Cherubin (1967) found that quinine could also produce skin abscesses suitable for the growth of the bacteria transmitting tetanus.

Tick borne relapsing fever

Lopez-Cortez *et al.* (1989) reported an incident in Spain, where four men 'shared venepuncture equipment' and were subsequently diagnosed with tick borne relapsing fever. They stated this to be the first reported case of infections by *Borrelia* species in intravenous drug abusers and suggested that 'transmission could have occurred via venepuncture equipment, as has been reported in malaria cases'.

Sexually transmitted infections and other infectious diseases

Sexually transmitted infections (STIs) are seen more frequently in injectors. Cherubin and Sapira (1993) reported that, 'these increases have been attributed to sexual promiscuity associated with drug abuse', giving injecting a relatively minor role in the transmission of STIs.

Cherubin and Sapira (1993) also reported needle sharing to be involved in skin and soft tissue lesions local to the site of injection. Other infections reported in intravenous drug abusers include endocarditis, an inflammation of the inner lining of the heart brought about by infection (Luttgens, 1949), and infections in almost every other organ system of the body. These may arise from injection in unusual sites (breast, penis, neck, chest wall, etc.) or from organisms entering the blood stream and then colonising almost any part of the body: brain, bone, or other organ.

Non-infectious health problems associated with injecting

Table I.1 in the Introduction to this book lists the non-infectious complications of injecting, many of which are self explanatory. The frequency with which many of these problems arise is largely unknown, as most published information about them is in the form of case reports.

Perhaps the most obvious of these problems is trauma to the tissues at the site of injection. Sharp, fine-gauge needles inserted skilfully into healthy superficial veins or healthy muscle minimise the likelihood of problems. If the equipment, skill level, site and vein fall short of these ideals, the risk of trauma to arteries, nerves, soft tissue and underlying structures (for example, puncturing the lungs leading to pneumothorax) rapidly increases (Lewis et al., 1980). Arterial injury is perhaps the most high risk relatively common problem, sometimes resulting in the loss of parts of limbs because of termination of the blood supply. Chronic damage to veins can also lead to poor circulation and long-term swelling of arms and legs.

The introduction of particulate matter – emboli – is addressed in Chapter 3, but the needle itself has sometimes been reported to snap off, then being swept along in the circulation, sometimes with a fatal outcome (Thorne & Collins, 1998).

Deep vein thrombosis in legs and arms, with the risk of pulmonary embolism, is strongly associated with injecting drug use, although the immediate causal connection is sometimes difficult to establish.

Rare conditions such as heroin associated nephropathy (HEN), a chronic disorder of kidney function, is linked to injecting drug use, although the causal agent remains to be identified (Cunningham et al., 1984).

Conclusions

Injecting drug use is associated with a wide range of disorders and diseases that vary very greatly in their frequency. Common problems such as infections at the site of injection and damage to surface veins contribute significantly to the morbidity and long-term risks of injecting. More serious adverse events are comparatively rare, but should not be completely forgotten despite the priority necessarily given to HIV and hepatitis.

References

Anonymous (1876) Tetanus after hypodermic injection of morphia. Lancet, 2, 873.

Bartley, J. (1991) Infection control strategies for managing intravenous drug abusers. In D.P. Levine (ed.), Infections in Intravenous Drug Abusers, pp. 51–67. New York: Oxford University Press.

Biggam, A.G. (1929) Malignant malaria associated with the administration of heroin intravenously. Transactions of the Society of Tropical Medicine and Hygiene, 23, 147–153.

Brettle, R.P. (1992) Infection and injecting drug use. Journal of Infection, 25, 121–131.

Cherubin, C.E. (1967) The medical sequelae of narcotic addiction. Annals of Internal Medicine, 67, 23–33.

Cherubin, C.E. & Sapira, J.D. (1993) The medical complications of drug addiction and the medical assessment of the intravenous drug user: 25 years later. Annals of Internal Medicine, 119, 1017–1028.

Cherubin, C.E., Millian, S.J., Palusci, E. & Fortunato, M. (1968) Investigations in tetanus in narcotics addicts in New York City. *American Journal of Epidemiology*, **88**, 215–223.

Crane, L.R. (1991) Epidemiology of infections in intravenous drug abusers. In D.P. Levine (ed.), *Infections in Intravenous Drug Abusers*, pp. 3–26. New York: Oxford University Press.

Cunningham, E.E., Venuto, R.C. & Zielezny, M.A. (1984) Adulterants in heroin/cocaine: implications concerning heroin-associated nephropathy. *Drug and Alcohol Dependence*, **14**, 19–22.

Derricott, J., Preston, A. & Hunt, N. (1999) *The Safer Injecting Briefing*. Liverpool: HIT.

Dover, A.S. (1971) Quinine as drug adulterant, and malaria transmission. *Journal of the American Medical Association*, **218**, 1830–1831.

Eulenburg, A. (1865) *Die hypodermatische Injektion der Arzneimittel*, Berlin: Hirschwald.

Faget, G.H. (1933) Malarial fever in narcotic addicts: its possible transmission by the hypodermic syringe. *Public Health Report*, **18**, 1031–1037.

Gonzalez Garcia, J.J., Arnalich, F., Pena, J.M., Garcia-Alegria, J.J., Garcia Fernandez, F., Jimenez Herraez, C. & Vazquez, J.J. (1986) An outbreak of *Plasmodium vivax* malaria among heroin users in Spain. *Transactions of the Royal Society of Tropical Medicine and Hygiene*, **80**, 549–552.

Helpern, M. (1934) Epidemic of fatal estivo-autumnal malaria among drug addicts in New York City transmitted by common use of hypodermic syringe. *American Journal of Surgery*, **26**, 111–123.

Howard, J. & Borges, P. (1971) Needle sharing in the Haight: some social and psychological functions. *Journal of Psychedelic Drugs*, **4**(1), 71–80.

Howard-Jones, N. (1947) A critical study of the origins and early development of hypodermic medication. *Journal of the History of Medicine and Allied Sciences*, **2**(2), 201–249.

Hunt, N. (1995) *'38' Injected Drug Use Study*. Maidstone: Cornerstone Research Services, Priority Care NHS Trust.

Hunt, N., Holland, J. & King, A. (1996) *South Kent Drug and Alcohol Team Syringe Exchange Evaluation: Final Report*. Maidstone: Cornerstone Research Services, Priority Care NHS Trust.

Hunter, C. (1858) On narcotic injections in neuralgia. *Medical Times and Gazette*, **2**, 408–409.

Hutin, Y.J.F., Hauri, A.M. & Armstrong, G.L. (2003) Use of injections in healthcare settings world wide, 2000: literature review and regional estimates. *British Medical Journal*, **327**, 1075–1078.

King, W.W & Cave, D.R. (1991) Use of Esmolol to control automatic instability of tetanus. *American Journal of Medicine*, **91**, 425–428.

Lewis Jr., J.W., Groux, N. & Elliott Jr., J.P. (1980) Complications of attempted central venous injections performed by drug abusers. *Chest*, **78**, 613–617.

Lopez-Cortez, L., Lozano de Leon, F., Gomez-Mateos, J.M., Sanchez-Porto, A. & Obrador, C. (1989) Tick-borne relapsing fever in intravenous drug abusers. *Journal of Infectious Diseases*, **159**, 804.

Luttgens, W.F. (1949) Endocarditis in 'main line' opium addicts. Reports on eleven cases. *Archives of Internal Medicine*, **83**, 653–664.

MMWR (1998) Tetanus among injecting-drug users – California 1997. *Morbidity and Mortality Weekly Report*, **47**(8), 149–151.

Ruttenber, A.J. & Luke, J.L. (1984) Heroin-related deaths: New epidemiologic insights. *Science*, **226**, 14–20.

Senaldi, G., Castelli, F., Chelazzi, G. & Piccinelli, O. (1985) *Plasmodium vivax* malaria in a drug addict in Italy. *Transactions of the Royal Society of Tropical Medicine and Hygiene*, **79**, 739.

Thorne, L.B. & Collins, K.A. (1998) Speedballing with needle embolisation: case study and review of the literature. *Journal of Forensic Sciences*, **43**(5), 1074–1076.

Wood, A. (1858) Treatment of neuralgic pains by narcotic injections. *British Medical Journal*, **1858**, 721–723.

Chapter 10

Transitions to and from Injecting

Matthew Southwell

Definitions

Transition

A passage or change from one place or state or act or set of circumstances to another.

Concise Oxford Dictionary

Change or passage from one state or stage to another.

The period of time during which something changes from one state or stage to another.

Collins English Dictionary

Any transition serious enough to alter your definition of self will require not just small adjustments in your way of living and thinking but a full-on metamorphosis.

Martha Beck (2004) *O Magazine, Growing Wings*

Drug transition

Transitions in route of administration of a drug refer to a phenomenon whereby a person who begins using a substance by one particular route subsequently substitutes that route for another; thereafter this new route is used in preference to the previous one.

(Dunn & Laranjeira, 1999)

Introduction

With the advent of HIV/AIDS in the 1980s, harm reduction was provided with a crucible within which the three dominant harm reduction strategies of needle and syringe exchange, outreach and methadone maintenance programmes, would be publicly tested and shown capable of meeting this public health challenge. Despite this undeniable success, injectors remained a population exposed to a wide range of acute and chronic health conditions. The identification of hepatitis C caused some to question whether widespread injecting drug use would continue in the long term (Wodak, 1997).

From the early 1990s, researchers began investigating the differential risks to which drug users are exposed when the dose and frequency of illicit drug use remains consistent but the route of administration varies. This evidence highlighted that non-injectors were exposed to lower levels of risk from blood borne virus transmission, overdose and problems of dependency. Additionally, non-injecting drug use was not associated with the range of acute or chronic health care problems associated with injecting.

The study of drug transitions is a relatively new stream of research in the harm reduction field, although Strang et al. (1992) acknowledge, 'that the study of changes in route of administration should always have been an important area of study in the drugs field'.

Understanding drug transitions

Initially, the term drug transition was employed simply to describe the switch between non-injecting and injecting routes of administering heroin (see Figure 10.1). In some national settings non-injecting routes of administration were almost non-existent in the early 1990s (e.g. Italy, Spain, France and Ireland). At the same time, in those countries with significant populations of non-injecting heroin users, the preferred alternative to injecting was by no means consistent (chasing the dragon in the UK and The Netherlands, sniffing in the USA and smoking cigarettes in Pakistan) (Strang et al., 1997).

The choice of 'gateway route' seems informed by two factors:

- Culture: The dominant mode of administration within a local heroin subculture, which Strang et al. (1997) suggest creates a stronger sense of *identity* than the more general characteristics of being a heroin user.
- Market: The type of product available within a drug scene given that brown heroin (base heroin) lends itself to smoking while china white (salt heroin) tends to be injected or sniffed.

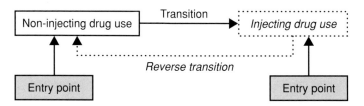

Figure 10.1   Drug transitions.

Such variations also exist at a regional level within countries. This is illustrated in the UK by the prominence of chasing in the Wirral (95%), compared with South London (50%) and Edinburgh (5%). This creates very different opportunities for engagement with drug transitions work.

The most common transition follows the predictable, though not inevitable, trend from non-injecting routes of administration towards injecting. Bravo *et al.* (2003) contend that, 'the two main reasons for changing the URHA [usual route of heroin administration] were the superior effectiveness (better or greater effect) and efficiency (same effect for less money) of injection compared to other routes'. Underlying these two main reasons are three themes that significantly inform drug transitions work: career progression and identity, demographic features and individual characteristics.

Career progression and identity

Dependent drug users are likely to experience changes in their engagement with substances as their drug taking 'career' progresses. Such changes may be informed by the physical consequences of sustained drug taking, which may become exacerbated over time. When non-injectors experience chronic problems, such as 'green phlegm lung' (bronchial tract irritation caused by smoking heroin), or nasal damage (linked to sniffing cocaine), this may reduce their attachment to such options and encourage transitions to injecting.

Another key issue linked to career progression is the time-consuming nature of both sniffing and smoking (either on silver foil or in cigarettes). Given the low dose nature of these methods of administration, using becomes increasingly laborious as tolerance and dose escalate. Users may initially have been put off by the thought of injecting; Hunt *et al.* (1998) have highlighted how these resistances can be eroded over time if non-injectors are exposed repeatedly to peers talking about injecting and its effects, or witness the act of injecting.

As a drug user progresses through their drug-using career, so they may also change their self-perception or sense of engagement in the drug scene. Concerns that becoming an injector will lead to a 'junkie identity' may dissipate if their wider behaviour patterns (e.g. offending, homelessness, etc.) are already leading to such an association.

Such factors can create a momentum among non-injectors towards injecting, demonstrated by one- to two-thirds of non-injectors transferring to injecting within a year of commencing heroin use (Bravo *et al.*, 2003). While many heroin chasers do transfer to injecting, others are resilient and seem set resolutely against such a progression, holding strongly to a positive identity as a non-injector. It is clear that the experience of heroin chasing is more than a simple precursor to injecting (Gossop *et al.*, 1988). Those with robust identities as non-injectors are sustained by two key factors: concerns about negative health consequences (blood borne virus infection and heightened overdose risk) and a fear of the act of injecting or a dislike of blood (Bravo *et al.*, 2003).

Drug transitions most frequently occur with the adoption of injecting, but there are those who achieve *reverse transitions* (i.e. movement back up the slope). Reverse transitions are predominantly motivated by health considerations such as a fear of blood borne virus transmission, becoming aware of a blood borne virus infection, or a deterioration in the condition of the person's injecting sites. This capacity for stepped change among injectors is consistent with similar successful reductions in the patterns of needle sharing and the reductions in frequency of injecting.

Reverse transitions may also reflect changes in the user's self-identity, reflecting a desire for a more moderate or measured engagement with heroin, or a desire to use drugs in a controlled manner to avoid the need to use drug services (Dolan *et al.*, 2004). Blackwell (1984) described this group of 'recovered' controllers as 'overcomers', and for many a switch in the route of administration is a critical component in this adaptive behaviour.

Others may return to heroin use after a period of abstinence and see the switch to non-injecting as an important step in breaking free from deeply embedded learned behaviour patterns.

I was drug-free for about 12 months after rehab but I missed heroin. I allow myself the treat of a boot [cockney rhyming slang: 'boot lace' to chase (chase the dragon)] once a fortnight when my shift pattern gives me a weekday off. I use with a mate from the old days and we help each other keep inside our boundaries. (Male, 39, non-dependent heroin chaser, ex-injector)

Reverse transitions were often related to personal crises, which generated a major change in attitude to drugs and/or life more generally.

Breaking free from injecting was about changing my lifestyle after being diagnosed with Hep C. It also coincided with getting married, becoming a father, developing my career and wanting to get drug services off my back. All these factors seemed to come together around the same period. (Male, 43, ex-injector who switched to mix of sniffing and chasing)

Unfortunately, those with a history of injecting may relapse into a second transition to injecting. This is probably facilitated by their existing desensitisation, their technical know-how and the likelihood that they will be mixing in peer groups containing other injectors. After a period of abstinence from injecting, some injectors may also find that their veins have recovered, offering a renewed opportunity to inject.

I returned to injecting for a number of reasons. I was feeling really down and I wanted to block everything out and to do it quick. One of my reasons for quitting with injecting was the loss of all my veins but ten years on a few had come back in my arms. It's still not something I want to go back to full time. (Female, 38, heroin and amphetamine user, mixed history of injecting and chasing)

Further, it is possible that some of these 'ex-injectors' may not have established strong personal identities as 'non-injectors', thus reducing internal ambivalence when contemplating the act of injecting. This may be compounded by poor technical know-how for those whose transition to chasing (the most technically challenging of the alternatives to injecting) corresponds with a switch away from daily or dependent using. Infrequent using and limited pool of chasing peers can combine to leave the user with the discomfort of remaining 'consciously incompetent'.

> I haven't injected for three years but I still feel really clumsy as a chaser. I don't really think about myself as a chaser. After all I injected for nearly two decades. (Male, 45, ex-injector now combines heroin chasing with street supply of dihydrocodeine)

Demographic features

Gender
Gender is a key demographic feature that informs drug transitions. Women appear highly influenced by the behaviour of their sexual partners. Entering a relationship with either an injector or a non-injector informs choices around transitions to and from injecting (van Ameijden *et al.*, 1994). When unaffected by the choices of sexual partners, women are less likely to choose injecting as a preferred route of administration (Griffiths *et al.*, 1994).

Black and minority ethnic communities
Another key demographic feature is ethnicity. Many black and minority ethnic (BME) communities in the developed world hold strong value systems that strongly disapprove of injecting (Strang *et al.*, 1992). Such value systems support drug users from BME communities to sustain non-injecting routes of administration, even when white drug users in the same geographic area predominantly inject. Historically this was linked to strong ties with non-injecting cultures in the user's country of origin. It is worthy of note that injecting drug use is spreading rapidly through many of the countries to which these BME communities can trace their roots.

Deprivation
Overall, epidemiological studies highlight that injecting is associated with entering drug use at a younger age, and is most often entered into by those experiencing a range of socioeconomic problems such as homelessness, unemployment, lower levels of educational achievement and 'addiction'. This highlights the strong correlation between injecting and problematic drug use, and may reflect different underlying motivations for drug taking among those selecting different routes of administration.

While many injectors may simply desire the enhanced 'rush' associated with injecting, others may be attracted by a desire to suppress negative feelings (Darke *et al.*, 1994). Traditionally, these have been attributed to individual features, such as personal trauma or psychological difficulties, which inform the 'self medication' psychopharmacological approach to drug taking. More recently, Friedman (2002) has described an alternative perspective, 'sociopharmacology', and proposes that problem drug use may be more prevalent among marginalised communities because of a collective search for analgesia in the face of poverty, deprivation and restricted opportunities.

Studies do indicate that those achieving reverse transitions cite their improved economic position and changing life circumstances as supportive factors in the transition to healthier and more controlled drug taking.

Individual characteristics

Side effects of non-injecting
Some non-injectors may be encouraged to inject because they have negative experiences with non-injecting routes: most commonly sniffing or chasing. For some, immediate acute problems such as nausea (smoking heroin) or allergic reactions (sniffing powdered drugs) may lead them to break with local trends if the only alternative is to abstain from drug taking altogether.

Desensitisation to injecting – special cases
While a fear of blood or aversion to the act of inserting a needle into one's vein were significant barriers to the uptake of injecting for many, this is not universally true. For example, those used to taking blood or administering medications as part of their professional role in healthcare settings may have a very different engagement with the process of injecting.

> I'm a doctor. I don't sniff Ketamine! I use by the sterile, clean method of injecting. (Male, 48, surgeon and ketamine user)

> I've never used illicit drugs before, so this placement has introduced me to a different world. . .when I lived in the halls of residence, we went to parties with the student pharmacists and they would bring different medications for us to try. I remember injecting Omnopon at one party. (Female, 23, student nurse on placement in user-based drug agency)

Those with chronic healthcare conditions may become similarly desensitised by regularly having blood taken from them or receiving medications by injection. This process of desensitisation raises a particular problem for the integrity of those donated blood schemes that offer financial inducement to donors, as injecting drug users see such schemes as a simple means of generating income.

Others may have a personal fascination with the process of injecting, which may be part of their identity as an outsider, which might cut across wider cultural norms.

> I always knew I would inject. I've read all of William Burroughs' books and I bought a beautiful antique needle and syringe in its original case from eBay. It was also part of

the culture of so many of my musical role models. (Male, 25, professional musician and heroin user)

This highlights the importance of testing attitudes to injecting and experiences of side effects from non-injecting alternatives in assessing an individual's risk of taking up injecting.

A wider interpretation of drug transitions work

Transitions backwards and forwards between routes of administering heroin were the dominant focus of early work on drug transitions. Other types of transitions are increasingly being discussed because of their influence on risk behaviour.

Stimulants

High dose using was previously the exclusive domain of those willing to insert a needle into their vein. The arrival of crack cocaine piping has made high dose using available to a much wider audience. Research into 'non-deviant' cocaine users suggests that a diverse range of risk factors can be shown to be directly influenced by dose (Cohen, 1994), with risk rising and falling in severity depending how much the user consumes. This has led others to contend that dose is the most significant factor at play in the heightened problems faced by cocaine injectors and pipers, when contrasted with sniffers, chasers and those smoking cocaine in cigarettes (Southwell, 2003). The addition of stimulants into the study of drug transitions raises a new set of challenges for researchers. Given the impact of dose on risk behaviour, it will be important to distinguish between different methods of 'smoking' (i.e. piping, chasing the dragon or smoking drugs in cigarettes) given their different dose profiles.

In general terms, it is also important to compare and contrast samples taken from treatment settings with non-service using populations. For example, a study of drug transitions among cocaine users drawn from service settings in Brazil noted a 70% incidence of transitions from sniffing to either smoking or injecting, of which half had occurred within 3 years of initiation into cocaine use (Dunn & Laranjeira, 1999). The dilemma in interpreting these data is that the transition to injecting may be one reason for this group to have sought services, rather than presenting a true indication of underlying transition rates in São Paulo.

One challenge faced by users and practitioners working with stimulant users (cocaine in both forms, amphetamines and methamphetamine) is that while smoking is clearly less risky than injecting, high dose smoking (i.e. piping) is associated with unexpectedly high levels of blood virus transmission, overdose, loss of control and psychosis (Matsumoto et al., 2002). A much greater difference in relative risk has been found between studies comparing injecting and sniffing of methamphetamine, than in studies comparing injecting and smoking, possibly affirming the 'dose' hypothesis (Domier et al., 2000). The high incidence of vascular problems associated with injecting stimulants (given the frequency and intensity of dosing) is the major reason cited for transitions away from amphetamine use (Darke *et al.*, 1999). In cocaine users, the risk of vascular damage is increased by the local anaesthetic effect.

Frequency of use

Another significant factor affecting transitions work is the frequency with which the drug user administers repeated doses. Bruneau *et al.* (2004) demonstrated that the more frequently the user injects, the less likely they are to achieve a transition away from injecting. This suggests that interventions designed to reduce the frequency of injecting might be valuable as part of an intermediate strategy.

Brugal *et al.* (2002) have reminded us that as heroin users reduce their frequency of use, so their tolerance falls and the risk of overdose is heightened. While this risk profile is most noticeable among injectors, sporadic sniffers face a higher risk of overdosing than chasers. Darke & Ross (2000) further reinforce the risk of overdose faced by non-injectors, which should be addressed as part of drug transition interventions.

Baker *et al.* (2003) argue for attention to be paid also to the frequency of injecting among amphetamine users. In their Australian study they demonstrated a positive relationship between intensity of injecting episodes and mental health problems.

Transitions between drug types

Outbreaks of methamphetamine and crack cocaine use have been shown to have a destabilising impact on previously relatively stable heroin scenes and treatment populations in a number of national settings. These findings emphasise the importance of monitoring such trends between drug types as suggested by Darke *et al.* (1999).

Market level changes and drug transitions

The impact of drug 'droughts' on non-injectors has also been considered a risk period for transitions to injecting to occur. While there is some evidence of this, other studies have highlighted that non-injectors can demonstrate a range of coping strategies other than switching to injecting. The accessibility and responsiveness of treatment services may play a key role in such situations. For example, a drought in the UK in 2002 led 50 drug users from the local South Asian population to enter a low threshold and popular local treatment service in one area, while longer waiting times and an orthodox medical treatment model resulted in anecdotal reports from local drug user groups and outreach workers of a significant number of transitions to injecting in another, comparable area.

Market changes may have other effects on transitions between drugs. The arrival of new drugs may introduce injecting into previously non-injecting populations. For example, in Laos an estimated 5% of the population are daily opium smokers (rising to 10% among some ethnic minorities). This has left injected heroin use on the margins of the local drug scene. The arrival of amphetamines has been coupled with reports of some amphetamine being injected, raising concerns that Laos could be at the beginning of an outbreak of injecting.

Opium using drug cultures usually had a pattern of drug taking typified by low dose use, ritualised patterns of use and well-established protective cultural norms. Changes in international drugs policy, driven primarily by the US, have contributed significantly to the destabilisation of such opium using cultures around the world, to be replaced by heroin use that has escalated harm and undermined public health.

It is important to note the influence of such macro level influences on local drug transitions. Strang *et al.* (1992) noted that interventions designed to support individual or community level change around drug transitions are based on an assumption that there is such a thing as a 'health conscious drug user' (Stimson, 1992). Further, even accepting this premise (as this author does), this area of work, 'assumes a considerable degree of continued personal influence on the continued nature of drug use' (Strang *et al.*, 1992)

Case 35, now thirty-eight years of age, started smoking opium twenty years ago (in 1905). After the importation of smoking opium was prevented by law, he used morphine, and when this could no longer be secured, he changed to heroin.

(Kolb, 1925)

These types of macro changes are largely out of the control of local agencies and individual users. Users are not usually aware of these influences on their behaviour, but, once prompted, do identify changes in quality, product type and price as informing their choices. For example, the availability of brown (base) heroin in Western Europe informs the choice of users to chase the drug as a preferred alternative to injecting, while the availability of china white (salt) heroin in New York informs users' choice to sniff as the preferred alternative.

The economic position of the user and retail price of the product will inevitably influence the degree to which any user can make informed choices. At times these choices will inevitably be bound up with an acceptance of a higher level of risk taking. This is best illustrated by the absence, at the time of writing (autumn 2004) of powdered cocaine from most street scenes in the UK, while crack cocaine is widely available. This maximises the harm faced by injectors and restricts opportunities for drug transitions work.

One further market factor is the issue of supply routes. For example, one such supply chain has brought refined heroin, suitable for injecting, to a number of markets in South East Asia. This accidental bringing together of a drug using (opium smoking) population with a supply of heroin, has disrupted local drug use patterns and raised the prevalence of injecting drug use.

One downstream effect of this supply chain effect is faced by Australia. Australia is at the end of the supply chain for china white heroin. This heroin is increasingly diverted as it passes through countries with their own heroin scenes, leaving Australia with lower quality and higher priced heroin, militating against transitions away from injecting.

These observations call for consideration of a new set of interventions based on global lobbying of governments and international agencies, and provide a cautionary note for drug transitions work, particularly when the developing world is experiencing increasing levels of injecting drug use.

In summary, for non-injecting drug use to be supported and reverse transitions to be stimulated, the quality of drugs needs to be high, the prices relatively low and products suitable for sniffing or smoking to be consistently available.

Route transition interventions

Hunt *et al.* (1999) proposed the term route transition intervention (RTI) as a means of categorising the evolving series of interventions that seek to reduce harm by promoting or supporting transitions between different routes of drug administration. To have

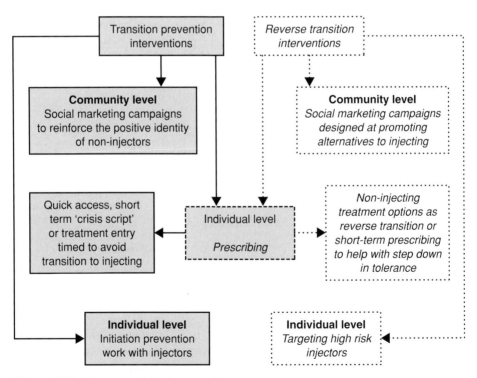

Figure 10.2   Route transition interventions.

maximum impact and to respond to the complexity described in this chapter, future work on drug transitions will need to be designed to impact at four different levels:

- individual
- community
- organisational settings
- public policy and practice.

A programme of RTIs operating at multiple levels would allow for a combination of strategies to address the range of challenges faced in implementing drug transitions work, in a manner consistent with the Ottawa Charter for Health Promotion. Interventions at each level should address both strategies for preventing transitions into injecting and those designed to foster reverse transitions.

Prevention – individual level

Individual risk factors
The evidence base indicates a range of risk factors that might trigger a transition to injecting:

- being exposed to discussions about the process and effects of injecting, or observing injecting itself
- entering into a relationship with an injecting drug user
- high dose usage
- multiple factors of deprivation
- early entry into drug taking
- having a history of past injecting practice
- a non-injecting drug using career of over 12 months.

A key step to integrating drug transitions work into mainstream practice is to incorporate the monitoring of such issues into baseline assessment and review tools, and subsequently to highlight such risk factors to non-injectors. The goal should be to reaffirm their identity as non-injectors, supporting them to enhance their efficacy as sniffers or smokers and to develop strategies for coping in desensitising situations. These ideas follow the principles of the 'break the cycle' intervention (Hunt *et al.*, 2002), but put the onus on the non-injector to protect their preferred drug using identity.

Organisational setting

- Specialist drug service should monitor non-injecting drug users for factors that might act as markers for future transitions to injecting. These should be included as a routine part of services' assessment and review procedures.

- Drug services should differentiate between different populations of non-injectors and prioritise for engagement with those at higher risk of crossing over to injecting.

Public policy and practice implications

- Public policy in a number of national settings places a priority on servicing the needs of injecting drug users over non-injectors because of their heightened risk exposure. A more sensitive approach may help protect non-injecting populations.

Prevention – community level

Community-level risk factors
The evidence base indicates that certain communities of non-injecting drug users may be at risk of a collective pressure to cross over to injecting. The key sub-cultures of drug users that should be of particular concern are high dose, dependent, heroin chasers or sniffers. The risk profile for this group will be enhanced if any of the following factors are also present:

- long-standing drug using careers
- co-existing stimulant use
- individuals who have injected previously
- high frequency usage
- non-service users
- multiple co-existing factors of deprivation.

   While the supply chain remains intact and the price and quality of drugs is stable, the collective cultural norms that support non-injecting are likely to remain stable. The following trends should be monitored, as they may act as markers of heightened communal risk of transitions to injecting:

- interruptions in the supply chain
- fluctuations in price or quality of drugs
- the re-routing of supply chains of drugs, making drug types suitable for injecting available to at-risk populations
- changes in the type of drugs available on the illicit scene.

Organisational setting

- Drug user groups and outreach teams should establish monitoring systems to identify changes in risk factors.

Public policy and practice implications

- Treatment services should have a 'contingency plan' to ensure rapid access to substitute prescribing in the event of a break in the supply chain (i.e. short-term, self-titrating buprenorphine or methadone programmes).

Reverse transitions – individual level

Individual promotional factors
The receptiveness of an injecting drug user to either a spontaneous or supported reverse transition is likely to be informed by two distinct but related processes:

(1)   The injector's attachment to injecting drug use may be reducing, perhaps as their vascular damage causes injecting drug use to become increasingly time-consuming, unreliable and a 'bloody business'.
(2)   The injector may be experiencing an increasing desire to change their engagement with drug taking, perhaps reflecting a desire for a more moderate, controlled and health conscious pattern of use.

When the user's decreasing attachment to injecting is matched by an increasing desire for change, then the conditions are set for a spontaneous reverse transition or a receptive response to a professional intervention.

The situation faced by needle exchange workers in promoting alternatives to injecting for those forced away from injecting due a breakdown in the user's veins is more problematic, particularly when even the highest dose alternative to injecting: 'up your bum' (Southwell, 1997) offers a lesser effect than injecting. In reality, the injector has usually already lost access to their desired effects by this stage, and the key to presenting such interventions is to focus on the user's actual comparative experience rather than their memory of an already lost effect.

It is for this reason that reverse transitions can be introduced helpfully during a crisis that may support a re-evaluation of the place of drug taking in a person's life. Nicolosi *et al.* (1991) demonstrated this in their successful attempts to induce 'a positive modification of injecting behaviour' as part of pre- and post-HIV test counselling engagement. The user's elevated awareness of the costs of continued injecting were employed to offset the costs of switching to a non-injecting route of administration.

For dependent opiate users, it is particularly important to give consideration to strategies that facilitate the step down from injecting to non-injecting alternatives. The same quantity of heroin will be one-third less effective if smoked, so that a brief reducing prescription of an opioid agonist can be an effective intervention during such a transition. An alternative platform for promoting reverse transitions arises on those occasions when heroin users find themselves drug free or with reduced tolerance. This might result from a period of incarceration, inpatient or home detoxification, or residential rehabilitation. Take 5, a pilot initiative in The Netherlands for crack cocaine users, recommended providing self-control training for all crack users leaving its programme, including those who had achieved a drug-free status. The self-control training was seen as a safety net for those who might relapse, based on a desire to reduce the negative consequences if such a relapse occurred. Providing behavioural training on self-regulation and non-injecting routes of administration could be seen as a similar 'safety net' type intervention.

Organisational setting

- The promotion of reverse transitions should be integrated into pre- and post-blood borne virus test counselling, safer injecting advice in needle exchanges (particularly as an alternative option for those discussing transitions to high risk injecting sites), and as part of the debriefing provided to users after a non-fatal overdose.
- Treatment services should consider the provision of 'step down' programmes to help users overcome the practical difficulties of switching from injecting to non-injecting routes of administration.
- Self-control programmes tied in with the promotion of non-injecting routes of administration should be introduced as one of the exit strategies from residential rehabilitation programmes, prisons and inpatient detoxification centres.

Public policy and practice implications

- There is a need to expand the research base into self-control models and their potential to support reverse drug transitions.
- The models for supporting reverse transitions have been developed by researchers in one-off studies and more informally through peer networks where 'step down' interventions have been developed on an experimental basis, with loaned medication, by peer educators. Bringing this work together is a key next step in creating viable models that can be more widely promoted.

Reverse transitions – community level

Community-level promotional factors
When drug users have witnessed the morbidity and mortality associated with injecting over many years, and have evolved new life goals, the conditions may be right for community level reverse transitions. Where this takes place in the midst of a rise in non-injecting routes of administration among younger users and a general rise in quality and lowering in price of their key drugs of choice, the conditions may be considered to be optimal.

Social marketing campaigns such as 'oi injectors: it's good to chase' (Southwell *et al.*, 1997) and 'the switch', which promoted heroin chasing as an alternative to injecting, have been supported by articles on this and other reverse transition options in drug user magazines in the UK, France, Australia, The Netherlands and the US. This demonstrates an increasing receptiveness among culture shapers in the drug users' community to such models.

Peer training schemes, such as 'the Mr Brown and Mr White tour', that set out to raise knowledge levels within drug using communities, and the more organic process of 'life outreach' among drug users, also require further investigation.

Organisational setting

- Drug user groups and community development agencies are key agents in bringing about change at this level, but this will still require 'fair' market conditions.

Public policy and practice implications

- The situation in Australia highlights the importance of market conditions also being in place if significant changes are to be achieved and maintained (see market level changes and drug transitions). Initiatives to stabilise the dealing scene have supported significant and sustained changes in The Netherlands. Attempts have also been made to employ consumer power to influence dealing networks (Carty, 2002).
- The funding of drug user groups to play roles beyond patient advocacy has already been embraced in Australia and is a key next step for funders and government agencies elsewhere.

Conclusion

Drug transitions work has reached a critical state of development, but tends to be fragmented and sometimes haphazard. Coordination under an international agency or other lead body will be required if the benefits of such work are to be translated into mainstream interventions and social marketing campaigns that are congruent with pioneering models and the evidence base.

A key issue that faces the field of intervention in general is how to translate the research findings for more widespread practice. . .Researchers alone should not take the lead in moving effective intervention components into the community. Bridge builders, language engineers who come from the community but who understand the research world need to translate the process and product and to smooth out the transference process while maintaining the fidelity and integrity of the intervention.

(Sloboda, 1998)

References

Baker, A., Lee, N.K., Claire, M. *et al.* (2003) Drug use patterns and mental health of regular amphetamine users during a reported 'heroin' drought, *Addiction*, **99**, 875–884.

Blackwell, J. (1984) Drifting, controlling and overcoming: opiate users who avoid becoming chronically dependent, *Journal of Drug Issues*, **13**, 219–235.

Bravo, M., Barrio, G., de la Fuente, L. *et al.* (2003) Reasons for selecting an initial route of heroin administration and for subsequent transitions during a severe HIV epidemic, *Addiction*, **98**(6), 749–760.

Brugal, M.T., Barrio, G., de la Fuente, L. *et al.* (2002) Factors associated with non-fatal heroin overdose: assessing the effect of frequency and route of administration, *Addiction*, **97**(3), 319.

Bruneau, J., Brogly, S.B., Tyndall, M.W. *et al.* (2004) Intensity of drug injection as a determinant of sustained injection cessation among chronic drug users: the interface with social factors and service utilisation. *Addiction*, **99**(6), 727–737.

Carty, P. (2002) Caned and able – crack cocaine users are self-destructive individuals with an incurable addiction. Not so, a new self-help group tells Peter Carty. *The Guardian* (http://www.guardian.co.uk/guardian).

Cohen, P. (1994) Cocaine use in Amsterdam in non-deviant subcultures. *Addiction Research*, **2**(1), 71–94.

Darke, S., Cohen, J., Ross, J. *et al.* (1994) Transitions between routes of administration of regular amphetamine users, *Addiction*, **89**(9), 1077–1083.

Darke, S., Kaye, S. & Ross, J. (1999) Transitions between the injection of heroin and amphetamines. *Addiction*, **94**(12), 1795–1803.

Darke, S. & Ross, J. (2000) Fatal heroin overdoses resulting from non-injecting routes of administration: NSW Australia 1992–1996, *Addiction*, **95**, 569–573.

Dolan, K., Clement, N., Rouen, D. *et al.* (2004) Can drug injectors be encouraged to adopt non-injecting routes of administration (NIROA) for drugs? *Drug and Alcohol Review*, **23**(3), 281–286.

Domier, C.P., Simon, S.L., Rawson, R.A. *et al.* (2000) A comparison of injecting and non-injecting methamphetamine users. *Journal of Psychoactive Drugs*, **32**, 229–232.

Dunn, J. & Laranjeira, R.R. (1999) Transitions in the route of cocaine administration – characteristics, direction and associated variables. *Addiction*, **94**(6), 813–824.

Friedman, S.R. (2002) Sociopharmacology of drug use: initial thoughts. *International Journal of Drug Policy*, **13**(5), 341–347.

Griffiths, P., Gossop, M., Powis, B. *et al.* (1994) Transitions in patterns of heroin administration: a study of heroin chasers and injectors. *Addiction*, **89**(3), 301–309.

Gossop, M., Griffiths, P. & Strang, J. (1988) Chasing the dragon: characteristics of heroin chasers. *British Journal of Addiction*, **83**, 1159–1162.

Hunt, N., Stillwell, G., Taylor, C. *et al.* (1998) Evaluation of a brief intervention to reduce initiation into injecting. *Drugs Education Prevention Policy*, **5**, 185–194.

Hunt, N., Griffiths, P., Southwell, M. *et al.* (1999) Preventing and curtailing injecting drug use: a review of opportunities for developing and delivering 'route transition interventions'. *Drug and Alcohol Review*, **18**(4), 441–452.

Hunt, N., Derricott, J., Preston, A. *et al.* (2002) *Break the cycle – preventing initiation into injecting*. Exchange Campaigns Department of Health (http://exchangecampaigns.org/ktsbtcbrieftext.html).

Kolb, L. (1925) Pleasure and deterioration from narcotic addiction, *Mental Hygiene*, **9**, 719–720.

Matsumoto, T., Kamijo, A., Miyakawa, T. *et al.* (2002) Methamphetamine in Japan: the consequences of methamphetamine abuse as a function of route of administration. *Addiction*, **97**(7), 809–817.

Nicolosi, A., Molinari, S., Musicco, M. *et al.* (1991) Positive modification of injecting behaviour among intravenous heroin users from Milan and Northern Italy 1987–1989. *British Journal of Addiction*, **86**(1), 91–102.

Reid, G. & Costigan, G. (2002) *Revisiting the 'Hidden Epidemic – a situational assessment of drug use in Asia in the context of HIV/AIDS*. Melbourne: Asian Harm Reduction Network.

Sibthorpe, B. & Lear, B. (1994) Circumstances surrounding needle use transitions among injection drug users: implications for HIV intervention. *International Journal of the Addictions*, **29**(10), 1245–1257.

Sloboda, Z. (1998) What have we learned from research about the prevention of HIV to drug abusers? *Public Health Reports*, **113** (Suppl 1).

Southwell, M. (1997) 'Up your bum' – a simple safer route of drug-taking or a squirt too far. *Presentation at 8th International Conference on the Reduction of Drug Related Harm*, Paris.

Southwell, M. *et al.* (1997) Promoting heroin and crack cocaine chasing as an alternative to injecting as harm reduction tools in the late 1990s. *Presentation at 8th International Conference on the Reduction of Drug Related Harm*, Paris.

Southwell, M. (2003) More than a pipe dream: reducing crack's harm. *Druglink*, **18**(3), 8–9.

Stimson, G. (1992) Minimising harm from drug use. In J. Strang & M. Gossop (eds) *Responding to Drug Misuse: The British System*, Oxford: Oxford University Press.

Strang, J., des Jarlais, D.C., Griffiths, P. *et al.* (1992) The study of transitions in the route of drug use: the route from one route to another. *British Journal of Addiction*, **87**(3), 473–483.

Strang, J., Griffiths, P. & Gossop, M. (1997) Heroin smoking by 'chasing the dragon': origins and history. *Addiction*, **92**(6), 673–683.

van Ameijden, E.J., Van Den Hoek, J.A.R., Hartgers, C. *et al.* (1994) Risk factors for the transition from non-injection to injection drug use and accompanying AIDS risk behaviour in a cohort of drug users. *American Journal of Epidemiology*, **139**(12), 1153–1163.

Wodak, A. (1997) Injecting nation: achieving control of hepatitis C in Australia. *Drug and Alcohol Review*, **16**, 275–284.

Chapter 11

Safer Injecting: Individual Harm Reduction Advice

Helen Williams and Mark Norman

The setting

Wherever there is provision for distribution of injecting equipment, there must be opportunities for giving safer injecting advice. The provision of needles in and of itself is not enough, but rather should be offered as part of a comprehensive treatment programme. There is often a wide range of professionals who come into contact with drug users during the course of their work, all with the potential to help in the reduction of injecting related morbidity and mortality.

Community pharmacists may provide a significant, and in some cases the only, point of contact with the intravenous drug user. They may therefore be in a unique position to offer advice, both written and verbal, about safer injecting, general healthcare and locally available treatment options.

Drug users are likely to present at accident and emergency (A&E) departments for a variety of reasons, ranging from drug overdose to consequences of injecting, e.g. local or systematic infections, thrombosis. The range of services offered by A&E departments will vary considerably depending on local policy; nevertheless, admission to A&E would appear to offer a unique window of opportunity to provide crucial harm reduction advice and onward referral to specialist services.

Primary healthcare practitioners, whether or not they are directly involved in treatment for substance misuse, are likely to see drug users presenting for care. They may be involved in the provision of vaccinations or treatment of injecting wounds. Drug users may present with a variety of medical and social problems. Harm reduction advice is consistent with the role of the primary healthcare team.

A potentially rich, but often neglected, setting for needle exchange and harm reduction advice is the prison service. The UK is not alone in its reluctance to utilise a harm reduction approach with incarcerated injecting drug users. However, a recent review of international prison based syringe exchange programmes found all had positive outcomes with no reports of negative consequences (see Chapter 6).

The specialist drug agency, whether statutory or voluntary, is likely to be able to offer the most comprehensive service for the provision of injecting equipment allied with safer injecting advice. Such services are more likely to be able to offer planned, detailed sessions specifically aimed at teaching and promoting safer injecting techniques. However, this does not negate the need for such services to remain open to providing more *ad hoc* and opportunistic advice as necessary and appropriate.

Whatever the setting, attention needs to be paid to health and safety issues and to maintaining privacy and confidentiality. Each individual service will have its own limitations, but, as a minimum, the environment should feel safe for both client and practitioner.

The process of advice giving

As noted above, different agencies and settings will provide varying opportunities for giving safer injecting advice. Advice can range from suggesting the rotation of injecting sites to an in-depth discussion of the risks and harms connected with the self injection of drugs or the teaching of self injecting techniques. Jargon and ambiguous language should be avoided. As with any health promotion activity, the use of a conversational style and simple language can help to create a non-threatening environment which is conducive to learning. In such an environment, a two minute conversation may provide both important harm reduction advice and the wish to learn more.

The aim of safer injecting advice is to reduce the risks associated with injecting drugs. Sharing any injecting equipment has been implicated in the transmission of blood borne viruses, including human immunodeficiency virus (HIV), hepatitis B and hepatitis C. Other problems may also occur such as blood poisoning (septicaemia), abscess both infected and non-infected, localised infections, endocarditis (infection of the inner heart lining), loss of needles, limb loss, ulcers and circulation problems, swelling to hands and feet and associated risk. Hence, the ramifications of sharing *any* injecting equipment must be addressed with *every* client, and poor injecting technique can lead to the problems listed above. Variations in purity, changes in tolerance levels and poly drug use can contribute to overdose. Comprehensive safer injecting advice should address all these areas.

The nature of safer injecting advice

Whatever the setting and however time limited the intervention, it is vital to reinforce the 'golden rules of safer injecting':

(1)   Always use your own injecting equipment. Injecting equipment means needles, syringes, water, spoons, filters and any other aspect of injecting paraphernalia.
(2)   Don't lend or borrow used equipment to or from *anybody* (including sexual partners).
(3)   Use the smallest bore needle possible.

(4) Don't inject alone. Try to do it with other people around, and try to make sure you all know what to do in an emergency.

(5) Use your own equipment once only and dispose of it carefully.

Such information can be provided both orally and in written form, and can be delivered in any setting. Where there is more time and expertise, the planned safer injecting harm reduction interview can provide detailed information and the opportunity to practise safer injecting techniques.

The safer injecting harm reduction interview

Practitioners should ensure that the environment is as comfortable and safe as possible. It is important to protect the privacy and confidentiality of the client, but the safety of both client and practitioner are of paramount importance.

One advantage of the planned interview is that the practitioner can have all the necessary equipment to hand. Such equipment may include pen, paper, assessment tools, educational materials and examples of injecting equipment. A range of learning materials, such as posters or models, can assist in making the session more enjoyable and stimulating. If these are not to hand when needed, the practitioner may appear disorganised and the session may be less effective.

The practitioner should begin by introducing themselves and reinforcing the reason for the session. It is the responsibility of the practitioner to ensure that the session remains focused on safer injecting unless a more urgent issue arises.

Safer injecting advice must, by necessity, be preceded by an assessment of an individual's injecting behaviour. In our clinical experience, clients are happy to provide this information if it is seen as part of the helping process. Use of open-ended questions allows the client to describe their drug use history and assists the practitioner in identifying current risks. Closed questions may elicit 'yes' or 'no' answers, increasing the possibility of missing vital information about potentially harmful practices. Assessment can also assist with raising the client's awareness of current and potential risks and harms. It is always worth bearing in mind that people tend to learn best in response to a perceived need. Following assessment, information gained should be fed back and summarised objectively in order to clarify the client's current knowledge and behaviour. Learning is more likely to take place when new material is related to old, and it is a good educational principle to build on what is already known.

When giving advice, it is usually most helpful to begin by addressing the riskiest behaviour. Should the interview end prematurely, this will allow for at least some harm reduction message to be given to the client. Safer techniques, which the client is already practising, can be reinforced towards the end of the session, allowing the interview to end on a positive note. As people tend to retain knowledge if it is put to immediate use, clients should be offered the opportunity to practise techniques with immediate feedback. Practitioners should never be afraid to inform the client of the potential risks and harms of their behaviour.

Risks associated with specific drugs

Injecting any drug carries risks. However, there are specific risks associated with certain substances and preparations: some of the most common are listed below. Clients may be injecting one or all of them. It is important to reinforce the message that injecting combinations of drugs carries an increased risk of overdose.

Injecting heroin

Injecting heroin always carries a high risk of overdose. This risk is increased when heroin is taken in combination with alcohol, other opiates, or benzodiazepines. Loss of tolerance can occur following a relatively short period of abstinence, thus increasing the risk of overdose. Dose fluctuation is a continual risk, and clients should be reminded that knowing their supplier is no guarantee of level of purity. It is always advisable to inject a small amount slowly in order to judge its effects. If there are no unusual effects, injecting can continue. It is advisable to inject with somebody else, so that they can call for emergency assistance in the case of overdose. The majority of fatal overdoses occur when the person is alone. Different agencies will have different policies regarding the provision of first aid and resuscitation advice to clients and their families. As a minimum, we would suggest that the professional has a duty to dispel myths and to ensure that the client is aware of how to contact the emergency services.

Injecting cocaine

Clients need to be aware that cocaine has local anaesthetic properties, which can lead to deadening of pain at the site of injection. Lack of pain may mean that they are unaware of damage to injection sites, leading to further trauma and the formation of abscesses. For this reason, it is particularly important to rotate injection sites. Cocaine effects are of a relatively short duration and clients may need to inject several times per day, leading to increased trauma. In addition, cocaine constricts blood vessels when injected, thus greatly reducing blood supply to the injured area and possibly leading to tissue necrosis.

Injecting amphetamine

Street amphetamine in Britain is usually no more than 5% pure. Injecting amphetamine will therefore involve injecting a high level of impurities, many of which are likely to cause vein trauma or may be harmful in and of themselves. Deaths from amphetamine use are rare, but are invariably related to injecting.

Injecting tablets

Injecting tablets is not advised and is considered to be extremely dangerous. Chalk from tablets is one of the major causes of collapsed veins, leading to infection, deep vein thrombosis and potential loss of limbs. Practitioners need to consider whether giving advice in this area is acceptable. If tablets are to be injected, they should be crushed to the finest powder possible and drawn up through a filter.

Injecting oral methadone

Clients should be advised that under no circumstances is it safe to inject oral methadone, which causes vein contraction and rapid vein collapse.

Preparing to inject safely

Safer injecting begins at the preparation stage. Clients should be informed that *all* equipment should be clean and sterile, and hands should be washed. New equipment is preferable in order to reduce the risks of infection, cross infection and needle trauma. If new equipment is not available, there are cleaning techniques which clients can be taught.

Clients need to be aware that the environment can be a means of transmitting infections including viruses such as HIV, hepatitis B and hepatitis C. It may be useful at this stage to offer brief information about blood borne viruses. Hepatitis C, in particular, has been known to survive for some considerable time outside the body in microscopic amounts of blood. An apparently clean surface may be anything but that. To create a clean field, we recommend the use of a clean piece of paper for laying out injecting equipment: clean newspapers or magazines are acceptable; as with any other equipment, these need to be disposed of safely. When choosing needles, the smallest bore possible should be used to minimise trauma to veins and/or surrounding area. Intramuscular injections will require a larger needle than intravenous injections. Sterile water should be used when possible, but is not always available. As an alternative we would recommend using cooled freshly boiled water. Water should not be shared.

In order to dissolve some drugs, such as brown street heroin, so that they are suitable for injection, an acidifier needs to be used. We strongly discourage the use of lemon juice as it can cause fungal infection with potentially serious consequences. Citric acid is recommended as the safer alternative, and clients are advised to use the smallest amount possible to minimise the risks of vein trauma. A burning sensation suggests that too much is being used. Effervescent tablets are not recommended, as they are likely to cause further vein trauma.

Drugs should be heated gently using a freestanding heat source, and for a short time only to prevent wastage through evaporation. Wastage leads to further injections and further vein trauma. If using spoons, it is not advisable to use silver spoons as these have a tendency to tarnish. Disposable metal containers are available in some areas and their use should be encouraged.

Filters are used to filter out particles and impurities. Cigarette filters are preferable to cotton wool, which is more likely to have loose fibres that risk being injected into the bloodstream. These may in turn lead to thrombosed veins. Filters should not be reused because of the risks of fungal infection. If the filter is cut, the cut side should be placed down to avoid drawing up loose fibres.

We would suggest that best practice would be to use different needles for drawing up and injecting, to minimise trauma from blunt needles. This is not always possible, however, and an alternative would be to take greater care not to hit the spoon with the needle when drawing up. To further minimise bluntness, the needle aperture needs to be pointed down when drawing up. Clients are advised not to lick the end of the needle, as this is likely to increase the spread of bacteria.

Safer intravenous administration

In order to inject safely, some basic knowledge of anatomy is necessary. Clients need to know the differences between veins and arteries and the way in which blood circulates around the body. Such knowledge may help to make safer injecting advice more relevant and meaningful. It is, of course, vital that practitioners are competent to give such information. Clients should also be taught what to do if they hit an artery. The needle should be withdrawn and firm pressure applied. It is always advisable to seek immediate medical assistance.

The safest site for intravenous administration is the cubital fossa or crook of the elbow. Veins in the hands and feet are particularly fragile, and injecting in these areas is likely to be painful. If using these sites, clients are advised to use the smallest needle possible, inject very slowly and take particular care. All jewellery should be removed. Women should be advised that injecting in the breasts carries particular risks. Veins may look prominent but have a tendency to collapse. Milk ducts can become blocked and mastitis is not uncommon. Men should be advised not to inject into the penis under any circumstances. Likewise, the neck and groin are both highly dangerous places to inject, and it is debatable whether any safer injecting advice is possible. In the neck, the carotid artery and jugular vein are in close proximity, and the same is true of the femoral artery and femoral vein in the groin. Whilst some agencies teach clients how to avoid arteries in these areas, individual anatomical differences mean that certainty cannot be guaranteed. Our view is that it is not possible to inject safely in these areas and that this should be reinforced to clients.

Clients may need reminding that injection sites need to be cleaned before administering the drug. Alcohol swabs may be used if there is no access to soap and water. If so, the alcohol should be left to dry after swabbing as it will not be sterile whilst wet. To minimise damage to veins, alternative injection sites need to be used. In order to raise a vein some clients prefer to use a tourniquet. If so, they should be advised to use one that is easy to release, not to tie it too tightly, leave it on for a short time only and release it before injecting. A tourniquet that is too tight will cut off blood flow. Asking the client to demonstrate how they would use the tourniquet may be a useful way of assessing practice and correcting as necessary.

A warm environment, warm baths or warm flannels around the limb will help to raise veins. However, excessive heat may lead to burns or scalds. Palpating the vein, tightening the fist and squeezing the biceps may all help to raise veins. It is often possible to feel a vein even when it is not visible, and feeling a vein increases the chance of hitting it. Anxiety can make it more difficult to raise a vein – injecting is easier if the client is able to relax. Clients are advised never to inject where a pulse can be felt, as this indicates an artery rather than a vein.

Remind clients to use the smallest needle possible and to make sure that the aperture is facing up. This ensures that the sharpest point of the needle pierces the skin and the aperture does not rest on the bottom of the vein thus causing further trauma. Needles should be pointed towards the heart, in the direction of blood flow, at an angle of 45 degrees. Demonstration of the correct angle by the practitioner is highly recommended. Care should be taken to ensure that needles do not go straight through the vein and into surrounding tissue, leading to pain and trauma. To minimise the risks, needles should be inserted slowly and clients advised to stop pushing when resistance is felt. Clients are advised to draw back gently to check the presence and colour of blood. Venous blood is dark red as opposed to arterial blood which is bright red. Use of coloured diagrams may help clients to distinguish between the two. If venous access is achieved, administration can continue. At this point, tourniquets should be released, if used, to prevent pressure on veins. Administration should continue slowly, as rapid injection can lead to overdose. The practice of 'flushing' or repeatedly pushing down and drawing back is strongly discouraged as it causes further trauma to the vein and increases the likelihood of infection. Following administration, the needle should be removed slowly to reduce trauma and prevent the vein collapsing. Pressure should then be applied to the site for approximately 1 minute to stem the blood flow. Clean cotton or tissue is preferred to alcohol swabs which can disrupt the healing process.

Safer intramuscular (IM) administration

Intramuscular administration should be discouraged. However, if venous access is difficult, clients may attempt IM administration. If so, the thigh is the least risky site. Clients should be advised to alternate legs and inject into different places within the front top part of the thigh where there is most muscle. Needles for intravenous use will generally be too small for intramuscular use and are more likely to break, potentially leading to embolism or infection. The leg should be in a comfortable position with the muscle relaxed. The tenser the muscle, the more painful the procedure. As with intravenous administration, the site needs to be clean and dry. The needle should be inserted at an angle of 90 degrees to ensure that the drug gets into the muscle. When drawing back, there should be no blood in the syringe as this would indicate that a vein or artery had been hit. If so, the needle should be withdrawn slightly and the plunger drawn back again. If no blood is present administration can continue. Keeping the leg relaxed, the plunger should be pushed in slowly. The needle should then be removed slowly and disposed of safely.

Safer subcutaneous administration

Subcutaneous administration (skin popping) carries a higher risk of infection because absorption is much slower than with the preferred intravenous route. Drugs which are contaminated with bacteria can cause particular problems when injected subcutaneously. If injecting subcutaneously, preferred sites are the stomach or upper thigh.

As with other routes, the site should be cleaned thoroughly. The needle should be inserted at a shallow angle of approximately 15–30 degrees to ensure that it enters the thin layer of fat beneath the skin. As with the IM route, blood should not be present when drawing back. If no blood is present, administration can continue slowly. Clients should be advised to inject no more than 50 ml in any one site; if there is more than 50 ml to inject, different sites should be used. Needles should be withdrawn slowly and the site cleaned. All needles should be disposed of safely.

If the subcutaneous route is chosen, clients need to be particularly alert for symptoms of infection, such as feeling hot, general malaise, swelling, redness or pain around the injection site. Clients should be advised to seek medical attention as a matter of some urgency. Whatever the chosen route, sites should be rotated and clients advised to be alert for symptoms of infection.

Safer disposal and cleaning of used injecting equipment

It is the responsibility of the user to dispose safely of all injecting equipment, a message that should be reinforced at every opportunity. Assisting the client to understand the potential consequences of discarding used equipment may be helpful; it is vital to do this in a way that is relevant to the client. Reinforcing the message regularly with every client will promote the diffusion of the message throughout the drug using community.

The safest way of disposing of injecting equipment is to use a sharps box which should be provided by the agency offering needle exchange. Sharps boxes are more likely to be used if they are relatively easy to obtain. Clients should be reminded of the need to store them out of the reach of children. When full, they should be returned to the issuing agency or approved facility, depending on local policy. If there is no sharps box to hand, needles and syringes need to be stored safely until they can be disposed of. Needles can be placed inside the syringe and then into a drinks can to prevent needlestick injury to others. Breaking the needle will discourage reuse.

The reuse of equipment should be strongly discouraged. However, in the real world some reusing of equipment is probably inevitable. As such, it is good practice to teach the safest method of cleaning whilst acknowledging the risks. Clients should be made aware that no cleaning method is completely safe, particularly if they continue to share equipment with others. The following cleaning method may help to prevent transmission of HIV, but offers little protection against hepatitis C.

Thin bleach should be drawn up with the used needle and syringe, left for a few seconds and flushed out into the sink. This step should be repeated twice before drawing up and flushing out cold water and repeating two or three times. Alternatively, equipment can be flushed out with cold water and immersed in bleach for up to an hour before flushing out again with cold water. Spoons may be cleaned in a similar way. There is no safe way of reusing filters and these should always be disposed of after use. Thin bleach is recommended as it may be impossible to draw thick bleach through needles. Cold water is used because warm water encourages blood to coagulate, thus making it difficult it flush out.

Training and supervision needs

Practitioners involved in teaching safer injecting techniques to drug users should ensure that they have the ability to do so. To provide wrong or inaccurate information is both unethical and potentially dangerous. Individual agency requirements will differ according to local protocols but a competent practitioner should have:

- knowledge and understanding of the subject, including drug effects and administration, basic anatomy and physiology, pharmacology and first aid
- communication skills – both verbal and non-verbal
- basic teaching skills and the ability to assess client's motivation and ability to learn.

Clear local standards, protocols and guidelines allied with good quality supervision should help to reduce the ethical dilemmas associated with this vital aspect of harm reduction.

Appendix: Rules and Guidelines for Safer Injecting

Six golden rules of self injecting

(1) Use your own injecting equipment.
(2) Don't lend or borrow used injecting equipment.
(3) Use your own spoon, water, filter.
(4) Use the smallest needle appropriate.
(5) Don't inject alone. Try to do it with other people around, and try to make sure you all know what to do in an emergency.
(6) Use your own works once only.

Safer preparation checklist	Reason for giving this advice
Wash hands	*Prevention of cross infection*
Use new equipment	*Prevent cross infection, sharp needle reduces local trauma*
Aim for sterile field	*Prevention of cross infection*
Lay out equipment on paper	*Prevention of cross infection*
Prepare smallest needle for area injecting	*Reduce trauma to skin and veins*
Sterile or pre-boiled water, allowed to cool	*Prevents infection and reduces vein trauma*
Use smallest amount of citric acid	*Reduces the risk of burning and vein trauma*
Put water into spoon slowly so as not to spill drug and only enough for powder to dissolve	*Wasting the drug means need for more injections*
Heat with free standing heat source	*Keeps hand(s) free to stir the drugs on the spoon*
Heat gently, do not boil	*Boiling leads to evaporation and therefore more drug needed*
Stir gently with needle sheath	*Mixes the drug into the liquid*
Use clean fibre coated cigarette filter broken lengthways in half	*Filter reduces some adulterants getting into the syringe*
Ensure needle aperture is pointing down when drawing up through filter	*Ensures more drug gets into the syringe*
Don't rub needle on bottom of spoon	*Blunting the needle will lead to trauma of vein and skin*
When drawn up expel air gently by pushing plunger up until a small droplet of drug *just* appears at needle end; *do not lick* end of needle	*Air can cause pain on injecting, licking the end adds more bacteria to the needle end and therefore to the skin and vein*
While waiting for solution to cool, clear up	*Avoid having paraphernalia around when intoxicated*
Keep a 'safe disposal bin' close by at all times	*Disposal of needles and sharps is the responsibility of the user*

Safer administration checklist

Remember all the preparation advice

Raise a vein; if using tourniquet don't have it too tight

An overtight tourniquet will cause veins to reduce in size as it cuts off the arterial flow

Ensure you have the smallest needle possible for your type of injection

Reducing trauma to the vein or area into which you are injecting

Ensure aperture is facing up

Point needle towards the heart, in direction of flow

If aperture is down it may rest on bottom of the vein and cause trauma

Pushing against the blood flow will cause pressure on the vein and cause trauma

Syringe at 15 to 45 degrees for intravenous injection (IVI)

Syringe at 90 degrees for intramuscular injection (IMI)

Syringe at 15 to 30 degrees for subcutaneous (SC) injection

Shallow angle prevents needle touching the vein walls

More upright angle ensures drug gets into the muscle

Angle needs to be shallow to get needle into the thin fat layer

Insert needle slowly, feel for reduction in resistance, stop pushing when this is felt

Reduction in resistance means vein is entered; more pushing may pass the needle through the vein into the tissue and cause pain and trauma

Draw back gently

IVI: blood present, if dark red continue, if bright red *stop*

For IMI and SC look for blood (not good)

Dark blood will mean vein access has been achieved; if bright red would mean an artery has been hit

IM drugs should not be inserted into blood directly; therefore stop and withdraw slightly, pull back again and if no blood continue

Release tourniquet if IVI

'Continue' to push plunger slowly; if there is any pain, unusual sensation or anything different *stop*

Injecting while tourniquet attached will cause pressure and trauma

Needle may have moved through the vein, or the strength of the drug may be stronger with risk of overdose

When finished, remove needle and syringe slowly

Use clean cotton or tissue to stem any blood flow

Slow removal will reduce trauma

Do not use finger to stem flow; dispose of tissue or cotton in a bin to prevent spread of blood borne virus and local infection

Immediately dispose of sharps in appropriate safe disposal receptacle, not just in a waste bin!

Prevents the risk of children or others injuring themselves on used sharp equipment

Advice on what to do when injecting intravenously

Ensure that you are:

- hydrated
- relaxed
- sitting or lying down.

Site preparation:

- vein prominent
- skin cleaned with swab
- allow alcohol to evaporate
- stretch skin below vein if another person is injecting.

Insert needle:

- in direction of venous blood flow
- aperture facing up (down if drawing up)
- 15 to 45 degree angle
- up and along the vein
- only part way in.

Raising veins in hand and arms

- Choose fullest looking vein
- raise less prominent veins, improving access, by:
  - being in warm environment
  - applying tourniquet, not too tight (Too tight will result in reduced size of veins; if client complains of tingling/pins and needles when applying tourniquet, it is too tight.)
  - palpating (gentle tapping) the area close to the entry point
  - lowering limb
  - clenching fist
  - applying warmth to site, not too hot as burning can occur and this will reduce chance of finding vein
  - massaging arm from wrist to elbow, with care and very gently
  - squeezing biceps
- Explore other sites: 'look with fingers', clients may feel a vein they cannot see.

Advice on what to avoid when injecting intravenously

Avoid:

- injecting standing and unsupported
- damaged or thrombosed/collapsed veins
- swollen skin or tissues
- rolling veins, ones that move easily
- arteries (bright red frothy blood)
- inserting needle too deep or too shallow (both lead to missing vein and then drug getting into tissue)
- pulling too hard on plunger
- pushing too hard on the plunger (the increased pressure can burst veins).

And remember:

- keep in good health
- inject less frequently
- learn which veins to access
- learn where to avoid
- learn to feel for veins
- rotate sites, so as not to overuse sites
- use sharp needles.

Suggested guide to safer injecting interview

- Have all necessary equipment with you.
- Make sure you are in a comfortable and safe environment.
- Introduce yourself and the purpose of the session.
- Allow person being interviewed to explain their use history and current risks.
- Don't interrupt with advice until they have finished.
- Keep the interview based on the subject agreed unless a more serious matter arises.
- Give the safer injecting advice from the risk perspective first. If client is displaying safer methods in daily practice then make sure you feed this back towards the end of the session.
- Leave the session with the client feeling they have had a positive experience, but *never* be afraid to inform the person that there is potential risk and harm from their behaviour.
- Record the information you have given and the client's history to help prevent repetition for the client when they return.
- *Store this information confidentially and ensure you obtain any permission from the client if you intend to use this information for any other purpose.*

Chapter 12

Overdose: Prevalence, Predictors and Prevention

Trudi Petersen and David Best

Introduction

Overdose is one of the greatest hazards encountered by injecting drug users and has been identified as the main source of the tenfold increase in mortality among drug users, notwithstanding the effect of HIV/AIDS (Advisory Council on the Misuse of Drugs, 2000). This chapter concentrates on the most reported injectable overdose drug in the literature – heroin. Stimulant overdose is addressed briefly, but available evidence in this area is limited.

Opiate overdose – definition

There is a need to differentiate between acute intoxication and overdose, although users' subjective experience may blur this distinction. The following symptoms are defined in the research literature for the latter (Darke *et al.*, 1996; McGregor *et al.*, 1998; Warner Smith *et al.*, 2002):

- suppressed breathing
- cyanosis
- collapse
- loss of consciousness
- an inability to be roused.

Epidemiology of overdose

Barnett (1999) estimated that, primarily as a result of overdose, between 7% and 8% of untreated opiate addicts die each year in the UK. According to the Office for National Statistics (2000), heroin overdose deaths doubled between 1994 and 1998. Overdose experiences appear to vary by population studied, but are commonplace. Best *et al.*

(2000) found that almost half (46.8%) of a sample of 155 drug users in out-patient methadone treatment had experienced overdose. Darke *et al.* (1996) reported that 68% of their heroin-using sample in Sydney had experienced overdose.

Witnessing others' overdoses is also a frequent occurrence. In the study of Best *et al.* (2000) 82.6% of the sample had witnessed overdoses: of the total 717 overdoses witnessed by the sample, 121 (16.9%) resulted in fatalities. These figures are similar to those reported by Darke *et al.* (1996) who found that 86% had witnessed at least one overdose.

Length of drug using career and route of administration mediate these results. Strang *et al.* (1999) reported that of 312 heroin injectors not in contact with treatment services, 38% had experienced an overdose and 50% had observed at least one overdose. Gossop *et al.* (1996) investigated heroin users early in their using 'careers' and found that just 22% had ever overdosed, and of the non-injecting sample, only 2% had ever experienced an opiate overdose.

Overdose is clearly an issue of importance. Hall (1999) has argued that opiate overdose is the cause of 76% of all the drug-related deaths among young adults in Australia, whilst Roberts *et al.* (1997) made the dramatic assertion that opiate overdose is now the most common cause of death among adolescents in the United Kingdom. Yet it is males in their late twenties and thirties who figure most significantly in mortality statistics.

Causative and protective factors

Most opiate overdoses occur over a 3-hour period after initial drug intake (Darke & Zador, 1996). Instantaneous death is rare and usually attributable to an anaphylactic reaction. Not all the mechanisms of overdose are, as yet, clearly understood, but respiratory depression has been highlighted as the prime cause of death (White & Irvine, 1999). There are a range of factors that may precipitate this.

Drug strength

Drug users and practitioners alike often relate overdose to drug strength. Just under half (49%) of the participants in one study of Australian heroin users (McGregor *et al.*, 1998) attributed their own non-fatal overdoses to drug strength, whilst 44% attributed others' overdoses to strength. If strength and/or purity were the central cause of overdose it would be expected that high levels of the drug would be detected in the bodies of those who have died from overdose, but this is often not the case. Studies of blood morphine levels amongst overdose fatalities have repeatedly shown low morphine concentrations (Zador *et al.*, 1996; Darke *et al.*, 2000). In some cases, morphine concentrations were below toxic levels. The comparison by Darke *et al.* (2000) of hair morphine levels in overdose fatalities and live heroin users found higher toxic levels amongst living subjects than among the deceased. It would appear that, contrary to popular belief, drug strength alone has little predictive power for overdose fatality.

Tolerance

Regular use of a drug results in an increasing capacity to cope with its euphoric and, to an extent, its toxic effects. Regular users may be relatively unaffected by amounts that would kill a neophyte. Tolerance fluctuates significantly and can decrease rapidly on cessation or from changes in drug use patterns. Substance misusers undergo periods of abstinence for a range of reasons, including constraints that may prevent the individual from accessing their drug of choice. Overdose following imprisonment has been reported (Seaman *et al.*, 1998; Darke *et al.*, 2000; Bird & Hutchinson, 2003), as has overdose following in-patient detoxification (Strang *et al.*, 2003). Sporer (1999) suggested that the risk of overdose death in the 2 weeks after leaving residential treatment is increased seven-fold.

The likelihood of tolerance playing a major role in overdose is supported by contemporary testing techniques. Blood morphine levels are limited, typically recording opiate use in the 72 hours before testing. Hair testing can provide a record of use over several months. Hair studies have demonstrated that morphine levels amongst overdose victims indicated lower than expected levels of use over time, supporting loss of tolerance as an impact factor (Tagliaro & DeBattesti, 1999; Darke *et al.*, 2000). It has been suggested that drug users naturally change their habits as they grow older, which may be consistent with 'maturing out' theories of addiction, or may relate to a decreased ability to inject due to venous damage or to treatment with substitute medication. Brugal *et al.* (2002) have suggested that intermittent heroin users have a higher cumulative risk of non-fatal and fatal overdose than daily users.

Tolerance is clearly an issue of importance that should be addressed during intervention, but it only offers a partial explanation. It still does not fully account for the over-representation of older, long-term heroin users in fatal overdose statistics.

Respiratory tolerance

One proposed explanation is that of respiratory tolerance (White & Irvine, 1999). Shifts in tolerance to the respiratory depressant effects of opiates occur at a slower pace than tolerance to the drug's psychoactive effects, leading to a narrower band between intoxication and respiratory depression.

Warner Smith *et al.* (2001) suggested that existing pulmonary dysfunction may predispose individuals to reduced respiratory tolerance. Nearly half (42%) of injecting heroin users have been reported as having impaired lung capacity and functioning (Overland *et al.*, 1980). Lung damage is more likely to be evident amongst older individuals, generally as a result of smoking: Harris *et al.* (2000) reported that 97% of a London in-patient drug detox sample were daily smokers. Cannabis smoking is also commonplace amongst heroin users (Best *et al.*, 1999) and carries the same (or greater) risk of respiratory damage.

Heroin may be smoked or injected, with many users choosing both routes of ingestion. Some opiate users will additionally use cocaine, in the form of smokeable crack cocaine. Crack has been reported to result in impaired lung function (Benson & Bentley, 1995) and there may be cumulative damage that increases risk.

Additional causes of pulmonary dysfunction include infective pulmonary disease, often precipitated by reduced immunity as a result of malnutrition and other negative health factors. Underlying chronic disorders, such as asthma, may be worsened by lifestyle and poor health.

Other diseases unrelated to respiratory functioning may play a part in overdose mortality. Hepatic diseases, such as hepatitis C, B and A, are frequently observed in injecting drug users (see Chapters 7, 8 and 9). Warner Smith *et al.* (2001) have dismissed the idea that liver disease in itself is a precipitating factor, but have suggested that liver damage may prolong periods of heavy intoxication thus increasing cumulative overdose vulnerability.

Use of other central nervous system depressants

Alcohol and benzodiazepines have been identified specifically as significant risk factors (Rutterber *et al.*, 1990; Hammersley *et al.*, 1995; Levine *et al.*, 1995). Darke *et al.* (2000) pointed out that alcohol is implicated in around half of all overdose fatalities; Warner Smith *et al.* (2001) noted a dearth of data on alcohol consumption patterns amongst heroin users, which makes it difficult to determine whether fatalities reflect alcohol consumption patterns, but it is clear that the role played by alcohol is significant.

Evidence of benzodiazepine use is also common among heroin overdoses (Darke & Zador, 1996), although current evidence suggests there is little relationship between blood levels and frequencies of use in fatal cases when compared to survivors. Oliver and Keen (2003), in a 4-year study of opiate deaths in Sheffield, found concomitant drugs of abuse in 61% of 94 deaths, with benzodiazepines featuring most often (48%). Blood levels tended towards therapeutic dosages rather than those that would be associated with 'binge' use; the authors point out that, unlike alcohol, benzodiazepines can fulfil a therapeutic purpose in drug treatment and that in lower dosages should be considered a feature rather than a risk factor. This assertion is supported by Guitierrez-Cebollada *et al.* (1994) who claim that only benzodiazepine concentrations above 900 ng/ml are of relevance in opiate overdose.

Amongst injecting drug users, younger individuals (mean age 22 years) and females have been shown to be more likely to use benzodiazepines regularly (Ross & Darke, 1997). These characteristics are inconsistent with the age and/or gender pattern generally reported for fatal overdoses. The interpretation of the role of concomitant central nervous system depressants in fatal overdose remains problematic.

Suicide/parasuicide

It is difficult to ascertain how many overdose deaths amongst substance misusers are attributable to suicide. Darke and Ross (2002) suggested that prevalence rates for reported suicides amongst heroin users range from 3% to 35% of cases. The suicide rate is estimated to be roughly 14 times that of the general populace (Harris & Barraclough, 1997). Methods employed by heroin users do not reflect their illicit drug use, with non-opiate prescription drugs being most frequently cited. Kjelsburg *et al.* (1995) have suggested one reason why heroin features rarely in deliberate overdose as being that users view it as 'survival orientated' rather than destructive.

It is possible that regular opiate users may believe their tolerance to be such that they would be unlikely to die from heroin. It is also possible that 'successful' deliberate heroin overdoses go unnoticed. Neale (2000) suggested that overdose in drug users may not be driven by an unambiguous desire to die. Some deaths may be described as 'sub intentional'. Rates of parasuicide and/or suicide amongst substance misusers are likely to be masked by uncertainty over motive in the overdose fatality statistics.

Substitute medication

Dependent individuals in treatment are less likely than their out-of-treatment counter-parts to die of drug related causes, including overdose. Hickman *et al.* (2003) reviewed the literature on methadone deaths and concluded that there was no evidence to support the assumption that opiate death rate increases resulted from increased availability of methadone, although there did appear to be more deaths over weekend periods, which may reflect prescribing patterns of weekend 'take homes'.

Zador & Sunjic (2000) reported an increased risk in the initial weeks of treatment (often attributed to inappropriate dose levels), but more significant risk is likely to result from sudden termination of methadone treatment, resulting in an uncontrolled return to the use of street drugs (Strang *et al.*, 1996). The key to safety is linked to dispensing practices and reductions in the opportunity for the diversion of methadone to vulnerable populations.

Buprenorphine has less respiratory depressant effects than methadone and plateaus at a level where there are no further effects. The drug has a good safety profile and fatalities are uncommon. Where death has occurred, this has been commonly related to the use of other central nervous system depressants and with injecting the drug (Merrill, 2002).

Post overdose mortality and morbidity

Injury and systemic complications

Negative health outcomes may be a result of long-term damage sustained during over-dose, but may not be evident until some time later. Even where death does not occur as a result of this damage, overall health and functioning can be significantly affected, adding to the general burden of ill health. Systemic complications include cardiovascular complications, renal failure and pulmonary complications. Aspiration of vomit during non-fatal overdose may result in pulmonary oedema, reducing overall vital capacity and enhancing the likelihood of bacterial pneumonia. Indirect complications include falls and burns, neuropathy, temporary paralysis and rhabdomyolysis (Warner Smith *et al.*, 2002).

Cognitive impairment

Prolonged hypoxia during overdose can lead to brain damage, and opiate overdose has been linked with cognitive impairment (Darke *et al.*, 2000). This may increase future overdose risk through impaired decision-making and may provide some explanation for the high levels of neurocognitive deficit reported among long-term drug users in treatment.

Effects of overdose on drug users and significant others

Heroin users have been identified as having low optimism regarding others' risk of overdose (McGregor *et al.*, 1998). Loss events have been identified as a specific risk factor for suicide in drug users (Murphy, 1988). Farrell *et al.* (1996) have suggested that loss may also precipitate risk of non-intentional overdose.

Family members are an under-researched group in relation to overdose. The impact of an overdose death in the family may be compounded by a range of factors, including conflicting feelings, an existing sense of loss for the pre-dependent family member, feelings of guilt and a perception that they (or others) could have done more to prevent the death. Additionally, the family may attempt to 'cover up' or downplay the death, perhaps attributing it to other, more socially acceptable, causes. The public and media attention that occasionally follows overdose deaths may stigmatise family members.

Practitioners working with this client group may frequently encounter death. Kadman-Telias (2001) suggests that the therapeutic relationship with 'addicts' [*sic*] can bring forth feelings of helplessness in counter transference. Practitioners must be able to access support from appropriate sources through such mechanisms as clinical supervision. A supportive and empathic team ethos is necessary to foster reflection and restitution of professional 'health'.

Stimulant overdose

Stimulant drugs, including amphetamine/methamphetamine and cocaine/crack cocaine stimulate the central nervous system, increasing alertness, raising blood pressure, cardiac rates and metabolism. In high doses, they can cause hypertension, hyperthermia, arrhythmia, seizures and infarction, together with altered mental states, confusion, anxiety, delirium, paranoia and psychosis. Toxic delirium usually prefaces collapse.

Space precludes a full discussion of stimulant overdose in this chapter and, compared to the literature on opiate overdose, there is a paucity of material on this topic. The reader is directed towards studies of cocaine overdose by Tardiff *et al.* (1996), Torralba *et al.* (1996), Coffin *et al.* (2003) and Mesquita *et al.* (2001). Heroin and cocaine in combination have been an increasingly reported finding in fatal overdoses (Coffin *et al.*, 2003). Methamphetamine has been related to coronary artery disease and subarachnoid and intracranial haemorrhage, suggesting that some stimulant users may be predisposed to an untimely death through physical catastrophe as a result of use (Karch *et al.*, 1999). Overdose by injection of other drugs such as Ecstacy and ketamine are too rare to warrant discussion here.

Overdose prevention

Naloxone

Naloxone hydrochloride is an injectable opiate antagonist that reverses the respiratory depression, sedation and hypotension associated with opioids, and, importantly, has no known abuse potential. Its use has become commonplace in emergency rooms and ambulance services. There have been calls to make naloxone more publicly available to the extent that Darke (1999) has even suggested that it should be available for every heroin user to keep at home. The main obstacle to widespread naloxone distribution in the UK is legal as, under the *Medicines Act 1968*, naloxone is available only on prescription and can only be administered to the person named on the prescription. This means that, technically, it is illegal to administer it to someone other than the named recipient.

A number of pilot projects have been carried out in other locations. In Berlin, 124 opiate addicts were trained in resuscitation and given naloxone to take home. Over a 16 month window, it was used on 29 occasions, with all 29 of the individuals recovering and clear evidence that it had a beneficial effect reported in at least nine cases (Dettmer *et al.*, 2000). Bigg (2002) reported on a Chicago initiative involving 550 drug users: their evaluation indicated 52 uses, all successful, although they did report that the administrators of the naloxone were disturbed by the experience.

Strang *et al.* (1999) found considerable enthusiasm for naloxone among UK opiate users, with the majority of respondents expressing a willingness to use the antagonist if it were available. However, a number of concerns persist, including the limited evidence base to date (Mountain, 2001), the possibility of adverse reactions, including violence (Osterwalder, 1996) and the potential for recreational 'flatlining' (Ashworth & Kidd, 2001). Further concerns include possible malicious use, storage safety, risk of needlestick injuries to administrator and recipient, and the possibility that those who do recover will not seek medical assistance afterwards. While each of these concerns has some merit, the naloxone initiative is firmly based within a harm reduction tradition, based on an ethos of the primacy of life and the necessity of developing effective applied interventions wherever possible. Some issues may be addressed by adminstration mechanisms, e.g. a naloxone nasal spray may be almost as rapidly efficacious with no percutaneous risk.

Overdose education

Most drug users express a willingness to intervene in overdoses, even those occurring among virtual strangers (Best *et al.*, 2000). This is a crucial resource in attempts to develop a strategy for early interventions. Fellow drug users will often be present at overdoses and may be in a position to save lives. However, this willingness to act is often undermined by a poor understanding of the most effective and appropriate techniques (Darke *et al.*, 1996). A number of myths persist which can be particularly harmful when they concern strategies for action. Best *et al.* (2000) found reports of inappropriate use of physical force, poor understanding of the recovery position, putting victims in baths or cold water, and a range of interventions that, although not harmful, would have little beneficial effect.

Darke and Hall (1997) and Strang *et al.* (1996) are among those who have emphasised the need for the systematic training of drug users in overdose recognition and interventions. This combines preventative training – simple messages such as do not use alone, do not use heroin when you have been drinking, take test doses, and so on – with basic skills for intervention (i.e. cardiopulmonary resuscitation). These are not intended to replace medical interventions, but to supplement these to maximise lives saved.

Conclusions

Overdose remains the single largest cause of mortality among drug users, but one that remains poorly understood. Although there are clear individual risk factors for opiate overdose (poor general health, social isolation, use of alcohol and other central nervous system depressant drugs) and situational risks (reduced tolerance, use of drugs by injection, depression and suicidal ideation), our ability to categorise and predict fatality remains poor. For stimulant drugs, our understanding of causes of death is even more limited.

There is a considerable need for programmatic research into the causes and correlates of both fatal and non-fatal overdose, and a commitment to evaluation for prevention and intervention programmes. We do know enough to develop improved intervention strategies – primarily in the community through increased training and awareness for drug users and by developing pharmacotherapies, such as naloxone, for peer use.

References

Advisory Council on the Misuse of Drugs (2000) *Reducing Drug Related Deaths*. London: The Stationery Office.

Ashworth A.J. & Kidd, A. (2001) Apparant advantages may be balanced by hidden harm. *British Medical Journal*, **323**, 934 (letter).

Barnett, P. (1999) The cost effectiveness of methadone maintenance as a health care intervention. *Addiction*, **94**(4), 479–488.

Benson, M.K. & Bentley, A.M. (1995) Lung disease induced by drug addiction. *Thorax*, **50**, 1125–1127.

Best, D., Gossop, M. & Greenwood, J. (1999) Cannabis use in relation to illicit drug use and health problems among opiate misusers in treatment. *Drug and Alcohol Review*, **18**(1), 31–38.

Best, D., Man, L., Gossop, M. *et al.* (2000) Drug users' experiences of witnessing overdoses: What do they know and what do they need to know? *Drug and Alcohol Review*, **19**, 407–412.

Bigg, D. (2002) Data on take home naloxone are unclear but not condemnatory. *British Medical Journal*, **324**, 678.

Bird, S.M. & Hutchinson, S.J. (2003) Male drug related deaths in the fortnight after release from prison: Scotland, 1996–99. *Addiction*, **98**, 185–190.

Brugal, M.T., Barrio, G., De La Fuente, L. *et al.* (2002) Factors associated with non fatal heroin overdose: assessing the effect of frequency and route of heroin administration, *Addiction*, **97**, 319–327.

Coffin, P.O., Galea, S., Ahern, J. *et al.* (2003) Opiates, cocaine and alcohol combinations in accidental drug overdose deaths in New York City, 1990–98. *Addiction*, **98**(6), 739–747.

Darke, S. (1999) Comments on Strang *et al.*'s 'preventing opiate overdose fatalities with take-home naloxone: pre-launch study of possible impact and acceptability': attacking overdose on the home front. *Addiction*, **94**(2), 205–206.

Darke, S. & Zador, D. (1996) Fatal heroin 'overdose': a review. *Addiction*, **91**, 1765–1772.

Darke, S. & Hall, W. (1997) The distribution of naloxone to heroin users. *Addiction*, **92**(9), 1195–1199.

Darke, S. & Ross, J. (2002) Suicide among heroin users: rates, risk factors and methods. *Addiction*, **97**, 1383–1394.

Darke, S., Ross, J. & Hall, W. (1996) Overdose among heroin users in Sydney, Australia. Prevalence and correlates of non fatal overdose, *Addiction*, **91**, 405–411.

Darke, S., Ross, J., Zador, D. & Sunjic, S. (2000) Heroin-related deaths in New South Wales, Australia, 1992–1996. *Drug and Alcohol Dependence*, **60**(2), 141–150.

Dettmer, K., Saunders, B. & Strang, J. (2000) Take home naloxone and the prevention of deaths from opiate overdose: two pilot schemes. *British Medical Journal*, **322**, 895–896.

Farrell, M., Neeleman, J., Griffiths, P. *et al.* (1996) Suicide and overdose among opiate addicts. *Addiction*, **91**, 321–323.

Gossop, M., Griffiths, P., Powis, B. *et al.* (1996) Frequency of non-fatal heroin overdose: survey of heroin users recruited in non-clinical settings. *British Medical Journal*, **313**, 402.

Guitierrez-Cebollada, J., Torre, R., Ortuno, J. *et al.* (1994) Psychotropic drug consumption and other factors associated with heroin overdose. *Drug and Alcohol Dependence*, **3**, 169–174.

Hall, W. (1999) reducing the toll of opioid overdose deaths in Australia. *Drug and Alcohol Review*, **18**(2), 213–220.

Hammersley, R., Cassidy, M.T. & Oliver, J. (1995) Drugs associated with drug-related deaths in Edinburgh and Glasgow, November 1990 to October 1992. *Addiction*, **90**(7), 959–965.

Harris, E.C. & Barraclough, B. (1997) Suicide as an outcome for mental disorders. *British Journal of Psychiatry*, **170**, 205–228.

Harris, J., Best, D., Man, L. *et al.* (2000) Changes in cigarette smoking among alcohol and drug misusers during in-patient detoxification. *Addiction Biology*, **5**, 443–450.

Hickman, M., Madden, P., Henry, J. *et al.* (2003) Trends in drug overdose deaths in England and Wales 1993–1998: methadone does not kill more people than heroin. *Addiction*, **98**, 419–425.

Kadman-Telias, A. (2001) Psychodrama and helplessness in the helper of addicts. *International Journal of Psychosocial Rehabilitation*, 5, 111–134.

Karch, S.B., Stephens, B.G. & Ho, C.H. (1999) Methamphetamine related deaths in San Francisco: demographic, pathologic and toxicologic profiles. *Journal of Forensic Sciences*, 44(2), 359–368.

Kjelsburg, E., Winther, M. & Dahl, A.A. (1995) Overdose deaths in young substance abusers: accidents or hidden suicides? *Acta Psychiatrica Scandinavica*, 91, 236–242.

Levine, B., Wu, S.C., Dixon, A. & Smialek, J.E. (1995) Site dependence of postmortem blood methadone concentrations. *American Journal of Forensic Medicine Pathology*, 16(2), 97–100.

McGregor, C., Darke, S., Christie, P. *et al.* (1998) Experience of non fatal overdose among heroin users in Adelaide: circumstances and risk perception. *Addiction*, 92, 1349–1352.

Merrill, J. (2002) In: Petersen, T. and McBride, A. (eds) *Working with Substance Misusers: A guide to Theory and Practice*, Chapter 11. London: Routledge.

Mesquita, F., Kral, A., Reingold, A. *et al.* (2001) Overdoses among cocaine users in Brazil. *Addiction*, 96, 1809–1813.

Mountain, D. (2001) So little evidence – such big conclusions. *British Medical Journal*, 323, 934 (letter).

Murphy, G.E. (1988) Suicide and substance abuse. *Archives of General Psychiatry*, 45(6), 593–594.

Neale, J. (2000) Suicidal intent in non fatal illicit drug overdose. *Addiction*, 95, 85–93.

Office for National Statistics (2000) Deaths related to drug poisoning: results for England and Wales, 1994–98, *Health Statistics Quarterly*, No. 7. London: Office for National Statistics.

Oliver, P. & Keen, J. (2003) Concomitant drugs of misuse and drug using behaviour associated with fatal opiate-related poisonings in Sheffield, UK, 1997–2000. *Addiction*, 98, 191–197.

Osterwalder, J. (1996) Naloxone for intoxications with intravenous heroin and heroin mixtures – harmless or hazardous? *Journal of Toxicology and Clinical Toxicology*, 34, 409–416.

Overland, E.S., Nolan, A.J. & Hopwell, P.C. (1980) Alteration of pulmonary function in intravenous drug abusers. Prevalence, severity and characterisation of gas exchange abnormalities. *American Journal of Medicine*, 68, 231–237.

Roberts, I., Barker, M. & Leah, L. (1997) Analysis of trends in deaths from accidental drug poisoning in teenagers, 1985–95. *British Medical Journal*, 289.

Ross, J. & Darke, S. (1997) *Benzodiazepine dependence and psychopathology among heroin users in Sydney* (NDARC Technical Report No. 50). Sydney: University of NSW, National Drug and Alcohol Research Centre.

Ruttenber, A.J., Katler, H.O. & Santinga, P. (1990) The role of ethanol abuse in the aetiology of heroin related death. *Journal of Forensic Sciences*, 35, 891–900.

Seaman, S.R., Brettle, R.P. & Gore, S.M. (1998) Mortality from overdose among injecting drug users recently released from prison: database linage study. *British Medical Journal*, 316, 426–428.

Sporer, K.A. (1999) Acute heroin overdose. *Annals of Internal Medicine*, 130, 584–590.

Strang, J., Darke, S., Hall, R., Farrell, M. & Ali, R. (1996) Heroin overdose: the case for take-home naloxone. *British Medical Journal*, 1435.

Strang, J., Griffiths, P., Powis, B. *et al.* (1999) Which drugs cause overdose among opiate misusers? Study of personal and witnessed overdoses. *Drug and Alcohol Review*, 18(3), 253–261.

Strang, J., McCambridge, J., Best, D. *et al.* (2003) Loss of tolerance and overdose mortality after inpatient opiate detoxification: follow up study. *British Medical Journal*, **326**, 959–960.

Tagliaro, F. & DeBattesti, Z. (1999) 'Heroin overdose' is often the truer description. *Addiction*, **94**, 973–974.

Tardiff, K., Marzuk, P., Leon, C. *et al.* (1996) Accidental fatal overdoses in New York City 1990–1992. *American Journal of Drug and Alcohol Abuse*, **22**, 135–146.

Torralba, L., Brugal, M.T., Villalbi, J.R. *et al.* (1996) Mortality due to acute adverse drug reactions: opiates and cocaine in Barcelona, 1898–1993. *Addiction*, **91**, 419–426.

Warner Smith, M., Darke, S., Lynskey, M., *et al.* (2001) Heroin overdose: causes and consequences. *Addiction*, **96**, 1113–1125.

Warner Smith, M., Darke, S. & Day, C. (2002) Morbidity associated with non fatal heroin overdose. *Addiction*, **97**, 963–967.

White, J. & Irvine, R.J. (1999) Mechanisms of fatal opioid overdose. *Addiction*, **94**, 961–972.

Zador D. & Sunjic S. (2000) Deaths in methadone maintenance treatment in New South Wales, Australia 1990–1995. *Addiction*, **95**(1), 77–84.

Zador, D., Sunjic, S. & Darke, S. (1996) Heroin related deaths in New South Wales, 1992: toxicological findings and circumstances. *Medical Journal of Australia*, **164**, 204–207.

Chapter 13

Supervised Injecting Rooms

Robert Haemmig and Ingrid van Beek

Introduction

Supervised injecting rooms (SIRs) have historically been established in areas with 'open drug scenes', where public health and public order problems had arisen in relation to the concentration of street-based injecting drug use. By accommodating injecting episodes that would otherwise have occurred in public places in SIRs staffed by appropriately qualified health professionals, it is hoped that these public health and public order problems will be reduced, benefitting both the street-based injecting drug user (IDU) population and the rest of the local community.

The primary aim of SIRs from a public health perspective is to reduce the morbidity and mortality which would otherwise result from later or no intervention when overdoses occur in public places and other unsupervised situations. Like needle–syringe programmes, SIRs also provide clean injecting equipment, which reduces the transmission of blood borne infections, including HIV and hepatitis B and C virus. The continuous education of IDUs about these risks is further facilitated by SIRs, where prevention messages are able to be integrated into the individual drug user's injecting behaviours in real time, also hopefully translating to safer injecting behaviour elsewhere at other times with other IDUs. In this way SIRs may also have a public health impact at a greater population level.

Other potential public health benefits accrue from the ability of SIRs to 'net widen' in terms of the proportion of the IDU population they bring into contact with the health and social welfare system. By being low threshold, easily accessible outreach posts, SIRs can engage the more marginalised, hard-to-reach parts of the IDU population. Such contact may then lead to further assistance, including referral to drug treatment and rehabilitation, earlier than otherwise, when such interventions are likely to be more effective. In this sense SIRs may provide a 'gateway' for IDUs to address the underlying issues associated with harmful drug use and drug dependence.

SIRs also have the capacity to respond in a timely way to new developments in the drug using population and can adapt their concepts easily. They provide 'early warning systems' regarding the availability of new drugs or more potent drugs on the streets, which can also be communicated to other relevant agencies, thereby reducing the risk of drug overdose and other harms, while also providing 'intelligence' regarding the patterns of drug supply in an area.

The potential public order benefits include reducing the 'public nuisance' associated with 'open drug scenes', including high visibility, public drug injecting, intoxication and overdose, and discarded injecting paraphernalia. Frequent ambulance call-outs to drug overdoses may also lead to anxiety among members of the local community concerned about the circumstances and outcomes of those drug overdose cases in these areas.

There are currently about 60 SIRs operating in three continents in the world, including Europe, Australia and North America. This chapter describes the history of their establishment and current issues regarding SIRs.

The first supervised injecting room in Bern, Switzerland

The first SIR was established in 1986 in Bern, Switzerland, as an HIV prevention measure in response to the rapid escalation in HIV/AIDS among IDUs; however, the initial concept was not a *de novo* invention. There had already been several attempts to integrate supervised injecting into projects for IDUs, including the AJZ (Autonomous Youth Centre in Zurich), the Perron 0 ('Platform Zero') at the railway station in Rotterdam, the Prinsenhof in Amsterdam and others. However, all these projects (like the more recent projects attempted in Brazil and France) lacked a professional interface between IDUs and the health bureaucracy that promoted the policy of allowing injected drug use as part of a general institutional policy.

The Bern SIR was initially designed as a simple café for drug users. The conceptual starting point was to provide a place for IDUs who had nowhere else to dwell, including the streets, where they attracted police attention, and in other cafés, where they were unwelcome. At the time of the initial service planning, the basic concept was to provide a café offering beverages and simple meals, information on safer sex and safer drug use, as well as clean needles and syringes, and condoms. Social workers were also available for people in need of counselling, social welfare advice and assistance.

It was not planned to include an injecting room in the café; however, the IDU clients soon started openly to inject drugs there, and this quickly became the most attractive aspect of the café. This injecting room operated covertly at the outset, but because it started to attract large numbers of IDUs, this could not be maintained. After negotiation with police and law makers, the café was allowed to continue its operation as an SIR on the condition that no underage drug users were admitted and drug trafficking did not occur on the premises.

Additionally, a drug counselling agency took responsibility for general order in such a facility, including the part of the facility where the injecting took place. As many of the IDUs had poor health, a primary healthcare service was added later (Haemmig, 1992a, b, 1995). In order to minimise public opposition to the first SIR in Bern, intensive work with the local community was also commenced.

While it has never been formally evaluated, new public management has recently imposed performance contracts requiring that various service activity data be collected and reported on a regular basis. But overall, the Bern SIR is considered to have already proven successful, with the facility still operating after more than 17 years.

Development of SIRs elsewhere

The first SIR in Bern served as a model for other SIRs subsequently established elsewhere in Switzerland, Germany, Spain, for some time in Austria, more recently in Australia, and now in Canada.

Different jurisdictions refer to SIRs differently: SIRs in Europe are also sometimes referred to as 'drug consumption rooms' or 'safe injecting rooms', whereas in Australia the legislation pertaining to its only facility uses the term 'medically supervised injecting centre' (MSIC). SIRs have taken on different names in different places, some of them relating directly to injecting while others avoid any allusion to injection due to the local political situation. Some used fantasy names and many have had double meanings which are lost when translated into English; for example, the first SIR was named 'Fixerstuebli', which translates into 'little junkie room' in English, while at the same time the word 'Stuebli', a Swiss diminutive, relates to Swiss cosiness.

There has also been a range of service models from the 'pure' model, which only incorporates a space to inject under supervision, to the 'comprehensive' model with various other related services including counselling and medical clinics, subsidised food, showers, personal lockers and laundry facilities (Dolan et al., 2000; Schneider & Stöver, 2000; Broadhead et al., 2002; Kimber et al., 2003). SIRs have also been co-located with methadone and other drug treatment services, and overnight accommodation facilities. The European models have tended to be less formal and clinical compared with what is probably the most formal and clinical model of the Sydney MSIC with a (part time) Medical Director and nurses trained to administer naloxone in the event of heroin overdose (van Beek, 2003). These service models have developed in response to local conditions, and the variation in models acknowledges that there is unlikely to be one model that would suit all situations across time.

Meanwhile there has been ongoing public debate about the potential role of SIRs in France, the UK and some other European countries.

Ideological background to SIRs

The ideological background to SIRs was (and still is) to approach drug use from a humanitarian perspective, encompassing the notion that IDUs should be respected as human beings and should not suffer as a result of drug policies prohibiting drug use. In this sense, the first SIRs were connected to the anti-prohibitionist movement.

There has been considerable change in medical ethics in recent decades, with a shift from a more paternalistic approach ('your doctor knows what it is good for you, and in the case of addiction it is abstinence') to one which respects the autonomy of the patient to make decisions about their own health. Beauchamp and Childress (2001) identified four main principles of a modern biomedical ethic: (1) respect for autonomy, (2) non-maleficence, (3) beneficence, and (4) justice in distribution of services; these are generally accepted by the medical profession today (ABIM Foundation et al., 2002). SIRs are the most radical application of these ethical principles in that they do not primarily aim to change the IDU's chosen lifestyle, but instead try to gain the IDU's informed consent for further possibly beneficial treatment and other interventions. SIRs have benefice by reducing the individual's suffering. There is no evidence for maleficence caused by them, and they embrace social equity in terms of who can utilise them.

Nowadays, some of the greatest supporters of SIRs emanate from the police service, because SIRs actually help police do their work in a more humane way. SIRs offer police an opportunity to refer for assistance IDUs that they come across during their work in the streets, especially after normal business hours, when most other services for drug users are closed. Police are required by law to regard IDUs as being criminal, yet through daily contact with IDUs they often develop an empathy for their situations, thereby creating an ethical conflict. Knowing that SIRs have the capacity to deal with many of the IDU's problems, this ethical conflict of the police is at least partly resolved. Visits to the Bern SIR are now part of the vocational education of the local police service.

The case against SIRs

There has been strong ideological opposition to SIRs from the advocates of strict drug prohibition who argue that SIRs should not be established because they are a new form of 'opium den', the extinction of the original opium dens being claimed as a major past success of the prohibitionist approach. They do not acknowledge any distinction between an opium den, which served its customers in total pleasure seeking, and an injection room, which is designed to serve a drug dependent IDU population that is generally considered as having a chronic relapsing health condition (O'Brien & McLellan, 1996; O'Brien, 1997; Leshner, 1999a, b). In contrast to providing drugs for maximal pleasure, the goal of SIRs is to preserve the health of its clients to the greatest extent possible, while they continue to engage in otherwise 'unhealthy' injecting behaviour.

In its 1999 report, the International Narcotics Control Board (INCB) of the United Nations Office of Drug Control (UNODC) based in Vienna, Austria contended that SIRs contravene Article 3 paragraphs 1 (c) (iii) and (iv) of the 1988 UN Convention by publicly inciting or inducing as well as aiding and abetting, facilitating or counselling the illicit use of drugs for personal use, and strongly urged countries to discontinue their operation (United Nations, 1988; INCB, 2000). All countries with SIRs are signatories to all UN drug control treaties (however, some have not yet ratified the 1988 Convention). The Prime Minister of Australia reiterated his Government's concerns that the UN might place sanctions on Australia's substantial pharmaceutical opium industry after a decision to extend its trial SIR in late 2003.

However, a report prepared by the Legal Affairs Section of the UNODC for the INCB in 2002 concluded that drug policy must come up with new strategies to cope with new health threats such as growing rates of intravenous HIV transmission. The report stated that, 'It could even be argued that the drug control treaties, as they stand, have been rendered out of sync with reality, since at the time they came into force they could not possibly have foreseen these new threats' (UNODC Legal Affairs Section, 2002). On SIRs it stated, 'It would be difficult to assert that, in establishing drug injection rooms, it is the intent of parties to actually incite or induce the illicit use of drugs, or even more so, to associate with, aid, abet or facilitate the possession of drugs. On the contrary, it seems clear that in such cases the intention of governments is to provide healthier conditions for IV drug [users], thereby reducing risk of infections with grave transmittable diseases and, at least in some cases, reaching out to them with counselling and other therapeutic options'.

Detractors of the SIR approach also often argue that it promotes drug use, sending 'the wrong message' to young people who do not inject drugs, that injecting drugs is 'safe', thereby encouraging their initiation to injecting drug use. However, there is no scientific evidence to suggest that this is the case. SIRs in all jurisdictions are integrated into national drug policies, all of which incorporate efforts to reduce the supply and demand for illicit drugs.

Conservative politicians and religious groups also frequently oppose the establishment of SIRs. The Roman Catholic church has reasoned that humans should not be allowed to damage themselves and to renounce the personal dignity that is given by God, arguing that drug use is against life and morals (Pope Johnnes Paul II, 1992). This equates with what some would judge to be a very un-Christian 'be abstinent or perish' approach. However, it has often been Christian church groups that have pioneered SIRs, sometimes as civil disobedience exercises prior to legislation being enacted to allow their legal operation: the Paulus Kerk in Rotterdam, The Netherlands, and the Wayside Chapel in Sydney, Australia, are examples of this.

Evidence for success

In the 1980s, scientific evidence to prove the efficacy of SIRs was rarely sought in the Swiss context. For the first 10 years of the SIR in Bern, the empirical evidence that the room attracted a lot of people who were among the most heavily drug dependent target IDU population was considered enough to justify its continuation. However, in 1992 the Federal Ministry of Internal Affairs required the conduct of scientific research for all parts of an overall package to stem the drug epidemic in Switzerland. All new approaches in this package, which became known as the 'four pillars drug policy' were approved for evaluation, including the SIRs and the results have since been published (Spreyermann & Flückiger, 1990; Benninghoff et al., 1996, 1998; Lanz et al., 1996; Ronco et al., 1996a, b; Minder Nejedly & Bürki, 1999; Reyes Fuentes, 2003).

Likewise in Germany, SIRs were established first, then later the Federal Ministry of Health in Germany mandated a major effort in research, mainly to prove that the SIR rules established by law were respected. However, the researchers also tried to demonstrate the impact of SIRs on fatal drug overdoses using a time series model (Bundesministerium für Gesundheit et al., 2003). The authors of the report were persuaded that the reduction of fatal overdoses measured across time was attributable to the SIRs.

However, in Switzerland, according to the official statistics of the Federal Office of Public Health, drug related fatal overdoses only declined after 1993, long after SIRs were first introduced. So the question remains as to whether this decline was a specific effect and if so, of which intervention.

The fact that there has not been a single death due to drug overdose in any SIR anywhere to date, defying all probability, can perhaps be considered an indication that they must prevent such events. However, it is methodologically impossible to calculate the total number of drug consumption events of all IDUs, which part of the total drug consumption took place in the protected environment of an injecting room, and how this supervised setting influenced injecting behaviour there and elsewhere.

Additionally, it should also be appreciated that prevention of fatal overdoses is only one of the aims of SIRs. Probably even more important from a public health perspective is the role of SIRs in the prevention of irreversible damage to the brain and other vital organs due to hypoxia (Hämmig, 1997), damage that may be progressive among IDUs who sustain multiple non-fatal overdoses across time. This is because in SIRs, unlike in community settings, basic life support measures are administered immediately from the first onset of symptoms of drug overdose. So while it is difficult, if not impossible, to quantify, it is self-evident that SIRs prevent significant morbidity.

The Australian experience

Australia had a different sequence of events. After several heroin overdose deaths occurred in the churchyard, the Wesley Mission in Melbourne, Victoria, decided to initiate an SIR. Purpose-built premises were constructed, staff were employed and trained by a Swiss team; however, the legislation necessary to operate the SIR was blocked after an unexpected change in state government. Finally, the project became embroiled in the maelstrom of neighbourhood resistance and was completely dismissed in favour of the establishment of primary health care services for IDUs in several suburbs where injecting drug use was prevalent.

While legislation was passed in the Australian Capital Territory to enable the operation of an SIR in Canberra in 2000, funding to establish the facility was blocked pending the outcome of the Sydney SIR trial.

Meanwhile there had been several years of wide-ranging public debate about the potential role of SIRs in Sydney, New South Wales (NSW), and a parliamentary inquiry into safe injecting rooms in 1997 (Parliament of New South Wales, 1998). However, it was a civil disobedience exercise wherein a mock SIR was operated for several sessions at the Wayside Chapel, a Protestant parish church in Kings Cross, which placed SIRs on the agenda of the NSW Parliamentary Drug Summit held in May 1999. Amongst 172 other resolutions, this Summit passed a resolution recommending that a 'medically supervised injecting centre' (MSIC) be established as a 'tightly controlled trial' (Parliament of New South Wales, 1998) and legislation to trial one SIR for 18 months was passed by the NSW Parliament in late 1999 (Parliament of New South Wales, 1999).

The Sydney MSIC commenced operations in May 2001. The initial 18-month trial was later extended by 12 months to enable the finalisation of the evaluation report. In October 2003, the MSIC trial was extended again, by a further 4 years, based on the findings of what has been the most rigorous attempt to scientifically evaluate a SIR to date (Kaldor *et al.*, 2003). Despite the New South Wales Government's assessment that there was evidence of success in terms of demonstrating that deaths had been averted, drug users had been referred to drug treatment, public amenity had improved, with high and increasing levels of local community support and no negative consequences, this was nonetheless disputed by the various detractors of the SIR approach. So the challenge remains as to how to conclusively prove the utility of SIRs through scientific research.

Methodological challenges in evaluating SIRs for success

It is, in fact, very difficult to measure the impacts of an intervention like SIRs. Drug users are necessarily a 'hidden population' given their inherently 'criminal' lifestyles, so it is hard to determine with any certainty how the users of a SIR relate to this population overall. While IDUs probably use SIRs randomly, this randomisation cannot be controlled by the researcher. Additionally, it is neither feasible nor ethically acceptable randomly to recruit a control group for this type of intervention, or create a 'placebo-room' or blind the service providers or participants, all considered the gold standards for research.

Therefore, the best that researchers can do is to observe certain key indicators over time and assess as best they can whether any changes that eventually occur can be attributed to the SIRs as opposed to other environmental variables, including other harm reduction interventions, which likewise cannot easily be controlled for. Because the hoped for shifts in injecting behaviour among the SIR's target IDU population resulting from this intervention are likely to take place over a considerable period of time, the observation period should ideally last from well before the intervention until SIR utilisation has reached a representative level for several years. But the reality is that researchers do not usually plan studies over many years; what is more, given the reality of short electoral cycles, the political imperatives usually need to be answered in a very much shorter time frame than that needed for research.

Safer smoking rooms?

Today in Europe, heroin and cocaine are often not administered by intravenous injection. Some IDUs switch between the different modes of use (intravenous, smoking, snorting, oral). Any form other than injecting is considered to be safer in terms of HIV transmission, but not necessarily for the transmission of hepatitis C virus (Brunton *et al.*, 2000). There are some reports of hepatitis C exposure among non-injecting drug users (Baozhang *et al.*, 1997; Santana Rodriguez *et al.*, 1998). Heroin overdose also continues to be a risk regardless of the mode of administration, especially when other drugs such as benzodiazepines, barbiturates and methaqualone are used concurrently.

The practice of smoking 'crack cocaine', the base form of cocaine suitable for smoking, started much later in Europe than in the US. However, the acid form, cocaine hydrochloride, is still sold in many street drug markets, and needs to be converted to base form if it is to be smoked. There are two main ways currently used to produce it: the ammonia method (also known as 'freebasing') and the bicarbonate method (also known as 'crack'). When the ammonia method is used, small amounts of ammonia remain in the cocaine, which can damage the lung. So from a harm reduction perspective it is better to use the bicarbonate method which produces 'crack'.

These considerations led to the recent establishment of smoking rooms as harm reduction measures in several cities in Switzerland (Haemmig & Buerge, 2003). The basic concept of smoking rooms is to prevent fatal overdoses and hepatitis C transmission and advocate safer modes of drug administration. Evaluation of their operation will elucidate their potential public health role further in coming years.

Finally

SIRs are a balanced approach to addressing both the public health and public order issues arising from street-based injecting drug use. SIRs would appear to have a place at the sharp end of the continuum of approaches to illicit drug use in terms of reducing the immediate and sometimes fatal harms associated with public drug use. However, it seems likely that philosophical debate about their merit will also continue and that scientific evidence will have a limited role in resolving this debate. Ultimately, perhaps state and national jurisdictions should be encouraged to pass enabling legislation for SIRs to be established, but it should be left to local communities to decide if this approach is an acceptable way to manage their particular local drug issues, with outcomes monitored to ensure that community goals are indeed achieved.

References

ABIM Foundation; American Board of Internal Medicine; ACP-ASIM Foundation; American College of Physicians – American Society of Internal Medicine; European Federation of Internal Medicine (2002) Medical professionalism in the new millennium: a physician charter. *Annals of Internal Medicine*, **136**(3), 243–246.

Baozhang, T., Kaining, Z., Jinxing, K., Ruchang, X., Ming, L., Caixia, Z. & Li, T. (1997) Infection with human immunodeficiency virus and hepatitis viruses in Chinese drug addicts. *Epidemiology and Infection*, **119**(3), 343–347.

Beauchamp, T.L. & Childress, J.F. (2001) *The Principles of Biomedical Ethics*, 5th edn. New York: Oxford University Press.

Benninghoff, F., Gervasoni, J.P. & Dubois-Arber, F. (1996) Monitoring des activités des structures a bas-seuil d'accès pour consommateurs de drogues en Suisse: remise de matériel d'injection stérile, résultats pour 1993 et quelques exemples cantonaux [Monitoring of the activities of low-threshold access structures for drug users in Switzerland: distribution of sterile injection equipment, results for 1993 and various cantonal examples]. *Sozial- und Praeventivmedizin*, **41**(Suppl 1) S5–S14.

Benninghoff, F., Gervasoni, J.P., Spencer, B. & Dubois-Arber, F. (1998) Caractéristiques de la clientèle des structures a bas seuil d'accès pour toxicomanes mettant a disposition du matériel d'injection stérile en Suisse [Characteristics of attenders of low threshold syringe-exchange centers providing sterile syringes in Switzerland]. *Revue d'Epidémiologie et de Santé Publique*, **46**(3), 205–217.

Broadhead, R.S., Kerr, T.H., Grund, J-P.C. & Altice, F.L. (2002) Safer injection facilities in North America: their place in public policy and health initiatives. *Journal of Drug Issues*, **32**(1), 329–356.

Brunton, C., Kemp, R., Raynel, P., Harte, D. & Baker, M. (2000) Cumulative incidence of hepatitis C seroconversion in a cohort of seronegative injecting drug users. *New Zealand Medical Journal*, **113**, 98–101.

Bundesministerium für Gesundheit, Poschadel, S., Höger, J., Schnitzler, J. & Schreckenberg, D. (2003) *Evaluation der Arbeit der Drogenkonsumräume in der Bundesrepublik Deutschland*, Baden-Baden: Nomos.

Dolan, K., Kimber, J., Fry, C., Fitzgerald, J., MacDonald, D. & Trautmann, F. (2000) Drug consumption facilities in Europe and the establishment of supervised injecting centres in Australia. *Drug and Alcohol Review*, **19**(3), 337–346.

Haemmig, R. (1992a) The overseas experience: Switzerland. In R.W. Fox & I. Mathews (eds), *Drugs Policy. Fact, Fiction and the Future*, pp. 206–209. Annandale, NSW: Federation Press.

Haemmig, R.B. (1992b) The streetcorner agency with shooting room ('Fixerstuebli'). In P.A. O'Hare *et al.* (eds), *The Reduction of Drug-Related Harm*, pp. 181–185. London: Routledge.

Haemmig, R.B. (1995) Harm reduction in Bern: from outreach to heroin maintenance. *Bulletin of the New York Academy of Medicine*, **72**(2), 371–379.

Haemmig, R.B. & Buerge, I. (2003) La salle d'inhalation: développement logique de la salle d'injection. In: B. Lebeau, M. Dheur & M. de Andrés (eds), *Deuxième Conférence Latine de Réduction de Risques liés aux Usages de Drogues, Livre de Communication*, p. 26. Perpignan: CLAT2.

Hämmig, R.B. (1997) Möglichkeiten der Gesundheitsversorgung in Druckräumen – Erfahrungen aus dem 'Fixerstübli' in Bern. In Deutsche AIDS-Hilfe e.V. & J. Klee (eds), *Akzeptanzorientierte Angebote in der Drogen- und AIDS-Selbsthilfe – Gesundheitsräume in der aktuellen Debatte*, Vol. 27, pp. 153–160. Berlin: Deutsche AIDS-Hilfe e.V.

INCB (2000) *Report of the International Narcotics Control Board for 1999.* pp. 26–27 (http://www.incb.org/e/ind_ar.htm).

Kaldor, J., Lapsely, H., Mattick, R., Weatherburn, D. & Wilson, A. (2003) *Final Report on the Evaluation of the Sydney Medically Supervised Injecting Centre*, Sydney.

Kimber, J., Dolan, K., van Beek, I., Hedrich, D. & Zurhold, H. (2003) Drug consumption facilities: an update since 2000. *Drug and Alcohol Review*, **22**(2), 227–233.

Lanz, A., Sempach, R. & Scholz, G. (1996) Evaluation der Kontakt- und Anlaufstellen, ein niedrigschwelliges Tagesstrukturangebot in der Stadt Zürich [Evaluation of contact and care centers, a low-threshold daytime source in the city of Zurich]. *Sozial und Praeventivmedizin*, **41**(Suppl 1) S35–S43.

Leshner, A. (1999a) Science is revolutionizing our view of addiction – and what to do about it. *American Journal of Psychiatry*, **156**(1), 1–3.

Leshner, A, (1999b) Science-based views of drug addiction and its treatment. *Journal of the American Medical Association*, 282(14), 1314–1316.

Minder Nejedly, M. & Bürki, C.M. (1999) *Monitoring HIV risk behaviours in a street agency with injection room in Switzerland*. Thesis, Medical Faculty of the University of Bern.

O'Brien, C. (1997) A range of research-based pharmacotherapies for addiction. *Science*, 278, 66–70.

O'Brien, C. & McLellan, A. (1996) Myths about the treatment of addiction. *Lancet*, 347, 237–240.

Parliament of New South Wales (1998) *Report on the establishment or trial of safe injecting rooms. Joint Select Committee into Safe Injecting Rooms*.

Parliament of New South Wales (1999) *Drug Summit Legislative Response Act, No 67*.

Pope Johnnes Paul II (1992) Ansprache des Heiligen Vaters Papst Johannes Paul II. An die Teilnehmer der Internationalen Konferenz zu Drogenmissbrauch und Alkoholismus, durchgeführt vom Päpstlichen Rat für die Pastoral im Krankendienst vom 21. bis 23. November 1991 in Rom, Vatikan. In *Ansprache des Heiligen Vaters Papst Johannes Paul II*, Verein zur Förderung der Psychologischen Menschenkenntnis (VPM), pp. 9–16. Zürich: Verlag Menschenkenntnis.

Reyes Fuentes, V. de C. (2003) *15 Jahre Fixerraum Bern. Auswirkungen auf soziale und medizinische Aspekte bei Drogenabhängigen*. Thesis, Medical Faculty of the University of Bern.

Ronco, C., Spuhler, G., Coda, P. & Schopfer, R. (1996a) Evaluation der Gassenzimmer I, II und III in Basel [Evaluation of street facilities I, II and III in Basel]. *Sozial und Praeventivmedizin*, **41**(Suppl 1) S58–S68.

Ronco, C., Spuhler, G. & Kaiser, R. (1996b) Evaluation des ‚Aufenthalts- und Betreuungsraums für Drogenabhängige' in Luzern [Evaluation of a stay and care center for drug addicts in Lucerne]. *Sozial und Praeventivmedizin*, **41**(Suppl 1) S45–S57.

Santana Rodriguez, O.E., Male Gil, M.L., Hernandez Santana, J.F., Liminana Canal, J.M. & Martin Sanchez, A.M. (1998) Prevalence of serologic markers of HBV, HDV, HCV and HIV in non-injection drug users compared to injection drug users in Gran Canaria, Spain. *European Journal of Epidemiology*, **14**(6), 555–561.

Schneider, W. & Stöver, H. (2000) *Guidelines for the operation and use of consumption rooms*. Materialien Nr. 4. Münster & Oldenburg: Akzept e.V & Carl von Ossietzky Universität.

Spreyermann, C. & Flückiger, M. (1990) *Aidsprävention bei Drogenkonsumenten/innen. Praxisauswertung der Aktion Sprützehüsli in Basel*. Lausanne: Institut Universitaire de Médecine Sociale et Préventive.

United Nations (1988) *United Nations Convention against Illicit Traffic in Narcotic Drugs and Psychotropic Substances*. Adopted by the Conference at its 6th plenary meeting, on 19 December 1988 (http://www.unodc.org/unodc/en/un_treaties_and_resolutions.html).

UNODC Legal Affairs Section (2002) *The flexibility of the treaty provisions as regards harm reduction approaches*. Document E/INB/2002/W.13/SS5.

van Beek, I (2003) The Sydney Medically Supervised Injecting Centre: a clinical model. *Journal of Drug Issues*, 33(3), 625–638.

Chapter 14

Injecting Drugs – The User's Perspective

Jimmy Dorabjee

I am an ex heroin user who has used drugs for a long, long time. For the past 12 years I have been working in the drug treatment and HIV prevention field. There used to be a time when I misused drugs; lost control, lost jobs, lost love, lost my family – indeed I lost everything I ever had, and I had plenty. I lost everything before I came to terms with myself: that I am a drug user and I needn't be ashamed of that; that I am a human being, with a lot of dignity and pride in myself and a lot to offer the world – and please don't tell me that I don't, because all through my life that's exactly the message I got. If you use drugs, you are a pariah, a useless human being, and are unworthy of trust, love or respect. An absolute loser!

This is a story, my story, and is about my journey through life. A life that has taken me through what seemed to be the endless depths of addiction to illicit drugs and its associated illegality and lawlessness, an overwhelming sense of hopelessness, and my reluctant but often desperate attempts to overcome it. It is about the various treatment modalities I was subjected to, without ever asking me for my opinion, or at the very least, my consent. It is an attempt to be retrospective and analyse what could or should have been done and what actually happened to me. In short, it is my story that spans 57 years, most of which has been a struggle to conceal my drug use, to lie and deceive everyone except fellow drug users, to be forced to live a life of multiple identities, and finally, after many years of struggle and self-searching, to be able to come to terms with my drug use.

My preferred name is LUCKY, all in capital letters, because that's what I am. I have used drugs for 40 years, and injected for most of that time. I have shared needles and syringes with friends and strangers, and have regularly had unprotected sex. Yet, in spite of these risky behaviours, I have not been infected with HIV or hepatitis B/C, nor have I ever had a sexually transmitted infection. This may be because during my early injecting career, HIV was not yet around. It also may be that, as I grew older, I began to use my own syringe and needle and never really shared. Sure, I got really physically sick many times, with a bloated liver, jaundice, TB – but more serious for me was the fact that I have had to endure and suffer the sickness associated with withdrawals that most opiate users needlessly undergo. *But* I didn't get HIV: when I look around me today, I see many young people getting infected with HIV within the first few months of starting to inject.

I was born in 1948 in a middle class Parsi family, in a middle class hospital in Bombay. Christened Jimmy by my parents, I lived a life of middle class comfort, well mannered, respectful and obedient to my elders; what some may call a 'normal' existence. The Parsi's are followers of the prophet Zarathustra, the religion of ancient Persia (Iran). I had many friends, was popular and fun loving, and went through my childhood doing all the normal things with my middle class friends.

I was educated in Christian schools, and by the time I was in High School, my friends and I would go out to smoke hashish during our lunch breaks. It began one day, while I was in the ninth standard in school, when a friend and I went to lunch at a small restaurant near the Mazagaon Dockyards in Bombay. Just before lunch, my friend took out a cigarette and lit it up. A pungent smell enveloped the private room in the restaurant where we ate lunch, and after a few puffs, he handed the cigarette to me. Taking a few drags, I felt a sense of relaxation and an easing of tension. In fact, the few drags livened up the dull and boring history class that occurred that afternoon, filling my mind with vivid images of the heroic figures and countless wars from ancient India. This was my introduction to hashish, known to all in Bombay as 'charas', and I thoroughly enjoyed the feeling.

At 17, I began smoking opium, often spending days lying around in the opium dens that were scattered all over Bombay, alongside other older, ordinary working men and some women who came to the dens for their dose of relaxation after a hard day's work. A year later, a Jewish friend who smoked opium with me introduced me to morphine and injecting, and after that there was no turning back. I was hooked, absolutely and irrevocably; morphine awakened something that was missing deep within my inner self that I didn't realise till I began injecting.

In the 1960s and 1970s, very few people injected drugs in Bombay. Injections were something you received to heal and cure you when you were ill. No doubt, injecting morphine did heal and make me feel better, though the illness was not understandable to me back then. Not confident of injecting myself in the early days, I would go to an old retired doctor who lived near the pharmacy where we bought the morphine ampoules and he would inject me and my friends for a small fee. With a large alcohol habit, he would be quite uncoordinated, doddery and drunk whenever we went to his house. Two of his daughters were nurses at a large public hospital, and would assist him at times when his permanently trembling hands shook too much. Each time he brought the syringe near my arms I would wince and pray for an early strike, but the near instant effects of the morphine would more than compensate for the anxiety I felt before being injected.

Later, I began to inject myself with the glass syringes that were available in those days. As my habit increased, I had to inject using larger syringes. Each 2 ml ampoule contained 30 mg of morphine; as I was injecting 150 mg a shot, this meant 10 ml of liquid several times a day.

At that time and till today, one could go to many pharmacies in India and buy any drug you wanted, with or without a doctor's prescription. With regular supplies of pure, pharmaceutical morphine easily available at chemists and enough money to pay, you could have continued to use opiates without the need to search for pushers or dealers; consequently, only a few of my friends who also experimented or used drugs knew, and there was no stigma attached to my habit.

Between 1967 and 1972, I was a lead guitarist and singer in one of India's most popular rock and roll bands, and was speeding, literally and figuratively, down life's fast lane. To play long sessions, or simply to be faster and more adept on our instruments, we would take methedrine or dexedrine (amphetamines) bought from pharmacies, and later, in order to come down and sleep, we would use mandrax (methaquolone) or other downers.

While playing at jam sessions at one of Bombay's most popular nightclubs, I met my first wife, a princess from the royal family of a princely state in Gujarat, India. After going out together for a few years, we got married in London where I was trying to get into the music circle in 1972. While in the UK, I tried unsuccessfully to stop injecting morphine at a residential clinic in Harrow on the Hill where I was treated with doses of methadone. For me, coming from India where my experience of treatment for opiate dependency consisted of pumping patients with chlorpromazine, thioridazine and diazepam till you felt lethargic and exhausted just waking up each morning, methadone was a wonder drug that adequately managed the severe withdrawals associated with my heavy morphine dependency.

However, during my stay at the clinic, I was introduced by another resident to heroin that was now flooding the UK markets. We would drive down to Gerard Street in Soho during the day to buy heroin, and I used to inject in the underground public toilets around that area. One day, coming out of the toilet still flushed and scratching my body, two policemen came out of the janitor's room and, on searching me, found the needle and syringe in my pocket, along with a small piece of hash. To my immense relief, I was let off with a caution and told not to be seen in the area for a month. Here I was, caught red handed with a freshly used syringe and some hash, and was being let off so lightly. I thanked my lucky stars but continued to visit the area to score heroin, though I never used the public toilets to inject again, preferring rather to use toilets of the numerous business offices in that area.

I returned to Bombay in 1974, and immediately began to use morphine again. Almost every time I returned to India from abroad, the final few hours of the journey would be filled with a delicious sense of anticipation of buying and using morphine again. Even when I had no intention of using drugs, the impulse would jump out and strike me out of the blue and I would head straight for the dealer, even before I reached my home.

My experiences with treatment

Between 1968 and 1971, my family had me admitted to the psychiatric wards of five different hospitals in Bombay for treatment of my morphine dependence. The duration of these admissions varied between 15 days and 6 months, depending on how convincing I was at manipulating the doctors into believing I was now 'clean', and no longer had a desire to use drugs. But all the time during my stay, I would plot and plan and dream of how I would use drugs the moment I got out or could escape. I never really wanted to stop, and remained in the institutions only to pacify and please my family. The only way for me to leave these institutions was to be signed out by the person who checked me in. I saw many who languished in the institutions for years together.

I was put into police lockups dozens of times by my now desperate mother, who probably was ill advised by well meaning friends, in the hope that I would be frightened into stopping drugs. The police lockup in the area consisted of four small cells that housed 30 to 40 inmates. The cells were always overcrowded and it was difficult to stretch your legs to sleep at night. During the day we sat around and every night the police patrols would round up more vagrants, thieves and any 'suspicious' persons, adding to the crowd. Rather than persuading me to quit, the environment was highly conducive to drug use. Drugs were easily available in the lockup and were often of a better quality than outside. Some of the drugs that we got while in the lockup were confiscated stocks from the police evidence rooms. Others were bought from the numerous drug dealers that did business on street corners in the area. Some policemen would bring the drugs to you if you had the money to pay. Who would dare to sell 'poor quality' drugs to a policeman?

After 2 or 3 weeks, my mother would come and 'bail' me out. By this time I would carry the 'battle scars' of the lockup: lice and nits in my hair, sores from bed bugs and other parasites, and raw wounds all over my body from scratching. I would be thin, having lost a lot of weight due to the insufficient food that was provided, and angry at the way I had been treated by my family and the police. But I also appreciated the fact that I was going back 'home' to have private space, something that was impossible in the police lockup.

As with hospital admission, these frequent periods of detention did little to discourage me from using drugs; rather they made me even more determined to enjoy the effects of the drugs that I took. For a while after each period of detention I would be careful to conceal my drug use from everyone, but I could not do so for long.

On the advice of a police inspector, I was admitted to a psychiatric institution in the garden city of Bangalore called the National Institute for Mental Health and Neuro Sciences. I spent another 3 months unsuccessfully undergoing yet another 'cure'. A year later in 1976, I was committed to the Thane Mental Hospital where I stayed for a total of 13 months, broken by my escaping for 8 days before being 'captured' by the police and sent back. Admission to the mental hospital was for treatment of my drug problem. Unfortunately the doctors at the hospital were at a loss to suggest a line of treatment except to put me on chlorpromazine and diazepam. During those days the administration of electroconvulsive therapy to 'cure' drug dependence was widespread in many Asian countries.

In 1978, in a frenzied bout of chaotic, drug induced anger and madness, I killed someone. I was attacked, and used a small kitchen knife to defend myself and to hurt the person assaulting me. I exploded with the long repressed anger and bitterness at being treated badly and subjected to verbal and physical violence. After a day on the run I walked into the police station where I had spent so many periods in the lockup.

Arrested and charged with murder under Section 302 of the Indian Penal Code, I was sent to the Bombay Central Prison, where I spent a total of 2 years and 8 months as an 'under-trial' prisoner. Those charged with serious crimes in India often have to wait several years for their trial in the Sessions Courts. At the trial, due to the 'extenuating circumstances' and my 'good background' I was convicted of 'over exceeding my right of private defence' and sentenced to 4 years' imprisonment. On appealing the decision in the High Court, I was released in late 1980. During my stay in the prison, I worked as a typist/clerk for the jailers and so had the privilege of free movement within the prison walls. All other inmates, except those who worked in the kitchen or as warders, were allowed only a few hours a day outside their barracks for exercise or washing and bathing at the community taps. All the time I was in prison, I had access to drugs and never stopped using them. Instead, I became friends with some of the deadliest hard-core criminals and gangsters, some of who still dominate the Asian drugs and crime scene.

While in prison, my mother died and I was left with a considerable inheritance. But within a few years, I had given away or spent most of the money on drugs. By 1985 I had sold my house, car and whatever valuables and jewellery my family had left me.

So what is it about heroin that is so enticing?

Heroin was one of the best experiences that happened to me. I fell in love with her – she was my lover, my beloved. She took care of my deepest aches and pains. I just couldn't live without her. Imagine your best orgasm, the best sex you have ever had. That's the effect heroin gives you when you use it, only a 1000 times better. And you get the same feeling time and again, every time you use her. And I loved her dearly. In such circumstances, how can one resist something that is so enticing and pleasurable?

And then people say, 'Why don't you just quit?' Unfortunately, it's not that simple. When you find yourself finally wanting to quit, there are a few things you need to do and prepare for. For me it was like this. I walked up to her(oin), held out my hand and shook hers and kissed her one last time saying, 'I'm leaving you and this time I'm not coming back'. She knew I would though; I had done this so often in the past. Then you turn around and start walking away from her, and you don't look back. She stands there, looking at you walking off and whispers, 'Jimmy darling, where are you going? Come back, I need you!' But you can't turn around and look at her because, if you do, you will almost certainly go back to her. She's that alluring, sexy and desirable and you have loved her absolutely, over anyone or anything else. So you just keep walking on, not looking back, desperately hoping and praying that the monkey is finally off your back.

A little later she starts to shout out, 'Hey you bastard! Don't go! I love you and I need you. You need me, I know, and you cannot live without me. Hey Jim, come on back.' But, you don't look back. And you start to walk a bit faster because you are now afraid: really afraid that if you slow down or look back, your resolve to leave is doomed and you will go back to her. And then she begins to rant and rave. 'Fuck you Jimmy, why are you deserting me? I am your lover and your best friend.' She pleads, 'don't go – please come back'. But go you must, you can't stop now as you feel you have almost got away. Just a little more distance and a little more time and she will be out of your life, this time forever. At least that's what you honestly think and believe.

The days creep past: slow, dreary and dull days, filled with a sick, lethargic existence. For the first few weeks and months you seem to have no life in you and there's no colour; everything is grey and black. It's as if you are sleep walking through life. You have no interest in anything except the physical pain and sorrow of leaving her. Many times you feel like just going back and feeling her immersed into your veins, the warmth of her love. But you still resist. Time goes by and you think you are now finally over her. But you're wrong. She still creeps into your subconscious states of mind. She filters through your every thought and action. When you sleep, you have this vivid dream that some-body just gave you a small paper bag of heroin. You are holding it in your now trembling hands and you desperately want to use. So, with a feeling of delicious anticipation you get together the instruments you need. Now, sweating and breathless, with shaky hands, you slowly open up the packet of heroin and see the powder there before your eyes. And just as you put it into the spoon, an uncontrollable coughing spasm hits you. The powder is blown all over the floor and there goes your anticipated high. You jerk back, with a sick sense of doom and wake up with a start. Hell, this was a dream, thank God! But that's how real it is. She appears when you least expect her to and for many long years, doesn't leave you alone. If you don't watch out now, you definitely will go back to her, and all the effort you made to try and stay away will be wasted. Once more you will have to go through the whole painful process again, unless some other relationship that is much more fulfilling and attractive begins with someone or something else.

And you start to think, 'What is it about her? Why did I have this special relationship with her? She is a whore, and is available for anyone who can afford her. She's not mine, and never was! She will go with anyone who can pay the price.'

So what changed?

Looking back at my life I often think about what led me to this change. What happened to make me the person that I am today? And I realise that many factors have contributed to shape the person I am now. The most important was the fact that I had access to and began to use buprenorphine as a substitute for heroin, just as methadone is used in many countries. Without the protecting and reinforcing effects of buprenorphine, I probably would still be there, out on the streets of Bombay, hustling and scoring heroin. Or I may have been dead. It has been a slow process of maturation out of the drug's charisma.

In 1991 I made a last ditch attempt to change my life and try and quit using heroin. Sahara House, a therapeutic community in Delhi was the first treatment centre I entered where the doors were never locked. For them it was important to keep people in the centre using persuasion, personal relationships and humane treatment. I responded very well to this approach, and within a few months was able to regain my health, lost dignity and pride, as well as maintain a drug free life. A few months later I began to work for

Sahara and later joined a sister organisation called SHARAN, where most of the staff were ex drug users. At SHARAN, we provided community based detoxification services for street and slum based heroin users, but the relapse rates were very high. Recognising the failure of the service, we changed our approach and began providing services with a harm reduction philosophy, including the provision of sublingual buprenorphine substitution. After a literature search on buprenorphine, we began services as a pilot programme, and this soon became a fully fledged harm reduction service, the first of its kind in India. The pilot phase of street- and home-based buprenorphine substitution began in 1993, 3 years before France introduced large-scale buprenorphine prescribing. In 1994, I broke my leg playing football and began to use buprenorphine to dull the pain. I also found that it provided me with a level of protection from relapsing back to heroin use. I have been on buprenorphine ever since.

Today, with much support and input, I am called various things. No, not a junkie, an addict, or any of these judgemental terms. Today, I am seen as an expert in drug treatment in India/Asia, a researcher, trainer, consultant, and a specialist – in short, a worthwhile human being. But I still use buprenorphine and I lead a very 'normal' life. My life is going well and I have a wonderful family and work that I love. This has been made possible through my introduction to and association with the Harm Reduction Movement, a growing evidence based and scientific community that has at its essence, compassionate and humane philosophies.

I hope that I have conveyed my journey appropriately. It has been a journey through a sometimes self inflicted hell and more often, a hell inflicted by circumstances beyond my control, a struggle to be recognised – as a human being, a good person, one who has something to offer. After jails, police lockups, hospitals and mental institutions, finally, a realisation of my SELF. I am what I am and PROUD OF IT!

Scene 1

It was dark, really dark, and the blood was pounding in my brain. I felt like I was in a deep pit, and no matter what I did, I just couldn't clear my head or eyes. I rubbed my eyes with my fingers (hand), but could not feel my hand though I felt something brush my eyes. Slowly my vision returned and I started to see things around me. I was lying on the ground, just below a parapet in a compound at the back of a five-storey building. The ground was muddy and I could taste the mud in my mouth. As my mind cleared slowly, I looked down and saw the syringe stuck in my left arm – still a quarter full of a dark brown liquid stained with blood. Oh yes, I was having a fix, I remembered and then things went black. I tried to sit up, but my head was pounding, shrieking at me in a tuneless scream, and my legs felt rubbery. I remembered X and Y were with me just a moment ago and wondered where they had gone. The throbbing in my head was now accompanied by flashes of bright light that accentuated the pain I felt in my brain. The sun had almost set and the twilight, or the heroin, played tricks on my vision. Using all my strength, I pushed myself off the ground, clutched the parapet and steadied myself. My breathing was shallow, noisy, and I could feel a wheeze each time I exhaled. With shaking hands, I lit a cigarette and took a few deep drags. If I shot up the rest, I thought, I might feel better. But doing that was harder than I thought and it took a concerted effort for me to manage to squeeze the plunger all the way in, and I experienced another slight rush of the heroin in my brain. My lips felt swollen, my feet felt as if I was walking on a cushion or air. I pulled the syringe out from my arm, pulled off the needle and packed them into the cigarette packet that was its home. After what seemed a long time I rose to my feet and started to walk out to the street. A few people were walking down the street and they paid no attention to me. Leaning against a wall I thought that the stuff was really strong. And realised that I had, once again, almost overdosed.

A day in the life

It was late evening when he walked into the house and his daughter opened the door for him. His 2-year-old son was crying in the lounge and he went in to comfort and quieten him. His wife called out from the kitchen, asking whether he wanted a cup of tea. He switched on the TV and flicked the channel to the cartoon network. His son grew quiet and smiled at the screen. Walking out, he went to the bedroom and came back with a small leather pouch. Unzipping the bag, he brought out a 2 cc syringe with a needle attached. A spoon and distilled water followed, along with a small cellophane packet of some white powder – heroin. Measuring a small portion into the spoon, he squirted some water into the spoon and watched the powder dissolve. His daughter came to the lounge and asked him for some money to go to the movies. Reaching into his hip pocket, he drew out his wallet and gave it to her. Carefully drawing the solution in the spoon into the syringe through a small ball of cotton, he asked her which movie she was going to. His daughter looked at him and said, 'Dad, some people at school were talking about drugs, and how they were really bad for you. They said that drugs kill you, and if you use drugs you are sick.'

He looked at her and gently asked whether she thought he was dead. 'No' she replied. 'I guess they are trying to frighten young people from experimenting with drugs', he said, putting down the unused syringe on the lounge tea table. 'Not that it works too well. People should have access to accurate information on the effects of drugs, and how they can destroy lives if you are not careful. Look at that family across the road and all the problems they have almost every night, fighting and shouting. That's because he is drunk and spends a lot of money on his alcohol. Did they tell you about alcohol and cigarettes at school?' 'No, they talked about marijuana and heroin, and also ecstasy', she replied. 'Anyway, I'm off now. Bye Mom. Don't keep dinner for me as I'll be home late.'

He waved goodbye and picked up the syringe. She's a mature girl, he thought. Just 19, but so much older than her years. Cleaning a spot on his arm with a swab, he fastened the tourniquet and gently pushed the needle into the vein. A trickle of blood entered the barrel of the syringe, and, unfastening the tourniquet with his teeth, he slowly pushed the solution into his vein.

His wife brought in the tea just then and put it onto the coffee table. 'How was your day?' she asked. Nodding, he smiled at her through the rush that he was experiencing. 'You really must stop doing this in front of the children', she said. 'You never know what they might accidentally say to someone, and you don't want to get into trouble.'

He smiled again, and looked at his family. He loved them dearly, and would do anything for them. 'Yes' he replied, 'it's not safe', just like any other responsible family man.

The alarm clock went off and I awoke.

Index